THE SECULAR IMAGINARY

Given the popularity and success of the Hindu right in India's electoral politics today, how may one study ostensibly 'Western' concepts and ideas, such as the secular and its family of cognates, like secularism, secularisation and secularity, in non-Western societies without assuming them to be simply derivative or colonial legacies or contrast cases of Western societies? In other words, what is the discourse of secularity in modern India? While recognising that the dominant language of political modernity of Western societies is not easily translatable in non-Western societies, *The Secular Imaginary* elaborates upon an intellectual history of secularity in modern India by focusing on the two most influential political leaders – M. K. Gandhi and Jawaharlal Nehru. It is an intellectual history of both idea(s) and intellectuals which sheds light on Indian narratives of secularity – the Gandhian *sarva dharma samabhava*, Nehruvian secularism and 'unity in diversity'. It revisits this dominant narrative of secularity of the twentieth century, which influenced and shaped the imagination of the modern nation-state.

Sushmita Nath is a postdoctoral fellow at Cluster of Excellence, Contestations of the Liberal Script (SCRIPTS), Freie Universität, Berlin. Her research engages with issues in Indian political thought and Indian politics, such as secularism, nationalism and populism, in relation to the emerging field of comparative political theory.

THE SECULAR IMAGINARY

GANDHI, NEHRU AND THE IDEA(S) OF INDIA

SUSHMITA NATH

CAMBRIDGE
UNIVERSITY PRESS

University Printing House, Cambridge CB2 8BS, United Kingdom

One Liberty Plaza, 20th Floor, New York, NY 10006, USA

477 Williamstown Road, Port Melbourne, vic 3207, Australia

314 to 321, 3rd Floor, Plot No.3, Splendor Forum, Jasola District Centre, New Delhi 110025, India

103 Penang Road, #05–06/07, Visioncrest Commercial, Singapore 238467

Cambridge University Press is part of the University of Cambridge.

It furthers the University's mission by disseminating knowledge in the pursuit of education, learning and research at the highest international levels of excellence.

www.cambridge.org
Information on this title: www.cambridge.org/9781009180290

© Sushmita Nath 2022

This publication is in copyright. Subject to statutory exception and to the provisions of relevant collective licensing agreements, no reproduction of any part may take place without the written permission of Cambridge University Press.

First published 2022

Printed in India by Avantika Printers Pvt. Ltd.

A catalogue record for this publication is available from the British Library

ISBN 978-1-009-18029-0 Hardback

Cambridge University Press has no responsibility for the persistence or accuracy of URLs for external or third-party internet websites referred to in this publication, and does not guarantee that any content on such websites is, or will remain, accurate or appropriate.

CONTENTS

Preface vii
Acknowledgements ix

   Introduction 1

1 Debating the Secular beyond the West 20

2 Gandhi's *Ashram* and Political Thought: A Counter-narrative of Secularity 47

3 Gandhi's Associationalism: A Non-state Alternative to Liberal Secularism? 98

4 Was Nehru Nehruvian? Religion, Secularity and Nehruism 141

5 Nehru and the Politics of Liberalism of Fear 192

   Conclusion 231

Bibliography 237
Index 253

PREFACE

December 2019 was a season of faith's perfection when India saw country-wide protests in response to an Act passed by the parliament which challenged the secular spirit of the Indian constitution.[1] Many of these peaceful protests were accompanied by ritualised reading of the preamble of the Indian constitution, and with this simple act, 'We, the people of India' sought to reaffirm the idea of India as a secular democratic republic. The post-colonial state in India today shows alarming impunity towards individual and minority rights, accompanied by a disregard for and dismissal of norms and values on which the 'idea of India' stands.[2] One such value that has increasingly become marginal and seemingly only of symbolic importance to the state in contemporary India, most visibly after the demolition of the Babri Masjid in 1992, is secularism. This political ideal, which found expression in the 'Gandhi–Nehru tradition' through popular slogans like 'unity in diversity' and *sarva dharma samabhava* during the Indian national movement and in Nehruvian secularism after independence, from being dominant and indeed one of the defining features of Indian nationhood, stands at the margins today. One may even go as far as to argue that today India is a 'secular republic' only nominally. Right-wing politics today does not simply reject secularism.

---

[1] The Citizenship (Amendment) Act, 2019.
[2] I borrow this famous phrase from Sunil Khilnani's book, where he argues that the founding idea of India, based on pluralism and democracy, was not simply a commitment to abstract values but borne out of and rooted in a practical understanding of the compulsions and constraints of Indian politics. Sunil Khilnani, *The Idea of India* (New Delhi: Penguin, 2012 [1997]).

It has re-defined the secular ideal; it is homogeneous and majoritarian. The Gandhi–Nehru tradition, by contrast, is based on ideals of pluralism and equality. The unfolding crisis in India's post-colonial history makes it urgent for us to revisit the inclusive ideas and ideals that marked the beginning of this nation. By examining Gandhi and Nehru's thought and politics on the question of the religion–state–society relationship, this book revisits the Gandhi–Nehru tradition in order to gain moral and political insights that may guide contemporary India's imperilled secular imaginary. Both the intellectual and political decline of the Gandhi–Nehru tradition of secularity, from a dominant one in the twentieth century to a marginal one in the twenty-first century, are tinged with irony when seen through the lens of intellectual history. On the one hand, late-twentieth-century writings on Gandhi and Nehru are replete with hagiographical accounts. On the other hand, many contemporary writings have moved in a direction where a defence or a critical appraisal of secularism in India is closely tied to a defence or criticism of the personalities of Gandhi and Nehru themselves. In this book, I attempt to move away from such academic proclivities and polemical arguments. By locating the Gandhi–Nehru tradition in the global intellectual history of secularity, in this book, I wish to draw attention to the possibilities as well as the limitations of Gandhian and Nehruvian thought and practice. My hope is that, instead of outright dismissal of ideas and thinkers, we may engage with concepts and ideas in ways that can question and challenge contrived binary narratives, such as those positing religion/tradition/Indian/Gandhian against secular/modern/Western/Nehruvian, and thereby effectively respond to the post-colonial state's irreverence towards constitutional secularism.

ACKNOWLEDGEMENTS

In writing this book I have accrued several unrepayable debts. I owe immense gratitude to my PhD supervisor at Jawaharlal Nehru University (JNU), Rinku Lamba, as the first iterations of this book emerged as a doctoral dissertation under her supervision. Her patience and willingness to enthusiastically and critically engage with my ideas trained me to nourish an idea instead of chasing it. I would like to thank my PhD examiners, Tridip Suhrud and Vasanthi Srinivasan, who provided crucial insights which helped refine my arguments in the book. Tridip's show of humility and generosity gave me the confidence to stay the course despite some unexpected challenges. I would also like to thank my teachers at the Centre for Political Studies, JNU: Shefali Jha, Rajarshi Dasgupta, Anupama Roy and Amir Ali, who transformed a master's student into a scholar.

This book would not have been possible without the generous support of KFG 'Multiple Secularities – Beyond the West, Beyond Modernities', Leipzig University, where the majority of the revisions to the manuscript were undertaken between 2019 and 2021. I cannot think of a more fitting environment than KFG in writing this book as I have gained immensely from the rich intellectual discussions with my colleagues in weekly colloquiums, workshops and conferences. The joint coffee-break on Tuesdays, the delectable *Eranos* and the monthly 'Screening Religion' added colour to an already engaging and interactive environment. At KFG, I found the opportunity to interact with scholars whom I have read and admired, and learnt about secularities around the world, across time. Here I also learnt how one may sincerely engage in comparative social and political theorisation. I would like to thank the Fritz Thyssen Foundation for granting a year-long postdoctoral fellowship which enabled me to return to KFG, 'Multiple Secularities' in 2019. I would especially like to thank the directors of KFG, 'Multiple Secularities' – Monika Wohlrab-Sahr and Christoph Kleine – for not only granting the fellowship which gave me the opportunity and time to work on the manuscript, but also for their unwavering support and encouragement. Revisions to the manuscript were done during the unprecedented circumstances of a pandemic. Words fall short as I wish to express my gratitude to my friends and colleagues at KFG who, during this time, were a home away from home. The friendship, concern and continuous support of Monika, Markus Dreßler and Judith Zimmerman made this place more than a research institution for me. Without Judith's support I would not have been able to navigate German academia. Lucy, Foteine, Pavel, Anja and Hannah turned KFG into a lively place of work. I would also like to thank my colleagues at KFG, André and Jill, Nader, Peter, Mohammad, Elliot, Lena, Sana, Elisabeth and Mariam, for their camaraderie. Johannes Duschka sacrificed days from his Christmas holidays to read a very long chapter. I have gained immensely from his detailed comments and critique on two of the chapters. I would also like to thank my colleagues and intellectual interlocuters, Florian Zemmin and Vanya Bhargav, both of whom read portions from this book and provided their invaluable feedback. Thanks is also due to the two anonymous reviewers of Cambridge University Press for their detailed comments and critique which helped me revise and sharpen the arguments in the book.

As a non-NET fellowship holder, during my PhD it was impossible to attend international conferences unless the organisers agreed to cover all the expenses. This, as I have come to realise over the years, is difficult to arrange for most conference organisers. That is why I would like to thank the conference organisers of 'Public Life and Religious Diversity' (2017) at Oxford University, 'Worldviews in World View: Particularizing Secularism, Secularity and Nonreligion' (2018) at King's College, London, and 'Patterns of Distinction, Paths of Differentiation' (2018), at KFG, 'Multiple Secularities', Leipzig University, for ensuring funds to attend the conference. Portions of the papers presented in these conferences have been incorporated in the book. I would like to thank the participants in these conferences for their helpful comments. During my PhD, a teaching job in Ashoka University, Haryana, provided the much-needed financial stability, as well as my first teaching experience. I thank Ravindran Sriramachandran and Ali Khan Mahmudabad for the trust and respect they exhibited towards an early career scholar. I also thank my students at Ashoka University who taught me how to be a better teacher.

ACKNOWLEDGEMENTS

Max Kramer has been a constant friend and colleague in conversation as both of us traverse between India and Germany, and fortuitously continue to work on related themes. In Delhi, Surajit Chakravarty always found time to meet up. Growing up in a Bengali *para*, our childhood friends were more like family than friends. I am grateful to Deepanjana Chakravarti for coming to our family's rescue during a very difficult time in Delhi. In Germany, Maruan has made sure by his presence in my life that I always have an alternative perspective on things. You amuse and inspire me in equal measure.

In the course of writing this book, new lives greeted us and brought immense happiness to our family. My niece and nephew, Ira and Niyor, are hope and happiness. I am ever so grateful to my sister, Arpita, whose support, kindness and generosity I often take for granted. Thanks for always being there. My parents, Rekha and Swapan, continue to support their daughter's unconventional life. I am grateful for their unconditional love and support. *Baba*, you will always be the better teacher. *Ma*, with your unrelenting strength, you continue to awe and inspire me. Lastly, how does one thank someone when they, as your fiercest critic and most ardent admirer, are the ones with whom you started the journey into adulthood and academia together? Deep, you always enthusiastically engaged with my first random thoughts to the final idea, and this book is as much yours as mine.

Berlin
March 2022

INTRODUCTION

Despite the seeming inferiority present in its nomenclature, Indian Political Thought has largely worked itself out in its sociopolitical operation rather than in normative justification and conceptual clarification as found in Western Political Theory. That is why a study of the political in India is always a 'thought' and never the enviable cogent theory of the West. By considering what seems to be a weakness as a strength, in this book, I first take up the task of elaborating upon an Indian intellectual history of a so-called Western conception – secularity. Drawing on recent debates on secularity, I wish to address the problem of understanding histories or narratives of secularity in context. Conceptually, I broadly follow recent studies, which through the framework of 'multiple secularities' challenge the claim of cultural embeddedness and historical specificity of secularity.[1] In this book, I understand secularity to connote a modern epistemological characterisation of the social world wherein religion and secular are distinguished in terms of conceptual distinctions as well as structural or institutional and symbolic forms of differentiation of social spheres.[2] It is also a 'historical category' in so far as such distinctions and differentiations develop as a response to social change brought in by new or unique conditions created by modernity.[3] Second, through the lens of secularity, I also undertake an exercise in an intellectual history of modern India's two leading political leaders – M. K. Gandhi, the leader of India's non-violent nationalism, and Jawaharlal Nehru, the first prime minister of independent India – whose thought and politics had a defining impact on the 'idea of India' as a multireligious nation-state.[4] This book is thus an intellectual history of both idea(s) and intellectuals, which revisits the narrative of secularity in modern India.[5] Lastly, as a self-avowed secular and democratic nation-state,[6] post-colonial India faces challenges of majoritarianism and extremist Hindu nationalism, where we see a simultaneous rejection and appropriation of secularism in the political field.[7] With the popularity and electoral success of right-wing Hindu nationalist groups challenging the 'Gandhi–Nehru tradition'[8] of a nation built on the secular ideal, I revisit dominant narratives of secularity in the twentieth century, as exemplified in *sarva dharma samabhava* (equality of all religions) and unity in diversity, which in Indian politics today have been reduced to empty rhetoric.

This book pursues a question that has confounded explorations in Indian Political Thought which engage with the Gandhi–Nehru tradition of secularity. How can we speak of a unified, single tradition of secularity in modern India, when the leaders who lent their names to this tradition had different, even opposing, ideas of India? In this book, I will argue that two distinctive, indeed contrapuntal, narratives of secularity emerge from the thought and politics of Gandhi and Nehru which influenced post-colonial India's constitutional secularism. While Gandhi's thought and politics elicit, what I call, a counter-narrative of secularity, Nehru's ideas and politics, I maintain, express the ideal of secularity in terms that are simultaneously Indian and modern. Despite this, both Gandhian and Nehruvian narratives nevertheless come together on the question of a secular state in independent India.[9] Both reject the Westphalian model of a confessional state, and this commitment is reflected in rhetorical ideals and nationalist slogans, such as *sarva dharma samabhava* and 'unity in diversity'.[10] In other words, although Gandhian and Nehruvian ideas are grounded in fundamentally different views of the world, it may be argued that on the question of a secular state 'their practical precepts and their historical tendency are miscible'.[11] Thus, the broader aim of the book is to demonstrate that although in modern India influential political ideas have sought both differentiation and integration of social spheres, the Gandhian 'holistic vision' of society does not elicit an adversarial position towards political secularism, and the Nehruvian 'secularist ideal' does not envision the radical secularism of the French *laïcité*, where the secular public sphere is freed from religion.[12] This broader argument needs to be highlighted, given the influence of critical discourses in the study of secularism.[13] Post-colonial studies have rightly shown the inadequacy and normative violence of the language of political modernity of the West in non-Western societies.[14] At the same time, arguments about derivativeness of ideas have also sometimes buried the ingenuity that non-Western sociopolitical actors and institutions brought to (seemingly) Western ideas. This problem is acute in studies in secularity because while it is acknowledged that the 'secular age' may be unique to the North Atlantic world,[15] the argument that ideas travel in interconnected histories and lend themselves to new interpretations and challenges gets shrouded by the culturally embedded character of the term 'secular'.[16] As a result, political secularism and secularity in general are denied their socio-historical specificity and therefore their applicability and relevance in non-Western societies.

Today, a historically contextualised study in secularity in India is necessitated by the challenge of religious majoritarianism on a multireligious nation-state and the consistent inability of this state to sustain and safeguard its secular principles in the face of this majoritarian challenge. In securing massive mandates in two successive general elections (2014 and 2019), the right-wing national party, the Bharatiya Janta Party (BJP), has successfully demonstrated its ability to garner votes based on exclusionary politics of Hindutva,[17] that is, on an anti-secular agenda. By locating the 'enemy' within the nation-state, most evidently the minority Muslim population, and by altering the secular character of Indian nationhood,[18] the BJP-led government has disseminated a new idea of India based on majoritarian nationalism. This idea of a 'new India', it must be noted, does not seek to remove but *alter* the meaning of secularism in India. In the current popularity of right-wing politics, in mainstream politics, there is no demand to remove the 'word' secular from the preamble of the Indian constitution. Instead, in a perverse Orwellian doublespeak, the Hindu right's claim is that it is they who are truly secular, such that those who defend minority rights are 'pseudo-secular' because they are supposedly motivated by the politics of minority appeasement and vote-bank politics. To put it differently, it has been argued that a certain 'dominance of nationalist habits of thinking' influenced Indian social science discussions in the twentieth century.[19] This nationalist influence was reflected in the sociopolitical field in the dominance of the Gandhi–Nehru tradition, which asserted the normative and ethical value of equal respect for all religions, and historically justified in the traditional 'tolerant,' 'secular' and 'plural' culture that was claimed to have existed in the pre-colonial past.[20] Given today's political climate, it may be argued that this Gandhi–Nehru ideal of secularity based on a multireligious nation stands marginalised, its relevance reduced to a symbolic value.

This study also emerges in the context of a renewed interest in religion (at least since the late 1980s and especially in the West), with its assumption of public-political roles and its new visibility in the public domain, including its discursive and political presence, as well as its visual and media manifestations. In the domain of academia, this has reopened debates about religion's engagement with society and politics found in influential ideas such as Jürgen Habermas's 'post-secular society', Charles Taylor's 'secular age' and José Casanova's 'public religions'.[21] The 'resurgence of religion'[22] in the public domain has prompted debates in the Western world about the viability of secularism as a philosophical ideal and as a set of political prescriptions.[23] This renewed debate on religion's role and relation to modern state and society has also called into question the theory of secularisation as a world-historical and social process of modernisation, which purported a decline of religion and its retreat from the public sphere.[24]

In the Indian context, these renewed academic debates on secularity seem belated for at least two reasons. First, in its transition from a modernising colonial to a post-colonial state, Indian political leaders and thinkers had to perforce engage with questions of religion's relationship to state and society philosophically, discursively and politically. The clearest example of these engagements, contestations and debates can be found in the Constituent Assembly debates (1946–1949), wherein independent India's constitution took shape. In rejecting the Westphalian model of a confessional state, the Indian national movement challenged the claim of the colonisers that India could never be a nation because of its bewildering diversity. In the Constituent Assembly, the members went on to ensure that the British Raj would not be replaced by a 'Hindu Raj'. Second, as opposed to the Western experience, a socio-historical examination of the religion–state–society relationship in modern India demonstrates a longer engagement with inter- and intra-religious diversity, domination and conflict.[25] Although religious diversity became philosophically and politically a central concern in Europe after the Reformation in the eighteenth century, this issue was internal to Christianity, in the sense that it was a concern within the ambit of diversity found within Judeo-Christian traditions.[26] The nature of conflict that arose from such diversity was thus intra-religious or internal to the religious field. It was only in the late twentieth century when Islam entered the European subcontinent in a major way, as a stable demographic and political entity, that the nature of religious diversity and conflict took the shape of inter-religious strife.[27] By contrast, in the Indian subcontinent, both inter- and intra-religious diversity was a social and political issue for a much longer period of time. In ancient India, internal religious diversity arose from a schism between Vedic religions and heterodox traditions of Buddhism and Jainism. Inter-religious diversity emerged with the arrival and entrenchment of Islam on the Indian subcontinent during the medieval period. The major presence of Islam as a religion from outside, from the thirteenth century onwards, brought social and political issues of accommodating inter-religious difference.[28] Evidently, in the debates on secularity in India, this history of inter- and intra-religious diversity and conflict has played an influential role in conceiving the relationship between religion, state and society in the modern period. In engaging with the works of Gandhi and Nehru, the assumption in this book is that such influences shaped their narratives of secularity as well. Indeed, Gandhi and Nehru's ideas are often invoked to defend or decry the value of secularism in contemporary India.[29] Furthermore, the influence of both these political figures on Indian society extends beyond the time inhabited by them. Thus, the aim of this book is to explore these narratives of secularity in their sociopolitical context, that is, as they have developed in modern India, as opposed to their place of origin – namely, Euro-America or the West.

THE GANDHI–NEHRU TRADITION

The notion of social imaginary was used by the political philosopher Charles Taylor to express the idea of how a given people imagine their collective social life under conditions of modernity.[30] By calling this book 'the secular imaginary', I wish to convey the idea of a modern social imaginary of Indian sociopolitical life, where 'secular' came to connote both societal tolerance and an impartial secular state.[31] To be sure, this social imaginary, to borrow Ranajit Guha's formulation, may be characterised as a dominance without hegemony constantly at loggerheads with another modern formation – popular sovereignty expressed in democracy.[32] Although Gandhi and Nehru's imprimatur on this tradition may be evident, it nevertheless also developed under the influence of other twentieth-century thinkers and politicians in the Indian subcontinent.[33] This Indian social imaginary is also not without shortcomings. To begin with, it was largely elite-driven and often seemed to neglect the centrality of caste (that is, intra-religious difference and inequality) on questions of religious tolerance and equality. In other words, this tradition draws more attention to concerns of intergroup equality and tolerance among religious groups (especially, Hindus, Muslims and Christians), rather than equality within a religious group.[34] Furthermore, conceptually speaking, the Gandhi–Nehru tradition can be confounding in its meaning as it signals dual connotations of tolerance (through notions such as *sarva dharma samabhava*) and secularism (state impartiality). This makes this tradition susceptible to the Hindu right's claim about the generosity and superiority of the Hindu tradition vis-à-vis other religions in the subcontinent visible in its long tradition of tolerance towards other religions and cultures.

However, the Gandhi–Nehru tradition crucially challenges forms of exclusionary ethnonationalist politics, visible in contemporary India, and central to this social imaginary is what Faisal Devji, quoting independent India's first president Rajendra Prasad, identifies as the 'unnational state':

> Instead, therefore, of seeking a solution of the Indian problem in the creation of national states of Hindus and Musalmans, in each of which there will remain a considerable minority of the other community, is it not better to allow India to continue as an unnational state that she is and has been?[35]

This idea of the unnational state, which emerged at a historical moment shrouded by the Western hegemonic conception of the Westphalian (mono-confessional) nation-state, evinced the possibility of a modern (liberal) post-colonial state in the presence of inter-religious plurality.[36] The distinguishing feature of the Gandhi–Nehru tradition is the coupling of the secular ideal, expressed in *sarva dharma samabhava* and 'unity in diversity', with the unnational state. A counterexample of an idea of the unnational state based on anti-secular ideals, which competed against the Gandhi–Nehru tradition, was articulated by the 'cosmopolitan nationalist' Vinayak Damodar Savarkar.[37] Savarkar, whose infamous essay[38] lent its title and influenced the BJP's ideological project of Hindutva, argued that the nation should be based on a common political project rather than on ethnicity, religion, culture or language. At the same time, Savarkar also articulated an imagination of the nation, where the minority Muslim community was the chief enemy of India. Given the existence and rejuvenation of such exclusionary nationalist narratives, I believe it is this coupling of the unnational state with the secular ideal of equality of religions which makes the time-worn Gandhi–Nehru tradition especially worthy of a revisit today.

The past three decades have amply demonstrated that modern democracy's majoritarian claims to legitimate right to rule come at the expense of the claims of self-determination of the minorities. In secular non-Western democracies, like India, the deepening of democracy has also meant the rise of popularity of political parties based on majoritarian religious ideologies. In contrast, the multinational state reflected in the Gandhi–Nehru tradition of the twentieth century emerged as a possible post-colonial alternative to the dominant idea of monocultural modern nation-states. Only partially realised (one may even argue imperfectly realised) in the post-colonial Indian constitution, a multinational state based on secular ideals provides a plausible alternative to dilemmas and challenges wrought by modern statecraft and majoritarian democratic politics that seem to have created permanent majorities and minorities in a democracy.[39] The social and religious minorities in India today are more visible and therefore vulnerable to communal and state violence than the 'fuzzy communities' in pre-modern India.[40] This idea of the unnational state, which will appear in various forms in the chapters that discuss the thought and politics of Gandhi and Nehru, along with the ideal of equality of religions makes it possible to talk about a Gandhi–Nehru tradition, despite the fact that these nationalist leaders had very different ideas of India.

NOTE ON METHODOLOGY

In order to shed light on how Gandhi and Nehru's thought and action influenced and shaped the dominant Gandhi–Nehru tradition of secularity in the twentieth century, this book follows a methodology broadly captured by intellectual history. With its focus on sociopolitical ideas and thinkers, in this book I follow a methodology established by studies in intellectual history of political ideas.[41] Where I depart from such studies is their excessive emphasis on linguistic contextualism, or 'speech acts'.[42] Here, I take inspiration from Aishwary Kumar's observation with regard to Gandhi's *Hind Swaraj* and Ambedkar's *Annihilation of Caste*.[43] Kumar argues that both these nationalist texts were 'equally untimely, addressed to an audience that was yet to be born'.[44] Gandhi's *Hind Swaraj*, written in 1909, was addressing a nationalist public that was yet to emerge and therefore engaging with epistemic questions, such as 'What is the political?' and 'How does one conduct politics under conditions of colonial domination and subjugation?'[45] His attempts at imbuing new meanings to common concepts, such as *dharma* (religion) and *ahimsa* (non-violence), and use of neologisms, like *satyagraha* (literally, insistence on truth; Gandhi's conceptualisation of passive resistance), cannot simply be understood by focusing on the linguistic conventions of the time. In other words, both his thought and politics may be better understood as an attempt to reinvent the political in early twentieth-century India.

Recent interventions in global intellectual history, which compare 'intellectuals or intellectual practices or ideas and concepts geographically or chronologically',[46] have also influenced this book's methodological commitments. These interventions have found it more constructive to respond to the colonialist lineages of the global by 'recovering resistance to the concept' rather than simply challenging the notion of the global 'as an artefact of imperial domination'.[47] In this book, an attempt is made to demonstrate how, despite a holistic worldview, the Gandhian narrative of the religion–state–society relationship aligns with the ethical commitments of Nehruvian secularism such that one may speak of a 'secular imaginary' expressed in the Gandhi–Nehru tradition. This argument goes much against dominant studies on secularity, mostly emanating from the experiences of Euro-America ('church-state separation') as well as reformist arguments from the Arab world,[48] where arguments of holism necessarily stand opposed to arguments for state secularism because secularism is and can only be understood as the separation of religion and state. Several Indian political thinkers and leaders, however, argued for a secular state which did not envisage separation. Thus, although Gandhi cannot be called a 'secularist', and Nehru was indeed a 'modernist', they both influenced a tradition where the boundaries between what constitutes religion and secular, tradition and modern, Indian and Western were questioned, challenged and reimagined in ways that do not adhere to dominant modular forms.

The exercise in intellectual history is also refracted through the new developments which have occurred in the field of comparative political theory. For instance, Rochana Bajpai's book *Debating Difference*, which examines group rights in post-colonial India by locating it in political theory discussions on multiculturalism, demonstrates how one may undertake an exercise in comparative political theory without relegating concepts to either derivative discourses or Indian exceptionalism.[49] By addressing India's experience of group-differentiated rights in a wider theoretical context and framework of liberal democracy, Bajpai shows the relevance of Indian experience beyond the ambit of area studies. Indeed, this remains one of the many challenges of the 'underdeveloped branch of comparative political thought' today[50] – to bring to attention non-Western political thought to Western audiences, where the non-West is central to exercises of theory-building and not simply treated as a place of exception or contrastive study. Methods in comparative political theory then seek to achieve the goal of conceptual and discursive comparison in order to decentralise some of the assumptions embedded in the analytical and ethical classificatory systems of Western political theory. Thus, in Michael Freeden and Andrew Vincent's opinion, one of the central problems of comparative political thought is 'the epistemological asymmetry that underlines assumptions of discursive equivalence'.[51] To illustrate this point, Freeden and Vincent give the example of 'the frequently asserted dichotomy between secular and religious cultures',[52] to demonstrate the problem of not accounting for the proportionately different weight assigned to various components of a system of ideas in comparative theorisation, as well as the multiplicity of approaches to common ideals, such as religious non-discrimination and state impartiality, also expressed by the ideology of secularism.

PLAN OF THE BOOK

In order to engage with the Gandhi–Nehru tradition of secularity in relation to the global intellectual history of secularity, the first chapter opens up a discussion on the so-called Western conception of the secular and its cognates – secularisation, secularism and secularity. The focus of this chapter is both an explanation of the aforementioned concepts and an engagement with the debates on secularism and secularisation, with a focus on India. This chapter thus clarifies the use of the family terms related to the secular throughout the rest of the book. In the rest of the following chapters, I frequently refer back to these debates to elaborate upon the narratives of secularity in India. Chapter 2 engages in an intellectual history of Gandhian thought with a focus on Gandhi's *ashram* observances to understand why religion was so central to his sociopolitical life. It seeks to forward an argument about how, despite his holistic vision, Gandhian thought and politics may be seen as compatible with value-based conceptions of liberal secularism. At the same time, the chapter also argues that Gandhian thought provides a counter-narrative to secularisation and secularity. Chapter 3 shifts attention to Gandhian politics to understand how Gandhi applied his religio-moral notions, such as *ahimsa* (non-violence) and *satyagraha* (Gandhi's conception of passive resistance), to politics. In that chapter, I discuss major political movements and issues with which Gandhi was associated to demonstrate how his politics cannot be understood through a liberal framework and language. Instead, I argue that Gandhi's politics can be better captured through, what I call, associationalism. I delineate three different types of associationalism in the sociopolitical field – namely, associational politics, associational activity and associational living – to argue how they create sociopolitical conditions for a society based on the principles of *ahimsa*. Chapter 4 is an intellectual history of Nehru's ideas of secularity. By focusing on Nehru's *The Discovery of India*, I argue that there are two different strands of arguments in his narrative of secularity. I call them the 'nationalist' and 'humanist-universal' arguments of secularity. I argue that these two arguments together give expression to Nehru's idea of secularity that is simultaneously indigenous and universal. In light of the insight gained through Nehruvian secularity, I go on to discuss Nehruvian secularism and distinguish it from the Nehruism of the 1970s and 1980s which emerged under Indira Gandhi's rule. Chapter 5, which is the last chapter in the book, focuses on how Nehru put his political ideals into practice and critically evaluates his engagement with politics both before and after independence. All the chapters together attempt to examine how embedded concepts, like the secular, whose origin is located in a different time and place, are challenged, appropriated and even reconceived by those who may be foreigners to such notions. Thus, the focus in this book is not the origin of concepts but the way political conceptions get articulated in their engagement with historical difference. This study of secularity in its context takes the following dictum seriously: '[that] formulae for living together have evolved in many different religious traditions, and are not the monopoly of those whose outlook has been formed by the modern, Western dyad, in which the secular lays claims to exclusive reality'.[53]

NOTES

1. In an eight-year-long project, the research group Kolleg-Forschungsgruppe (KFG) 'Multiple Secularities: Beyond the West, Beyond Modernities' at Leipzig University seeks to 'explore the boundaries between the religious and non-religious … in regions that differ greatly from the so-called "West" in the "Modern World"' in order to make a plea for comparative research, as well as highlight entangled histories. See Christoph Kleine and Monika Wohlrab-Sahr, 'Research Programme of the Humanities Centre of Advanced Studies (HCAS), "Multiple Secularities: Beyond the West, Beyond Modernities"', Leipzig University, 2016. https://www.multiple-secularities.de (accessed on 7 April 2021). Much of the revisions to the manuscript was done during my fellowship at KFG's Multiple Secularities. Some notable contemporary writings, which have explored the conceptual and historical possibilities and the presence of multiple secularities, are Ira Katznelson and Gareth Stedman Jones (eds.), *Religion and the Political Imagination* (New York: Cambridge University Press, 2010); Marian Burchardt, Monika Wohlrab-Sahr and Matthias Middell (eds.), *Multiple Secularities Beyond the West: Religion and Modernity in the Global Age* (Boston, Berlin and Munich: de Gruyter, 2015); Akeel Bilgrami (ed.), *Beyond the Secular West* (New York: Columbia University Press, 2016); Mirjam Künkler, John Madeley and Shylashri Shankar (eds.), *A Secular Age Beyond the West: Religion, Law and the State in Asia, the Middle East and North Africa* (New York: Cambridge University Press, 2018); Humeira Iqtidar and Tanika Sarkar (eds.), *Tolerance, Secularization, and Democratic Politics in South Asia* (New York: Cambridge University Press, 2018). For debates on secularity and Islam in contemporary India, see Anindita Chakrabarti and Sudha Sitharaman, *Religion and Secularities: Reconfiguring Islam in Contemporary India* (Hyderabad: Orient Blackswan, 2020).
2. Kleine and Wohlrab-Sahr, 'Multiple Secularities'. I engage with the concept of secularity in detail in Chapter 1.

3. Florian Zemmin, 'How (Not) to Take "Secularity" beyond the Modern West: Reflections from Islamic Sociology', Working Paper Series of the HCAS 'Multiple Secularities: Beyond the West, Beyond Modernities' 9, Leipzig University, 2019. For the theory of differentiation, see S. N. Eisenstadt, 'Social Change, Differentiation and Evolution', *American Sociological Review* 29, no. 3 (1964): 375–386.
4. To borrow this famous phrase, which is also the title of Sunil Khilnani's book. In the introduction to the 2012 edition, Khilnani notes, 'When I wrote *The Idea of India* in 1997, I wanted to show that the founding idea of India is anchored as much in resisting certain powerful seductions – the temptations for a clear, singular definition of nationhood, for the apparent neatness of authoritarian politics, for the clarities of a statist or pure market economy, for unambiguous alliances with other states – as it was in realizing declaratory visions.' One such declaratory vision of the founding leaders was the idea of India as a multireligious secular state. Sunil Khilnani, 'Introduction to the 2012 Edition', in *The Idea of India* (e-book), pp. 8–14 (New Delhi: Penguin Books, 2012 [1997]), p. 8.
5. Right at the outset, I would like to point out that the method of intellectual history followed in this book differs from contemporary studies in Indian Political Thought, where scholars have sought to 'retrieve' the philosophical and political foundations of Indian thinkers through a philological exercise. Ajay Skaria, for instance, contrasts Gandhi's Gujarati writings to his English translations to highlight the conceptual distance between Gandhi's thought and the liberal tradition. Ajay Skaria, *Unconditional Equality: Gandhi's Religion of Resistance* (Minneapolis: University of Minnesota Press, 2016). I discuss the methodology pursued in this book later in the chapter.
6. The word 'secular' was formally introduced to the preamble of the Indian constitution during Indira Gandhi's Emergency Rule in 1976 through the 42nd amendment and enacted by the Indian National Congress government.
7. I use the term '(political) secularism' to signify the ideology of state neutrality or non-discrimination towards religion. I discuss the term in detail in Chapter 1.
8. P. C. Joshi, 'Gandhi–Nehru Tradition and Indian Secularism', *Mainstream* 45, no. 48 (2007), https://www.mainstreamweekly.net/article432.html (accessed on 7 April 2021). Also see the section Stanley J. Tambiah, 'The

Gandhi–Nehru View on the Relation between Religion and State', in 'The Crisis of Secularism in India', in *Secularism and Its Critics*, ed. Rajeev Bhargava, pp. 418–453 (New Delhi: Oxford University Press, 2008 [1998]). I elaborate upon this dominant tradition of secularity later in this chapter.

9. Rajeev Bhargava notes that the secular state in post-colonial India was meant to 'impose limits on the political expression of cultural or religious conflicts between Hindus and Muslims, limits that were tragically transgressed immediately before and in the aftermath of the declaration of Independence in August 1947. The Nehru–Gandhi consensus on the secular state was grounded in the acceptance of the necessity of these limits and of the values they made possible'. See Bhargava, 'Introduction', in *Secularism and Its Critics*, p. 1.

10. It must be noted that the Westphalian system of states, where each state assumed absolute sovereignty vis-à-vis the other, were confessional states in the sense that each of them enforced religious confessionalisation over their subjects. For further discussion, see José Casanova, *Global Religious and Secular Dynamics: The Modern System of Classification* (Leiden: Brill, 2019). As such, what we today call a secular state has a very different meaning. For much of the nineteenth century, a person who merely denied 'the truth of Christianity in general, or of the existence of God' in England, could find himself behind bars for committing 'blasphemy'. Until the mid-1850s, students at the universities of Oxford and Cambridge had to take an oath subscribing to the thirty-nine articles of the Church of England. As late as 2015, a member of the royal family could be disqualified from succeeding to the Crown upon merely marrying a Roman Catholic. See Abinav Chandrachud, *Republic of Religion: The Rise and Fall of Colonial Secularism in India* (New Delhi: Penguin Random House India, 2020).

11. Sudipta Kaviraj, 'An Outline of a Revisionist Theory of Modernity', *European Journal of Sociology* 46, no. 3 (2005): 497–526, at 521–22, footnote 65. For a detailed argument, see Sudipta Kaviraj, 'Languages of Secularity', *Economic and Political Weekly* 48, no. 50 (2013): 93–102.

12. Although the Gandhi–Nehru tradition dominated Indian politics in the twentieth century, there were other competing secularist ideals, which did not gain traction. For instance, Vanya Bhargav argues that in the mid-1920s, the Hindu nationalist Lala Lajpat Rai espoused a 'radical' secular state and politics (that is, a hard-line position) free of religion

driven by a commitment to politico-moral ideals such as the prevention of religious conflict, promotion of equal citizenship, the protection of minorities from Hindu majoritarian domination, and respect for religious freedom and equality. I think Lajpat Rai's 'secular' ideas come close to the strict separation between religion and politics envisioned in French secularism. See Vanya Bhargav, 'Between Hindu and Indian: The Nationalist Thought of Lala Lajpat Rai', PhD dissertation, University of Oxford, 2018.

13. Talal Asad's *Formations of the Secular* remains one of the most influential books in the twenty-first century, which demonstrates the hegemony of the liberal Western discourse in 'the formations of the secular'. Talal Asad, *Formations of the Secular: Christianity, Islam, Modernity* (Stanford, CA: Stanford University Press, 2003).

14. For a critical engagement with the discourse of secularism as tolerance in India, see C. S. Adcock, *The Limits of Tolerance: Indian Secularism and the Politics of Religious Freedom* (New York: Oxford University Press, 2014). For a critical engagement with the discourse of religious freedom, see C. S. Adcock, 'Cow Protection and Minority Rights in India: Reassessing Religious Freedom', *Asian Affairs* 49, no. 2 (2018): 340–354. For an argument about the Eurocentric bias in the language of political modernity in general, see Dipesh Chakrabarty, *Provincializing Europe: Postcolonial Thought and Historical Difference* (Princeton: Princeton University Press, 2000).

15. For the story of the 'secular' from its foundational moment until today in the North Atlantic world, see Charles Taylor, *A Secular Age* (Cambridge, MA: Harvard University Press, 2007).

16. In arguing for 'multiple modernities', S. N. Eisenstadt points out how under conditions of modernity, non-western societies appropriate specific themes and institutional patterns of the 'original' Western modern civilization through 'continuous selection, reinterpretation, and reformulation' of these imported ideas. S. N. Eisenstadt, 'Multiple Modernities', *Daedalus* 129, no. 1 (2000): 1–29. Building upon Eisenstadt's argument, Sudipta Kaviraj draws attention to the role of 'improvisation' and 'reflexivity' in modernity. In arguing for multiple modernities, he points to the historical fact that the more modernity expands and spreads to different parts of the world, the more differentiated and plural it becomes. Kaviraj, 'An Outline of a Revisionist Theory of Modernity'. I find many recent scholarly accounts of 'multiple secularities' (see

note 1) to be undertaking a similar approach with regard to secularity or secularism.
17. The ideology of Hindutva, propagated by Hindu nationalists, seeks cultural and political domination of Hinduism in India. It is based on an exclusionary ideology and politics which identifies national identity with Hindu identity and considers Muslims and Christians as 'outsiders'.
18. The Citizenship Amendment Act, 2019 (CAA), explicitly excludes Muslims from the category of persecuted minorities in seeking Indian citizenship. In a detailed analysis of the CAA, Abhinav Chandrachud notes, 'In covering only some religious communities and not others, the CAA violates the principle of secularism which is a part of constitutional morality.' Abhinav Chandrachud, 'Secularism and the Citizenship Amendment Act', *Indian Law Review* 4, no. 2 (2020): 138–162, at p. 151.
19. Sudipta Kaviraj, 'Religion, Politics and Modernity', in *Crisis and Change in Contemporary India*, ed. Upendra Baxi and Bhikhu Parekh, pp. 295–316 (New Delhi: SAGE Publications, 1995), p. 300. Also see Rakesh Batabyal, 'In Search of Secular Template: History Writing in India in the First Decade of the Republic', *Studies in People's History* 3, no. 2 (2016): 216–228.
20. It was Nehru, more than Gandhi, who reconstructed the subcontinental history in this way. See Jawaharlal Nehru, *The Discovery of India* (Delhi: Oxford University Press, 1994 [1946]). In Gandhi's narrative such ideas are not central. Gandhi's reconstruction of Indian history, I argue in later chapters, is better understood through the lens of communal historiography. Despite this, his political thought does not lead in the direction of communalism.
21. Jürgen Habermas, 'An Awareness of What Is Missing', in *An Awareness of What Is Missing: Faith and Reason in a Post-Secular Age*, trans. Ciaran Cronin, ed. Jurgen Habermas et al., pp. 15–23 (Cambridge: Polity Press, 2010); Taylor, *A Secular Age*; José Casanova, *Public Religions in the Modern World* (Chicago: University of Chicago Press, 1994).
22. Casanova, *Public Religions*, p. 225.
23. For a critical appraisal of secularism, see Asad, *Formations of the Secular*; William E. Connolly, *Why I Am Not a Secularist* (Minneapolis: University of Minnesota Press, 1999); Saba Mahmood, *Religious Difference in a Secular Age: A Minority Report* (New Jersey: Princeton University Press, 2016). Also see the collection of essays on secularism in *Cultural Anthropology* 26, no. 4 (2011).

24. For a recent study on the debates of secularisation, see Casanova, *Global Religious and Secular Dynamics*.
25. Rajeev Bhargava, 'Political Secularism', in *The Oxford Handbook of Political Theory*, ed. John S. Dryzek, Bonnie Honig, and Anne Phillips, pp. 635–655 (Oxford: Oxford University Press, 2006). Also see Sudipta Kaviraj, 'Modernity, State and Toleration in Indian History: Exploring Accommodations and Partitions', in *Boundaries of Toleration*, ed. Alfred Stepan and Charles Taylor, pp. 233–266 (New York: Columbia University Press, 2014).
26. Thus, José Casanova observes that the plural term *religiones* was first used within Latin Christendom to refer to multiple Christian religious orders and *not* multiple religions. Casanova, *Global Religious and Secular Dynamics*, p. 11.
27. The religious minorities in post-colonial India are national minorities and not immigrant minorities, like in Europe. José Casanova notes that the debate on secularity has resurfaced in the heartland of secularisation – Western Europe – as a result of significant influx of 'new immigrant religions'. The dominating presence of Islam in Euro-America has opened up debates about what is called 'political Islam'. José Casanova, 'Public Religions Revisited', in *Religion: Beyond the Concept*, ed. Hent de Vries, pp. 101–119 (New York: Fordham University Press, 2008). For an argument about how the idea of political Islam is a modern notion, see Jocelyne Cesari, *What Is Political Islam?* (Boulder, CO: Lynne Rienner, 2018).
28. Kaviraj, 'Modernity, State and Toleration in Indian History'.
29. For instance, in the debate on secularism in India, both T. N. Madan and Ashis Nandy invoke Gandhi to criticise secularism. I discuss this 1990s debate in Chapter 1. For the 1990s debate on secularism in India, see Rajeev Bhargava (ed.), *Secularism and Its Critics* (New Delhi: Oxford University Press: 2008 [1998]).
30. Originally the term 'social imaginary' was introduced by Cornelius Castoriadis. Taylor distinguishes imaginaries from theories as follows: (*a*) imaginaries are how ordinary people 'imagine' their world. This is then not represented in theoretical terms but instead carried in images, stories and legends; (*b*) while theory circulates within a small number of people, imaginaries are shared by large groups of people; and thus (*c*) social imaginary is that common understanding that makes possible common practices and a widely shared sense of legitimacy. Charles

Taylor, *Modern Social Imaginaries* (Durham: Duke University Press, 2004).

31. For instance, see Nehru's articulation of a secular state in India in *Jawaharlal Nehru, An Anthology*, ed. Sarvepalli Gopal Sarvepalli (Delhi: Oxford University Press, 1980), p. 330 and pp. 332–333. If we literally translate 'secularism' as 'religious non-discrimination', then *dharmnirpekshata* (religious impartiality) or *panthnirpekshata* (sectarian impartiality) are the terms that signify this meaning of secularism in India. However, it is very common in India to understand secularism in terms of *sarva dharma samabhava* (equality of all religions).

32. I say that the Gandhi–Nehru tradition was dominant but not hegemonic because although this ideal was constitutionally embraced (via Nehruvian secularism), in political practice there has been no consensus.

33. There are, of course, other conceptions of secularity in contemporary India. Nadja-Christina Schneider, for instance, directs attention to visual media to show how cause marketing campaigns 'introduce or mediate an understanding of secularity as care for and connectedness with adherents of other religions'. Nadja-Christina Schneider, 'Tea for Interreligious Harmony? Cause Marketing as a New Field of Experimentation with Visual Secularity in India', Working Paper Series of the HCAS 'Multiple Secularities: Beyond the West, Beyond Modernities' 20, Leipzig University, 2020, p. 5.

34. This is reflected in the state policy towards affirmative action, which calls for representation of weaker communities (Scheduled Castes [SCs], Scheduled Tribes [STs] and Other Backward Classes [OBCs]) in legislatures, executives and government employment. For instance, the policy of reservation (as part of affirmative action) applies only to low-caste Dalit Hindus (SCs), and not to Dalit Christians and Muslims, because the state does not consider the existence of the caste system outside the fold of Hinduism. In reality, however, over centuries, many Dalits have sought to escape their sub-human status and socio-economic oppression sanctioned by the caste system by converting to other religions, particularly Islam, Buddhism, Christianity and Sikhism. Such religious conversions have resulted in the replication of caste-like hierarchy and discrimination within other religions.

35. Rajendra Prasad quoted from Faisal Devji, *Muslim Zion: Pakistan as a Political Idea* (London: Harvard University Press, 2013), p. 30.

36. Based on the principle of *cuius regio, eius religio* (meaning 'whose realm, their religion' in Latin), the Treaty of Augsburg, 1555, largely created mono-confessional states with relatively clear-cut religious boundaries which associated state with confession and territory. Later, the Peace of Westphalia, 1648, which is claimed to have provided the foundation for the modern state system, reiterated this principle. See Casanova, *Global Religious and Secular Dynamics*.
37. Janaki Bakhle, 'Putting Global Intellectual History in Its Place', in *Global Intellectual History*, ed. Samuel Moyn and Andrew Sartori, pp. 228–253 (New York: Columbia University Press, 2013), p. 233. In this essay, Bakhle has noted the influence of and similarities between Mazzini and Savarkar.
38. V. D. Savarkar, 'Essentials of Hindutva', in *Selected Works of Veer Savarkar*, vol. 4 (New Delhi: Abhishek, 2007).
39. In the ideal model of democratic politics, however, electoral voting creates temporary and conjectural majorities and minorities.
40. Kaviraj, 'Religion, Politics and Modernity', p. 299. Kaviraj argues how colonial modernity, through measures such as the census, transformed pre-modern and traditional identities, like caste, from 'fuzzy' to 'enumerated' communities.
41. Two most influential scholars of the history of political thought are the 'Cambridge School' historians Quentin Skinner and J. G. A. Pocock. See J. G. A. Pocock, 'The History of Political Thought: A Methodological Inquiry', in *Philosophy, Politics and Society (Second Series)*, ed. Peter Laslett and W. G. Runciman, pp. 183–202 (Oxford: Basil Blackwell 1964 [1962]). Also see Quentin Skinner, 'Meaning and Understanding in the History of Ideas', in *Visions of Politics, Vol. 1: Regarding Method*, pp. 57–89 (New York: Cambridge University Press, 2002 [1969]). For a criticism of Skinner's methodology, see Bhikhu Parekh and R. N. Berki, 'The History of Political Ideas: A Critique of Q. Skinner's Methodology', *Journal of the History of Ideas* 34, no. 2 (1973): 163–184. Also see James Tully, *Meaning and Context: Quentin Skinner and His Critics* (Princeton and New Jersey: Princeton University Press, 1988).
42. Quentin Skinner, 'Interpretation and the Understanding of Speech Acts', in *Visions of Politics, Vol. 1: Regarding Method*, pp. 103–127 (New York: Cambridge University Press, 2002).
43. M. K. Gandhi, 'Indian Home Rule or Hind Swaraj', trans. M. K. Gandhi, in *M.K. Gandhi: Hind Swaraj and Other Writings*, ed. Anthony J. Parel,

pp. 1–125 (New York: Cambridge University Press, 2009 [1997]); B. R. Ambedkar, 'Annihilation of Caste: Speech Prepared for the Annual Conference of the Jat-Pat-Todak Mandal of Lahore but Not Delivered', in *Annihilation of Caste: The Annotated Critical Edition*, ed. S. Anand, pp. 181–356 (London: Verso, 2014).

44. Aishwary Kumar, *Radical Equality: Ambedkar, Gandhi and the Risk of Democracy* (Stanford: Stanford University Press, 2015), p. 11.
45. I return to these questions with regard to Gandhi's political thought in Chapter 2.
46. Samuel Moyn and Andrew Sartori, 'Approaches to Global Intellectual History', in *Global Intellectual History*, ed. Samuel Moyn and Andrew Sartori, pp. 3–30 (New York: Columbia University Press, 2013), p. 7.
47. Ibid., p. 19.
48. For instance, with regard to Islamic reformism in the Arab world, Florian Zemmin notes, 'Islamic reformists have rejected secularism almost unanimously as an external political regime that evolved in Christian Europe and is alien to Islam.' Florian Zemmin, 'Secularism, Secularity and Islamic Reformism', in *Companion to the Study of Secularity*, ed. HCAS 'Multiple Secularities: Beyond the West, Beyond Modernities', Leipzig University, 2019, p. 1.
49. Rochana Bajpai, *Debating Difference: Group Rights and Liberal Democracy* (New Delhi: Oxford University Press, 2011). Karuna Mantena's article, 'Another Realism: The Politics of Gandhian Nonviolence', *American Political Science Review* 106, no. 2 (2012): 455–470, is another very good example of how one may undertake an exercise in comparative political theory.
50. Michael Freeden and Andrew Vincent, 'Introduction: The Study of Comparative Political Thought', in *Comparative Political Thought: Theorizing Practices*, ed. Michael Freeden and Andrew Vincent, pp. 1–23 (Oxon: Routledge, 2013), p. 15.
51. Ibid., p. 25.
52. Ibid.
53. Charles Taylor, 'The Polysemy of the Secular', *Social Research: An International Quarterly* 76, no. 4 (2009): 1143–1166, at 1150.

1
DEBATING THE SECULAR BEYOND THE WEST

INTRODUCTION

In the first half of the twentieth century, undivided British India saw a politically fractious and ultimately violent and bloody resolution to the question 'What is a nation?' Mirroring the Westphalian model, this political resolution came in the form of partition of India and the creation of two nation-states in 1947: India with a secular constitution and a Hindu majority population, and the Islamic state of Pakistan with a Muslim majority population. The Indian National Congress (hereafter, Congress), which led the movement for national independence, became the dominant national party in independent India. Although, after its independence from British colonial rule, India was declared a secular republic, the term 'secularism' itself was introduced very late in the official rhetoric of the Indian constitution.[1] The trauma and bloodshed caused by the partition, where thousands of Hindus and Muslims killed each other in the name of religion, aided in hardening a political discourse in post-colonial India, where 'secular' largely came to signify the universal homogeneous category of the citizen and 'communal' signalled all forms of communitarian politics based on religious identity. At the same time, this discourse also reflected, what has been called, 'the liberalism of fear',[2] where constitutional rights are not assumed to be given equally to every citizen. Rather, this kind of liberal politics actively seeks proper constitutional and institutional measures to safeguard citizens from the fear of 'abuse of power and intimidation of the defenceless'.[3] These concerns gave the Indian constitution a multicultural inflection such that protection of minority religious communities through constitutional and cultural safeguards became one of the defining features of Indian secularism. For instance, it provided the possibility to argue that changes in the personal laws of minority religious communities could only be brought about when these communities were themselves 'ready' for them. In contemporary Indian politics, it is this idea of protection of minorities through constitutional and cultural safeguards which has been increasingly attacked by the Hindu right as 'pseudo-secular', as it is seen as a means to garner votes through 'minority appeasement'. The right-wing groups in India see them as preferential policies that have inhibited the development of the idea of a universal citizenship and a common national culture. In order to shed light on the dominant secular imaginary of the Gandhi–Nehru tradition in relation to the debates in global intellectual history of secularity, in this chapter I will revisit the conceptual and theoretical debates on secular and its related terms, with modern and contemporary India as the point of reference. A whole chapter in respect to clarification of terms related to the secular seems imperative, although they have been extensively written about both within and outside India. A recently edited volume on South Asia noted that in both scholarly and popular usage, secularism is equated with secularisation, and both are made interchangeable with state and societal tolerance towards religious minorities.[4] The chapter is divided into five sections. The first four sections will elaborate upon the secular and its family of cognates, namely secularisation, secularism and secularity. The last concluding section will end with some remarks on the issue of the religion–state–society relationship in modern and contemporary India.

SECULAR

Etymologically, the word 'secular' comes from a notion of time in Latin Christendom; its root is to be found in the medieval Latin word *saeculum*, which means 'century' or 'age'.[5] José Casanova remarks that today the word 'secular' has become 'a central modern category – theologico-philosophical, legal-political, and cultural-anthropological – to construct, codify, grasp, and experience a realm or reality differentiated from the religious'.[6] Outlining the features of the secular, as it developed within Latin Christendom, Charles Taylor observes that, in the beginning, it was a non-oppositional dyad term. Here, the secular had to do with the century, that is, profane or ordinary time, which was contrasted with the eternal or higher time. While certain times, places, persons, institutions and actions were seen as related to the sacred or higher time, others were located in ordinary time, which was 'out there in profane time'.[7] Thus, in the beginning the word 'secular' was used for ordinary time as against higher time to distinguish two dimensions of the same temporal existence. From the seventeenth century onwards, however, a new possibility arose, where secular as profane or ordinary time was made independent of its dyad and thereby denied any relations to higher time. This gradually led to a new conception of social life, which asserted that 'secular was all there was'.[8] This is what Taylor has called the 'secular age' in the North Atlantic world ('the West'),[9] where the secular order was clearly separated from the higher or transcendent order. Here, the secular was opposed to 'claims on resources or allegiances made in the name of something transcendent to this world and its interests'.[10] As such, those who imagined a secular world in this new sense saw these latter claims based on a belief in the transcendent world as unfounded and deemed them to be tolerated so long as they did not challenge 'the interests of worldly power and well-being'.[11] Taylor notes that this clear-cut distinction which divided and opposed 'this-world' or the immanent from the transcendent was a product and invention of the development of Latin Christendom and has become 'part of our way of seeing things in the West'.[12] He further argues that, at first, the independence and self-sufficiency claimed by the secular was partial and limited, as in the eighteenth-century Deist version, where God was still seen as the 'artificer of the immanent order'.[13] Thus, in the Deist version, religion was still seen as necessary for a good social order. According to Taylor, the first unambiguous assertion of the self-sufficiency of the secular came with the radical phases of the French Revolution in the late eighteenth century, where a rational moral order was instituted and expressed in religion's separation from the state. The state for the radical republicans was to be founded on ideas of exclusion of religion from the sociopolitical domain. This is the spirit of *laïcité*, which, Taylor remarks, is still not entirely dead in contemporary France, as is evident in the discussions about banning the Muslim headscarf (*hijab*).

Taylor narrates the history of the secular in the West to show how its trajectory was complex and ambiguous such that in its evolutionary course the dyad religious and secular itself has undergone 'profound mutation'.[14] So while, to begin with, the dyad was 'internal' in that each term is impossible without its other (non-oppositional dyad), after the mutations the dyads became 'external' such that 'secular' and 'religious' are opposed to each other.[15] Taylor goes on to argue that in the post-Deist modes of secularism, humanist ideology is based on nature, and what has become unacceptable, in turn, is any form of public religion: 'faith must be relegated to the private sphere'.[16] Such a secular worldview claims a self-sufficient social morality, which generates another claim that there is such a thing as 'reason alone'.[17] Taylor calls this self-sufficient social morality 'exclusive humanism', which he argues is 'at the heart of modern secularity'.[18] It is from such a history of the secular that Western secularism gets its present inflection: first, the separation of religion and state, and, then, the relegation of religion to a private sphere, where it cannot interfere with the common life of the public-political. Taylor remarks that the final satisfactory solution is where 'religion is finally hived off and relegated to the margins of political life'.[19] He argues that today a commonsensical understanding of the term 'secular' refers to post-reformation and post-Enlightenment practices and institutions in the West that formally separated private religious belief from public and political life. Can this foundational idea of the secular with a clear-cut distinction and separation of 'this-world', from the 'other-world', travel to the non-Western world in more inventive and imaginative ways? According to Taylor, although secularism emerged as a response to the political problems of Western Christian societies of modern Euro-America, it is applicable to non-Christian and non-Western societies that have become modern.

Talal Asad's *Formations of the Secular* continues to remain one of the most influential critical studies of the concepts and practices related to the secular in the modern world.[20] His criticism of secularism is based on the observation that it 'presupposes new concepts of "religion", "ethics"," and "politics", and new imperatives associated with them'.[21] Asad's criticism of secularism is based on the argument that this ideology is not simply modern state's answer to a question of social peace and tolerance; rather, it is an 'enactment' by which the political medium of citizenship redefines and transcends 'particular and differentiating practices of the self', which are based on class, religion and gender.[22] He goes on to note that the distinctive feature of modern liberal governance is 'statecraft that uses "self-discipline", and "participation", "law", and "economy"' as its political strategy.[23] Furthermore, Asad shows how secularism, as a doctrine of the state, is based on a distinction between private reason and public principle, where religion is placed in the former. I reiterate this well-known criticism of secularism in this section on the secular because central to Asad's criticism is the premise that the secular cannot be understood independently of the religious, such that they are entangled in a dialectical relationship with each other. He notes, 'representations of "the secular" and "the religious" in modern and modernizing states mediate people's identities, help shape their sensibilities, and guarantee their experiences'.[24] As such, a major concern of Asad's book is not just secularism but the 'secular', which, he states, is 'conceptually prior to the political doctrine of "secularism"' because 'over time a variety of concepts, practices, and sensibilities have come together to form the "secular"'.[25] The following chapters on M. K. Gandhi will show how he almost seems to have anticipated the Asadian critique of the secular and modern statecraft. And yet, as these chapters will argue, the variety of concepts, practices and sensibilities that came together to give expression to Gandhian religious thought and politics do not lead in a direction where such politics can be said to be opposed to secularism as it came to be conceived in India. In Indian Political Thought, Gandhi is paradoxically seen to affirm both religious politics and secularism. In this book, I closely examine this paradox to argue that the Gandhian holistic vision of social life does not elicit an adversarial position towards Indian secularism. And that is why I claim that it is possible to talk, indeed common in India to hear, about the secular ideals of the 'Gandhi–Nehru tradition'.[26]

SECULARISATION

Half a century ago the theory of secularisation gained prominence in social sciences, and its dominance in the field influenced theories of secularism. This theory, which proclaimed the declining relevance of religion in modern societies, was based on two different propositions.[27] The first one laid out a series of empirically verifiable propositions based on the evidence of secularisation of European societies under modernity. The evidence of secularisation was based on the following observations: first, the long-term loss of power and prestige of religious institutions, such as churches, under modernity and the comparative dominance of modern secular institutions, such as nation-states, democratic politics, market-driven economy, and so on; second, the general decline of religious practices in European societies, such as falling church attendance and participation in religious rites like baptism, church marriages and funerals; third, the decline in religious belief, that is, the loss of belief in God. The second proposition, which has been rightly identified as the more problematic aspect of this theory and has been largely debunked, attributed this evidence of secularisation in Europe to a more general process of modernisation. It is this aspect of secularisation theory which relegated religious life to a pre-modern phase of human development and declared the triumph of secularisation under modernity. Secularisation, in this second aspect, was either seen as a 'normal' path towards modernity and progress, or forced on to a society due to conditions of modernisation. It was, in other words, seen as a feature of modernity itself. It was contended that the march of science, industrialisation, urbanisation, technological advancement, the emergence of an individualist and a capitalist society, and so on would eventually relegate religion to a marginal status in society.[28] Thus, Casanova remarks:

> What could have been a plausible historical narrative of particular European socio-historical developments was transformed into a universal teleological grand narrative of what was supposed to happen to all human societies as they became more modern. The theory of secularization postulated that all modern societies would become less religious and more secular.[29]

The re-emergence of religion in the public-political sphere in the 1980s, what Casanova calls 'public religion', has brought this grand narrative of secularisation into question.[30] By drawing on the writings of Taylor, in this section I will touch upon this triumphalist narrative of secularisation, prominently forwarded by theories of modernisation, through a brief excursion into this putatively ineluctable modernity. Taylor distinguishes between two kinds of theories of modernity – cultural and acultural.[31] A cultural theory of modernity sees transformations in the modern West in terms of the rise of a new culture, whereby contemporary Western society is seen as a culture, among others,[32] with its own specific understandings of person, nature, the good, and so on. It is usually contrasted to all others, including its own predecessor civilisation.[33] In contrast, an acultural theory of modernity describes these transformations in terms of some culture-neutral operation, where such transformation is seen as something which any traditional society could undergo and probably will even be forced to undergo. According to Taylor, a paradigm case of the acultural theory of modernity and secularisation is Max Weber's conception of rationalisation and disenchantment in the modern world. By rationalisation, Weber referred to a set of interrelated social processes by which the modern world had been systematically transformed into a rational system. For Weber, a result of rationalisation was the disenchantment of reality, which contemporary theorists have equated with the secularisation of values and attitudes.[34] Since such theories of secularisation are based on some universal principles – here, rationalisation of sociopolitical and economic spheres – which can be achieved by all human societies, Taylor labels them to be essentially acultural theories. When confronted with diverse socio-historical processes, theories of secularisation based on such Weberian insights either morph from a description of a historical process to a normative theory, where secularisation of society *ought to happen* for it to be modern, or declare the failure of secularisation in certain societies.

Such master narratives of secularisation, or what Taylor calls 'subtraction stories',[35] not only provide *a* lens through which one describes secularisation but also come with attendant claims of civilisational superiority and normalisation of certain values and attitudes, including the dominance of an empirical-scientific approach to knowledge claims, of individualism, negative freedom and instrumental rationality. The claim here is that a modern secularised society *will* be animated by these values because '... they are what we humans "normally" value, once we are no longer impeded or blinded by false or superstitious beliefs and the stultifying modes of life which accompany them. Once myth and error are dissipated, these are the only games in town.'[36] Such theories of secularisation, Sudipta Kaviraj notes, pre-commits one to write about the decline of religion, although the entire point of the analysis should be to ascertain whether religion has suffered a decline under modern conditions or not.[37] Thus, acultural theories of secularisation – which, seeing the Western trajectory, declared religion's decline and privatisation in modern societies – are incapable of explaining the resurgence of religions across the world since the late twentieth century and its marked visibility and relevance in the public-political sphere today. Until recently, this ahistorical theory of secularisation dominated social sciences. Unable to account for historical difference, this narrative of secularisation gradually came to be postulated as a normative theory which saw secularisation of spheres as both 'natural' and desirable, where the transition from a traditional religious to a modern secular conception of the world is a universal phenomenon that 'ought to happen' or 'will happen'. Thus, this theory of secularisation of society as a normative idea or a general universal process of human and societal development identified the Western path as the universal and inevitable path to modernity and secularity. Since this universal history of secularisation, with its normative overtones, has been shown to be problematic and largely debunked, I will not explore it any further in this book.[38]

Casanova has clarified that it is *not* the secularisation of European societies which is under question; rather, recent global developments, in the last forty years or so, have questioned the teleological projection of European secularisation onto the rest of the world. Thus, the understanding of secularisation as a process, whereby religion's role and place are accessed vis-à-vis modern conditions, has found greater acceptability.[39] In a revisionist understanding of secularisation, Casanova differentiates three aspects of this theory. According to him, the 'core' aspect of the secularisation theory is the conceptualisation of the process of societal modernisation as 'a process of functional differentiation and emancipation of the secular spheres – primarily, the state, the economy, and science – from the religious sphere....'[40] The two other 'subtheses' of this theory are the claims of decline and privatisation of religion that have been shown to be cases of European exceptionalism, rather than a universal trend. Casanova argues that it is this core aspect of 'differentiation' of spheres which is still defensible in the theory of secularisation. In other words, secularisation here is reconceptualised in terms of a theory of differentiation which claims that the process of modernisation leads to a functionally and institutionally differentiated society, where the main social functions and major institutional spheres, including religion, progressively become more specialised and therefore more differentiated from one another. Casanova's secularisation thesis thus retains a universalist claim as he maintains that there is a 'core' to secularisation which is that of functional differentiation of modern societies.[41] In this book, in Chapter 2 on Gandhi, we will see how Gandhi's holistic vision of society challenged this idea of functional differentiation as a feature of modern society. Gandhi's thought and politics, I argue, provide a counter-narrative to the secularisation thesis. If even the central basis of Casanova's secularisation thesis has been challenged in modern but non-Western societies like India, what remains of secularisation? I think it is here that Taylor's interventions become important, because in narrating the story of secularisation in the West he shifts attention away from theories of differentiation and does not make any universalist claims beyond the North Atlantic world.[42]

One of the most influential narratives of secularisation in the West has come from Taylor in his book *A Secular Age*. Through this narrative, he seeks to answer the question 'why was it virtually impossible not to believe in God in, say, 1500 in our Western society, while in 2000 many of us find this not only easy, but even inescapable?'[43] When Taylor reconfigures the conception of secularisation in this way, he also points out that his secularisation narrative does not extend to contemporary societies like Islamic countries, Africa and India. In an intellectual and philosophical enquiry, he traces the changes in the nature and sensibility of religious belief from a pre-modern 'enchanted' universe to a modern 'disenchanted' universe in the North Atlantic world.[44] Taylor asserts that it is this phenomenological experience that marks 'the secular age' in the West, irrespective of the extent to which people living in this age may still hold religious or theistic beliefs. In Taylor's analysis then secularisation in Euro-America is explained in terms of an evolutionary story of the phenomenological experience of elite unbelief in the eighteenth century to a process of mass secularisation in the twenty-first century.[45] He observes that the period from roughly 1500 to 1700 in Europe saw great confessional conflict, the banning of 'heretical' confessions, forced emigration and even armed clashes. All these events, however, did not offer a persuasive argument for the abandonment of the religious forms in dispute until an alternative social imaginary came on the scene that opened the possibility of living outside these religious forms. Taylor describes this emerging alternative in terms of an 'immanent frame' (IF).[46] According to him,

> ... the fullness of the IF comes when the new economic, social, educational, and political disciplines and practices end up entrenching a new social imaginary that projects our human social condition as the intersection of impersonal, this-worldly orders: cosmic (the universe understood in the terms of post-Galilean natural science), political (the modern state with a historically chosen constitution), and moral (universal human rights and equality).[47]

Taylor further outlines three types of secularity. In secularity 1, common institutions and practices including the state can function with no reference to God or a transcendent realm (that is, secularised public spaces). In secularity 2, people no longer believe and practise religious faiths (that is, the decline of belief and practice). Secularity 3, which is the focus of Taylor's book, refers to the 'conditions of belief' in which a multiplicity of beliefs as well as unbelief exist side by side such that faith in God is just one option among others and 'frequently not the easiest to embrace'.[48] He argues that the evolution of secularity 3 as conditions of belief required a complex interplay of factors, the crucial transforming move in the process being 'exclusive humanism'.[49] By exclusive humanism, he means the idea that modern secularity in the West was coterminous with the rise of a society in which a purely self-sufficient humanism became a widely available option. Exclusive humanism accepts '... no final goals beyond human flourishing, nor any allegiance to anything else beyond this flourishing. Of no previous society was this true'.[50]

Taylor's spatially and temporally limited narrative of secularisation in the Western world raises the question 'What happened elsewhere?'[51] According to Kaviraj, the most startling aspect of Taylor's narrative is a crucial revision which destabilises the conventional secularisation narrative: the claim that the establishment of the science-driven immanent frame does not inevitably lead people to a disenchanted universe of mandatory unbelief. Taylor's narrative shows that human beings in the modern West generally accept the immanent frame, but they may still remain undecided between a belief in God and disbelief. Kaviraj therefore argues that assent to a scientific view of the world does not necessarily force people into disbelief in God for the sake of pure logical consistency. Taylor's secularisation narrative has serious and complex implications for the study of secularity in non-Western societies as it moves away from universal claims where exploring secularities of the world may be seen as coterminous with a thesis on functional differentiation of spheres, or simply a search for exclusive humanism, or even a social imaginary dominated by the immanent frame. As Kaviraj notes, Taylor's revised version of European secularity allows us to think about what really happened in non-Western societies without a constant reference to the West. It opens up conceptual space to investigate 'multiple secularities'.[52] It thus becomes possible to ask: Is there a conception of Indian secularity? What does secularity mean in modern India?

SECULARITY

I discuss the concept of secularity next because Taylor's narrative of secularisation blurs conceptual boundaries, if any, between secularisation and secularity. In this book, I will use the term 'secularity' to distinguish it from both the *process* of secularisation (which may be one aspect of secularity) and secularism, which is an *ideology* of the modern state. I understand secularity to connote a modern epistemological characterisation of the social world wherein religion and secular are distinguished in terms of conceptual distinctions as well as structural or institutional and symbolic forms of differentiation of social spheres.[53] It is also a 'historical category' in so far as such distinctions and differentiations develop as a response to social change brought in by new or unique conditions created by modernity.[54] The notion of secularity is different from the doctrine of secularism because it is not an expression of modern state ideology of separation of church and state. Unlike state secularism, which is usually a top—down approach, where it is the state which determines the relationship among religion, state and society, expressions of secularity can emerge from below, such that it is the society which influences imaginations and articulations of the religion–state–society relationship.[55] As such, it need not be closely associated with the projects of modern state. Conceived this way, the term 'secularity' may be used to express ideas, actions and politics which may even be anti-state or anti-government. Furthermore, since it is not a state project of separation, there may be articulations of secularity which oppose the ideology of secularism.[56] One of the central arguments in this book is that although Gandhi's ideas and his religious politics evince a counter-narrative of secularity, they are nevertheless not against the idea of religious non-discrimination as articulated in Indian secularism. Secularity may also be distinguished from secularisation as it is simply not a universal description of the processual changes, understood in terms of functional and institutional differentiation, that a society under modernity undergoes. Taylor, for instance, uses the term to capture the coming together of a wide variety of ideas, practices and processes under the influence of modernity in a contingent manner, where it is 'the fruit of new inventions, newly constructed self-understandings and related practices'.[57] In other words, although 'secularity' belongs to the family of 'secularism' and 'secularisation', it may be conceived in relative independence to them. In recent years, scholars have also attempted to employ it as a 'heuristic concept' and not simply understand it only in relation to modernity.[58] For instance, in order to historicise secularity – both spatially (beyond the 'West') and temporally (beyond 'modernity') – Monika Wohlrab-Sahr and Christophe Kleine have used the term to identify forms of religious-secular distinctions in ancient and medieval periods. By defining secularity in terms of 'conceptual distinctions and institutional differentiations between the religious and the secular', they argue that 'forms of distinction and differentiation existed from early on, which, under certain conditions, could later be related to the secular-religious binary'.[59] In this book, however, I limit the conceptual reach of secularity to modernity because I use the terms 'religion' and 'secular' as modern epistemological categories.[60] Lastly, scholars have also used the term 'secularity' to distinguish it from 'atheism' and 'non-religion', where atheism refers to an explicit and principled rejection of religion, and non-religion signifies indifference to or even rejection of religion.[61]

In order to examine a concept like secularity in its historical and cultural context one has to engage with historical difference. If secularity is understood in terms of a declined relevance of religion in society, then clearly it is not a familiar idea in Indian culture. To understand secularity in its historicity, it requires emendation. The framework of 'multiple secularities' provides such a possibility as it opens up conceptual and discursive space to investigate histories of secularity outside the modern West.[62] In this book, I use the conceptual idea of multiple secularities based on the insight that societies may undertake multiple paths to modernity and secularity, such that the content of the modern and secular is determined by the sequence in which modern processes appeared in each society.[63] Here, I follow Kaviraj's revisionist theory of modernity, where he argues for a 'sequential' reading of the history of modernity, where the precise sequence in which the constituent processes of modernity appear in a particular society (like democracy, individualism, capitalism, secularism) determines the specific form of modernity in that context.[64] He states:

> If we accept the sequential view seriously, we should not treat modernity as a general, ubiquitous condition that has an emergently homogeneous character everywhere, but as a historically contingent combination of its constituent elements which tend to produce different histories of the modern.[65]

If one follows this revisionist account of modernity, an argument based on historical difference between Europe and India may be forwarded. As we know, in Europe, institutions of state secularism emerged and entrenched themselves in the aftermath of religious civil wars and long before the framing of democratic constitutions. Consequently, at the moment of its inception, secularism as a state principle did not undergo a democratic test in these societies. By contrast, in post-colonial India, democracy (via universal suffrage) and state secularism were established at the same time and through the same constitution. The history of partition of India further demonstrated that secular principles were contentious from the start in Indian politics. A dominant strand of Muslim nationalism formed the state of Pakistan rejecting that principle, and a large segment of nationalists in India remained unreconciled to it. As a result, Kaviraj notes that in post-colonial India, unlike in Europe, 'the whole question of the secular state ... was implicitly subject to a democratic test. Ever since, this has been a question that can be reopened if Hindu nationalists get a sizeable electoral presence'.[66] Thus, approaching the question of secularity through the conceptual framework of multiple secularities and a sequential reading of history opens up the possibility of diverse narratives or paths to secularity without treating Western history as a modular or contrast case to all non-Western histories.[67]

SECULARISM

The word 'secularism' is associated with the emergence of the modern state. Broadly speaking, secularism is a modern state ideology, which seeks separation of religion from political power, what is known as 'church–state separation'. It is a secular ideology which advocates the state's impartiality or non-discrimination towards religions. Scholars like Charles Taylor and Rajeev Bhargava have argued that secularism does not simply signify a doctrine of separation of church and state, where the state does not intervene with or in religion. This is simply a *feature* of secularism. These scholars also conceive secularism in terms of its *function* as a 'value-based' doctrine, which calls for religious non-discrimination in the name of protecting certain substantive values, such as liberty (of worship), equality (of faith) and fraternity or peace.[68] Bhargava states:

Just as without separation there is no secularism, just so a value-less separation does not add up to secularism. In this sense, secularism is a universal normative doctrine. But, it does not follow that these elements are interpreted or related to each other in any one particular way, or that there is a single ideal way in which they should be interpreted or related to one another.[69]

As we have already seen in the section on the secular, Taylor charts out the canonical background for a conventional understanding of a secularist regime in a three-stage history: first, the distinction between church and state; second, the separation of church and state; and finally, the sidelining of religion from state and public life. Taylor has argued that it is this crude idea with its deep assumptions of a clear immanent and transcendent world and a sharp public and private distinction that began to travel from the West to countries in Asia, Africa and the Middle East. His narrative of secularity in the Western world reminds the reader that even before the idea of secularism started travelling to the non-Western world, it was an ambiguous and deeply fraught conception in the West itself. The lively debate that we are witnessing today between the defenders of secularism and post-colonial critics may be narrowed down to an epistemological difference that Taylor describes as the contingent 'polysemy of the secular'.[70] His analysis of the secular opens up conceptual space and empirical possibility for varieties of secularism such that there is an American secularism, French secularism, British secularism, Turkish secularism, Indian secularism, *ad infinitum*. But for most critics, the concept of secularism is itself problematic because of its Christian origins and therefore its Western character. There is a deep uncritical assumption here about the relationship between the process of secularisation and the normative doctrine of secularism. By focusing on the debates on secularism in India, it is this unquestioned relationship between secularisation and secularism that I wish to focus on in the next section.

Usually, a criticism of secularism in India highlights the embedded cultural character of secularism and its historical association and emergence in the context of secularisation of Western society.[71] T. N. Madan, for instance, has argued that in South Asia, 'secularism is impossible as a shared credo of life, it is impracticable as a basis for state action and impotent as a blueprint for the foreseeable future'.[72] According to him, secularism cannot be a shared conception of social life because a majority of people in South Asia are active adherents of some religious faith. It is impracticable as a basis for state action because the stance of religious neutrality by the state is difficult to maintain. Lastly, secularism is also impotent as the basis for state action in future because it is incapable of countering religious fundamentalism and fanaticism. Bhargava identifies the first two arguments against secularism which attack the Western character of secularism as 'the cultural inadaptability thesis'.[73] Madan's criticism about secularism's cultural inadaptability is based on the observation that devoid of Western-style secularisation, secularism has come under crisis in India. He argues that the historical process of secularisation in the West is a condition for state secularism and both of them are dependent on a Christian culture. Secularisation and secularism, in this view, are 'a gift of Christianity', where the latter emerged from the dialectic of modern science and Protestantism.[74] Madan argues that unlike other religious traditions, Christianity underwent a process of secularisation because of the seventeenth-century scientific revolution and the rise of Protestantism. It is in such a historical context that secularism emerged as the separation between church and state. He contends that when modernisation introduces secularism to non-Western societies, where religious traditions are marked by their high degree of religiosity in the public domain, secularism's existence is weak in these societies. As a doctrine, it then exists only empirically and is not disseminated ideologically. Madan's argument therefore points out that secularisation of society is a necessary condition for state secularism to succeed.

Taylor's theoretical interventions regarding the secular, that I discussed earlier, however, show that Madan's criticisms may be misplaced. First, Madan's construal of secularism is based on an excessively theoretical reading the separation of religion and state. A historical analysis of state secularism in Western societies demonstrates that even there we find varieties of secular states, such that separation may range from an extremely hard-line understanding and institutional arrangement of 'strict non-interference', to 'mutual exclusion', to 'equidistance'.[75] Furthermore, Bhargava argues that a commitment to political neutrality for a secular state can also be understood in terms of 'principled distance' where state policy may require the state to follow a strategy where it intervenes and also abstains from religious practices.[76] In other words, a 'wall of separation' between religion and state may not be the only kind of political neutrality of a secular state.[77] Second, according to Bhargava, Madan's claim that secularism enjoins believers to leave their religious convictions in private when they step into public life conceptually confuses between two types of secularism: ethical and political secularism. This conceptual distinction between political and ethical secularism separates the doctrine of secularism from the process of secularisation. According to Bhargava, ethical secularism separates religion from politics for the sake of some ultimate ideal, such as democracy or autonomy, which promises a better life. In this sense, the notion of ethical secularism can be linked to the process of secularisation, where the promotion of a high ideal(s) by the state can eventually lead to a secularised society. Political secularism, on the other hand, simply requires 'a policy of restraint and toleration' from the state.[78] Bhargava argues that Indian secularism is based on the idea of political secularism, which only demands that the state should be politically neutral from 'all religious and non-religious ultimate ideals'.[79] His argument seeks to demonstrate that Indian state's principles are based on the notion of secularism which is compatible with a high degree of religiosity in the public domain. Lastly, apart from theoretical clarification, a socio-historical explanation may be advanced to argue why secularism became necessary for post-colonial India. It may be argued that as the sociopolitical situation in the Indian subcontinent drastically changed in the late 1940s, eventually leading to the partition in 1947, the political leaders saw the establishment of a secular state as an answer to that crisis. That is, the institution of a secular state was seen as normatively appropriate from the point of view of statecraft.[80]

Another criticism similar to Madan's argument about secularism's cultural inadaptability comes from Ashis Nandy, who, somewhat misleadingly, declares himself to be an 'anti-secularist'.[81] Like Talal Asad, Nandy's charge against secularism should be placed within a larger critique of modern statecraft. According to Nandy, modern conditions have transformed religion itself – from faith to ideology. Modernity has reconfigured religious faith, which is a way of life or tradition, into ideology, which, as a sub-national, national or cross-national identifier of populations, contests for or protects non-religious, usually political or socio-economic, interests.[82] Through a critique of modern statecraft, Nandy seeks to recover religious tolerance from 'the hegemonic language of secularism'.[83] His solution lies in sources of tolerance that may be found in pre-modern religious traditions. Nandy says, '... traditional ways of life have, over the centuries, developed internal principles of tolerance and these principles must have a play in contemporary politics'.[84] As Nandy perceives modern state to be responsible for the emergence of religious fundamentalism in society, his solution seeks to separate the goal of religious tolerance from the modern secular state. In doing so, he alludes to Gandhian tolerance, which does not require a secular state to manage religious conflict. Given the explicit and violent attacks on minority religious communities in India today, is a tradition of tolerance and co-existence enough to counter religious extremism and hatred towards minorities? In the following chapters on Gandhi, we will see that in the face of the emergence of the new nation-state which was increasingly mirroring a Westphalian solution, Gandhian thought and politics did not contest the need for a secular state. Thus, it may be useful to separate a general Gandhian critique of modern statecraft from the ideal of secularism as religious non-discrimination.

The problem with Nandy's criticism is that in delinking traditional forms of tolerance from the modern state, his solution to religious intolerance looks more idealistic than an alternative to state secularism. His unequivocal rejection of modern statecraft and political secularism, and an exclusive reliance on traditional forms of religious toleration, proffers an idealistic solution because it seeks religion's absolute independence from the modern state. Gandhi, on the other hand, I will argue in Chapter 2, seeks a solution to religious intolerance which demonstrates both religion's interdependence on politics and its relative independence from state power. Lastly, according to Kaviraj, Nandy and Madan's arguments against secularism in India are based on a strong binary between an undifferentiated modern and an equally undifferentiated traditional mode of thinking.[85] Kaviraj points out that modernity and tradition are not doctrinal positions but 'alphabetic languages' through the elements of which quite dissimilar doctrinal positions can be fashioned.[86] With regard to secularity in modern India, he notes that the elaboration of social thought in India leads to forms of argumentation that in one sense extended and in another moved away from the established corpus of (Western) social theory. This is also one of the aims of the book – to demonstrate how Gandhian and Nehruvian thought not only freely borrowed but also differed from canonical Western ideas.

CONCLUSION

The religion–state–society relationship, when seen in terms of the declining relevance of religion in society and its privatisation, has been critiqued, questioned and challenged, especially in regard to non-Western societies of Asia, the Middle East and Africa. The theory of secularisation has been viewed as problematic in India because, first, unlike Western secularisation, both privatisation of religion and decline of religion in the public sphere were not seen as essential to Indian secularity. The debates on secularism in modern India bring out this issue sharply into focus as the critics question whether this doctrine is suitable for a country with deep religious diversity and a society where, instead of privatised religion, there is a dominant public presence of religion. These critics claim that since secularism is essentially a Western concept based on privatisation of religion, it is unsuitable for Indian society. Due to the pervasive role that religion plays in the sociopolitical lives of people in India, this so-called Western import of secularism with a clear public–private demarcation is seen as unappealing to the faithful.[87] Thus, unlike the modern West, where a resurgence of religions in the public sphere in the 1980s brought the secularisation narrative into question, India, at no point, could partake in a secularisation process which either sought privatisation of religion or envisaged its decline in society. Critics of secularism in India, therefore, pointing at the impossibility of privatising religion or its decline, argued for seeking either alternative forms of secularism or alternatives to secularism. Defenders of secularism in India, however, insist that secularisation of society is inessential to a political conception of secularism. What is clearly at stake in these debates is not only the meaning of secularism in India but its assumed relationship to a secularised society. Second, secularism debates in India attack the church–state model of Western secularism, where the spheres of religious and state activity are clearly demarcated. Since Indian state's continuous engagement with religion (for example, the legal ban on the prohibition of Dalits[88] into temple entry) fails to adhere to this Western model of secularism, the nature of Indian secularism has come under criticism. Since both Gandhi and Jawaharlal Nehru are often invoked to defend or criticise secularism in contemporary India, examining how these leaders understood and influenced the idea of the religion–state–society relationship under conditions of modernity may provide us with possible resources to resolve the current political crisis, where secularism seems to be held hostage to majoritarian politics and Hindu nationalism.

Apart from the fact that as national leaders, Gandhi and Nehru had major influence on Indian society and politics, another reason to study their thought and politics in relation to the question of secularity is that it provides for a contrapuntal analysis. That is, if Gandhi insisted on religious politics, Nehru saw the importance of separation of religion and politics for secular politics and depoliticised religion. However, this apparent difference between Gandhi and Nehru gets complicated when one takes note of recent scholarship that has examined the relationship between religion and politics in the works of these nationalist leaders. For instance, until the 1930s, Gandhi insisted that there can be 'no politics without religion'.[89] However, from the late 1940s onwards, he began insisting for a separation of religion and politics.[90] Although this shift in Gandhi's opinion seems glaring, scholars like Ajay Skaria do not see a significant change in Gandhi's understanding of religion and politics. Skaria suggests that a chronological understanding of Gandhi's views on religion and politics – where, until the 1930s he called for religious politics, and from the 1940s onwards, he explicitly called for separation of religion and politics – fails to discern the divergent conceptual registers on which Gandhi affirmed both religious politics and secularism.[91] Similarly, Kaviraj points to an 'apparently odd agreement' between Gandhi and Nehru, where despite their divergent opinions on the question of social morality, they seemed to have similar views on political secularism.[92] Akeel Bilgrami holds a different opinion compared to Skaria. According to him, Gandhi's espousal of political secularism in the late 1940s emerged due to the increasing influence of majoritarian nationalism in the later period of the Indian national movement. In such a reading, Gandhi's affirmation of religious politics and political secularism belongs in different contextual backgrounds, such that to present Gandhi as a 'proto-secularist' in the early twentieth century would be a misreading of Gandhi's conception of secularism.[93] Nandy absolutely refutes the idea that Gandhi ever supported a notion of secularism. Gandhi was 'an arch anti-secularist', he declares.[94] Thus, we see that Gandhi is espoused to both defend and criticise secularism in India.

It may be asked, what purpose does such an exercise that examines the politico-philosophical ideas of India's sociopolitical thinkers serve in terms of the present predicament? Today, religion's (this includes the category of caste in India) engagement with politics has become so contentious that any discussion on this issue invokes binaries of secular versus communal, modernity versus tradition, minority versus majority, state versus community, where one of the binaries is invariably a pejorative term. Can these contrived binaries be challenged, revisited and reframed so as to be able to respond to the challenges of both Hindutva and majoritarian electoral politics in a more effective manner? Tracing these conceptions back to a time when they were more inchoate and malleable may provide us with resources to rethink and reconstruct the relationship among religion, state and society. Gandhi's politics, for instance, sought to infuse religion in politics, and yet it was quite different from today's Hindutva politics.[95] The point here is that there may be various ways of fusing religion and politics, and not all of them may be antithetical to secularism's ideal of state impartiality and religious non-discrimination. Moreover, the recent electoral success of the Bharatiya Janta Party (BJP) demonstrates that riding on the legitimacy of electoral success, right-wing groups, including the national political party BJP, do not shy away from even directly attacking Indian state's secular commitments, especially the protection of minority communities. While Partha Chatterjee rightly pointed towards a shift in the strategy of Hindutva politics since the mid-1980s, where the Hindu right's explicit attacks on secularism had faded away, it is also the case that these explicit attacks return as and when right-wing groups secure a majority consensus in electoral politics.[96] While the Hindu right's ideological goal has remained the same, namely the dominance of the Hindu national culture and polity, the 'linguistic shift'[97] in their political strategy assists them in deploying provisions in the constitution, like the common civil code in the directive principles, to argue that those supporting minority rights are actually 'pseudo-secular'. Thus, Chatterjee rightly notes that the political conception of Hindutva is unlikely to pit itself against the idea of the secular state.[98] What Chatterjee's remark in fact reveals is that political commitments that shaped India's constitutional secularism are divergently different from the so-called secular commitments of the Hindu right. Given this political scenario, it seems imperative that we take a closer look at ideas which influenced India's secular imaginary at the time of its emergence as a nation-state. And the Gandhi–Nehru tradition is one of the most influential secular ideals of the twentieth century that marked the beginning of this nation.

NOTES

1. The word 'secular' was formally introduced to the Preamble of the Indian constitution during Indira Gandhi's Emergency Rule in 1976 through the 42nd amendment enacted by the Congress government.
2. Judith Shklar, 'The Liberalism of Fear', in *Political Liberalism: Variations on a Theme*, ed. Shaun P. Young, pp. 149–166 (Albany: State University of New York Press, 2004).
3. Ibid., p. 155.
4. Humeira Iqtidar and Tanika Sarkar, 'Introduction', in *Tolerance, Secularization, and Democratic Politics in South Asia*, ed. Humeira Iqtidar and Tanika Sarkar, pp. 1–21 (New York: Cambridge University Press, 2018).
5. Charles Taylor, *A Secular Age* (Cambridge, MA: Harvard University Press, 2007); José Casanova, *Public Religions in the Modern World* (Chicago: University of Chicago Press, 1994).
6. José Casanova, 'The Secular, Secularizations, Secularisms', in *Rethinking Secularism*, ed. Craig Calhoun, Mark Juergensmeyer, and Jonathan VanAntwerpen, pp. 54–74 (New York: Oxford University Press, 2011), p. 54.
7. Charles Taylor, 'The Polysemy of the Secular', *Social Research: An International Quarterly* 76, no. 4 (2009): 1143–1166, at p. 1144. Also see José Casanova, *Global Religious and Secular Dynamics: The Modern System of Classification* (Leiden: Brill, 2019).
8. Taylor, 'Polysemy of the Secular', p. 1144.
9. Taylor, *A Secular Age*.
10. Taylor, 'Polysemy of the Secular', p. 1145.
11. Ibid.
12. Ibid.
13. Ibid., p. 1146.
14. Ibid., p. 1147.
15. Like 'true' or 'false'. Ibid.
16. Ibid., p. 1148.
17. Ibid.
18. Taylor, *A Secular Age*, p. 19.
19. Taylor, 'Polysemy of the Secular', p. 1149.
20. Another oft-cited critique of secularism is William Connolly's book *Why I Am Not a Secularist* (Minneapolis: University of Minnesota Press, 1999).

Also see Saba Mahmood, *Religious Difference in a Secular Age: A Minority Report* (Princeton, NJ: Princeton University Press, 2016).
21. Talal Asad, *Formations of the Secular: Christianity, Islam, Modernity* (Stanford: Stanford University Press, 2003), p. 2.
22. Ibid., p. 5.
23. Ibid., p. 3.
24. Ibid., p. 14.
25. Ibid., p. 16.
26. P. C. Joshi, 'Gandhi–Nehru Tradition and Indian Secularism', *Mainstream* 45, no. 48 (2007), https://www.mainstreamweekly.net/article432.html (accessed on 7 April 2021). I have discussed the Gandhi–Nehru tradition in the introduction to the book.
27. Casanova, *Global Religious and Secular Dynamics*.
28. For instance, see Bryan R. Wilson, *Religion in Secular Society* (London: C.A. Watts & Co. Ltd., 1966).
29. Casanova, *Global Religious and Secular Dynamics*, p. 3.
30. Ibid., p. 4.
31. Charles Taylor, 'Two Theories of Modernity', *Hastings Centre Report* 25, no. 2 (1995): 24–33.
32. The Atlantic world, for Taylor, is a group of closely related cultures.
33. Taylor's history of secularity in the West mostly includes examples from Western Europe (especially France, Germany, Holland and the British Isles) and North America (the United States and Canada). He has maintained that his story of secularity covers the North Atlantic area and the settler societies of Canada, Australia and New Zealand. Taylor, 'A Secular Age Outside Latin Christendom: Charles Taylor Responds', in *Beyond the Secular West*, ed. Akeel Bilgrami, pp. 246–260 (New York: Columbia University Press, 2016), p. 249.
34. Sudipta Kaviraj however points out that Weber's conception of rationalisation has two distinct meanings, one terminal and the other carrying a non-terminal meaning of the process. In its former construal, rationalisation can mean a process through which rationally untenable beliefs about the world are gradually undermined and rejected, thereby leading eventually to a terminal process of 'disenchantment'. In the latter process, however, the term 'rationalisation' can indicate a tendency towards a greater elaboration and analytic systematisation of ideas, without entailing a teleological movement towards disenchantment. See Kaviraj, 'On Thick and Thin Religions: Some Critical Reflections

on Secularisation Theory', in *Religion and Political Imagination*, ed. Ira Katznelson and Gareth Stedman Jones, pp. 336–355 (New York: Cambridge University Press, 2010), p. 338, note 5.
35. Taylor, *A Secular Age*, p. 22.
36. Taylor, 'Two Theories of Modernity', p. 26.
37. Kaviraj, 'On Thick and Thin Religion', pp. 336–355.
38. For further discussion on such normatively conceived secularisation theories, see Casanova, *Global Religious and Secular Dynamics*.
39. For instance, see Ira Katznelson and Gareth Stedman Jones (eds.), *Religion and the Political Imagination* (New York: Cambridge University Press, 2010); Marian Burchardt, Monika Wohlrab-Sahr, and Matthias Middell (eds.), *Multiple Secularities beyond the West: Religion and Modernity in the Global Age* (Boston, Berlin and Munich: De Gruyter, 2015); Akeel Bilgrami (ed.), *Beyond the Secular West* (New York: Columbia University Press, 2016); Mirjam Künkler, John Madeley and Shylashri Shankar (eds.), *A Secular Age beyond the West: Religion, Law and the State in Asia, the Middle East and North Africa* (New York: Cambridge University Press, 2018); and Humeira Iqtidar and Tanika Sarkar (eds.), *Tolerance, Secularization, and Democratic Politics in South Asia* (New York: Cambridge University Press, 2018).
40. Casanova, *Public Religions*, p. 19.
41. For a criticism of Casanova's secularisation thesis, see Asad, 'Secularism, Nation-State, Religion', in *Formations of the Secular*. Also see Talal Asad, 'Responses', in *Powers of the Secular Modern: Talal Asad and His Interlocuters*, ed. David Scott and Charles Hirschkind, pp. 206–241 (Stanford: Stanford University Press, 2006).
42. For the critique of the theory of functional differentiation, see Hans Joas, 'Dangerous Nouns of Process: Differentiation, Rationalization, Modernization', in *The Art and Science of Sociology: Essays in Honor of Edward A. Tiryakian*, ed. Ronald Robertson and John Simpson, pp. 149–162 (London and New York: Anthem Press, 2016).
43. Taylor, *A Secular Age*, p. 25.
44. Ibid.
45. Ibid., p. 437.
46. Ibid., p. 539.
47. Taylor, 'A Secular Age Outside Latin Christendom: Charles Taylor Responds', p. 247.
48. Taylor, *A Secular Age*, pp. 2 and 3.

49. Ibid., p. 19. But Taylor also warns us of equating modern secularity as being coterminous with exclusive humanism. He notes that the latter was not the only alternative to religion.
50. Ibid., p. 18.
51. Sudipta Kaviraj, 'Disenchantment Deferred', in *Beyond the Secular West*, p. 136.
52. See recent publications such as Ira Katznelson and Gareth Stedman Jones (eds.), *Religion and the Political Imagination* (New York: Cambridge University Press, 2010); Marian Burchardt, Monika Wohlrab-Sahr and Matthias Middell (eds.), *Multiple Secularities Beyond the West: Religion and Modernity in the Global Age* (Boston, Berlin and Munich: de Gruyter, 2015); Akeel Bilgrami (ed.), *Beyond the Secular West* (New York: Columbia University Press, 2016); Mirjam Künkler, John Madeley and Shylashri Shankar (eds.), *A Secular Age Beyond the West: Religion, Law and the State in Asia, the Middle East and North Africa* (New York: Cambridge University Press, 2018); Humeira Iqtidar and Tanika Sarkar (eds.), *Tolerance, Secularization, and Democratic Politics in South Asia* (New York: Cambridge University Press, 2018).
53. Christoph Kleine and Monika Wohlrab-Sahr, 'Research Programme of the Humanities Centre of Advanced Studies (HCAS), "Multiple Secularities: Beyond the West, Beyond Modernities"', Leipzig University, 2016, https://www.multiple-secularities.de/ (accessed on 7 April 2021). Also see Christophe Kleine and Monika Wohlrab-Sahr, 'Historicizing Secularity: A Proposal for Comparative Research from a Global Perspective', *Comparative Sociology* 20, no. 2021: 287–316.
54. Florian Zemmin, 'How (Not) to Take "Secularity" beyond the Modern West: Reflections from Islamic Sociology', Working Paper Series of the HCAS 'Multiple Secularities: Beyond the West, Beyond Modernities' 9, Leipzig University, 2019. For the theory of differentiation, see S. N. Eisenstadt, 'Social Change, Differentiation and Evolution', *American Sociological Review* 29, no. 3 (1964): 375–386.
55. For instance, Nadja-Christina Schneider draws attention to visual media in India to argue how cause marketing campaigns introduce and mediate an understanding of secularity as care for and connectedness with adherents of other religions. See Nadja-Christina Schneider, 'Tea for Interreligious Harmony? Cause Marketing as a New Field of Experimentation with Visual Secularity in India', Working Paper Series of the HCAS 'Multiple Secularities: Beyond the West, Beyond Modernities' 20, Leipzig University, 2020, pp. 1–31.

56. Florian Zemmin, for instance, argues that Islamic reformists rejected secularism 'almost unanimously' as an external political regime that emerged in Christian Europe and therefore considered it as alien to Islam. However, he also notes that these reformists also operated with the conceptual distinction between religion and the secular, articulated within an Islamic framework itself, such that Islam as a societal order (as opposed to it being conceived as religion) replaces secularity. See Florian Zemmin, 'Secularism, Secularity and Islamic Reformism', in *Companion to the Study of Secularity*, ed. HCAS 'Multiple Secularities: Beyond the West, Beyond Modernities', Leipzig University, 2019, pp. 1–14.
57. Taylor, *A Secular Age*, p. 22. Künkler et al. have employed a Taylorian understanding of secularity to study the relationship between religion and politics outside the West (or what Taylor calls the North Atlantic world) – in countries of Asia, North Africa and the Middle East. See Künkler, Madeley and Shankar (eds.), *A Secular Age beyond the West*.
58. Kleine and Wohlrab-Sahr, 'Historicizing Secularity', p. 288.
59. Ibid.
60. Robert E. Frykenberg, for instance, argues that Hinduism is a modern construction. See Robert E. Frykenberg, 'Constructions of Hinduism at the nexus of History and Religion', *Journal of Interdisciplinary History* 22, no. 3 (1993): 523–550.
61. Monika Wohlrab-Sahr, 'Secularity, Non-religiosity, Atheism: Boundaries between Religion and Its Others', *The Annual Review of the Sociology of Religion* 7 (2016): 251–271.
62. Marian Burchardt and Monika Wohlrab-Sahr, 'Multiple Secularities: Toward a Cultural Sociology of Secular Modernities', *Comparative Sociology* 11, no. 6 (2012): 875–909. Also see Kleine and Wohlrab-Sahr, 'Multiple Secularities'.
63. Sudipta Kaviraj, 'An Outline of a Revisionist Theory of Modernity', *European Journal of Sociology* 46, no. 3 (2005): 497–526. Also see Sudipta Kaviraj, 'Languages of Secularity', *Economic and Political Weekly* 48, no. 50 (2013): 93–102.
64. Kaviraj, 'An Outline of a Revisionist Theory of Modernity', p. 510.
65. Ibid., p. 514.
66. Kaviraj, 'Languages of Secularity', p. 96.
67. For an elaboration on the methodological aspect of comparative as opposed to 'contrastive' history, see Sudipta Kaviraj, 'The Curious

Persistence of Colonial Ideology', *Constellations* 21, no. 2 (2014): 186–198. Kaviraj argues that the enterprise of 'universal history' in the works of Hegel and Scottish Enlightenment gave rise to a strand of historical reflection, where different civilisations were placed on a hierarchical and a linear scale of progress. In this historical tradition, European writings about non-Western societies were an exercise in contrastive and not comparative history, because such theorisation set up a contrast in which attention to some large, supposedly essential features of Asian societies set the stage for a closer and detailed exploration of the history of Europe. For further discussion on comparative theorisation, see Michael Freeden and Andrew Vincent, 'Introduction: The Study of Comparative Political Thought', in *Comparative Political Thought: Theorizing Practices*, ed. Michael Freeden and Andrew Vincent, pp. 1–23 (Oxon: Routledge, 2013).

68. Rajeev Bhargava, 'Political Secularism', in *The Oxford Handbook of Political Theory*, ed. John S. Dryzek, Bonnie Honig and Anne Phillips, pp. 636–655 (Oxford: Oxford University Press, 2006), p. 642. Also see Rajeev Bhargava, 'Indian Secularism: An Alternative, Trans-cultural Ideal', in *The Promise of India's Secular Democracy*, pp. 63–105 (New Delhi: Oxford University Press, 2010); Taylor, 'Polysemy of the Secular'; and Akeel Bilgrami, 'Secularism: Its Content and Context', in *Secularism, Identity, and Enchantment*, pp. 3–56 (Cambridge, MA: Harvard University Press, 2014).
69. Bhargava, 'Indian Secularism', p. 65.
70. Taylor, 'Polysemy of the Secular'.
71. Two prominent edited volumes on secularism in India are Rajeev Bhargava (ed.), *Secularism and Its Critics* (New Delhi: Oxford University Press, 2008 [1998]); and Anuradha Dingwaney Needham and Rajeswari Sunder Rajan, *The Crisis of Secularism in India* (Durham: Duke University Press, 2007). More recently, Iqtidar and Sarkar's edited volume, *Tolerance, Secularization, and Democratic Politics in South Asia*, revisited the debates in these earlier volumes.
72. T. N. Madan, 'Secularism in Its Place', in *Secularism and Its Critics*, ed. Rajeev Bhargava, pp. 297–320, at p. 298.
73. Rajeev Bhargava, 'What is Secularism For?' in *Secularism and Its Critics*, ed. Rajeev Bhargava, pp. 486–555, at p. 522.
74. Madan, 'Secularism in Its Place', p. 307.
75. Bhargava, 'What Is Secularism For?' p. 520.
76. Ibid., p. 493. Bhargava clarifies that political neutrality does not mean a god's eye view, that is, a strict objectivist neutrality.

77. The metaphor of a wall of separation between church and state refers to the Jeffersonian idea of the relationship between religion and state in the United States of America.
78. Bhargava, 'What Is Secularism For?' p. 492.
79. Ibid., p. 494.
80. Kaviraj, 'Languages of Secularity'.
81. Ashis Nandy, 'An Anti-secularist Manifesto', *India International Centre Quarterly* 22, no. 1 (1995): 35–64.
82. Ashis Nandy, 'The Politics of Secularism and the Recovery of Religious Tolerance', in *Secularism and Its Critics*, ed. Rajeev Bhargava, pp. 321–344.
83. Ibid., p. 321.
84. Ibid., p. 336.
85. Kaviraj, 'Languages of Secularity'.
86. Ibid., p. 102.
87. Nandy, 'The Politics of Secularism'.
88. The ex-untouchables of the Hindu community who are deemed to be the lowest members in the Hindu caste hierarchy.
89. M. K. Gandhi, 'May God Help', 26 November 1924, in *The Collected Works of Mahatma Gandhi* (henceforth, *CWMG*), 98 volumes (New Delhi: Government of India), vol. 29, p. 374, https://www.gandhiashramsevagram.org/gandhi-literature/collected-works-of-mahatma-gandhi-volume-1-to-98.php (accessed on 14 March 2021).
90. Ajay Skaria, 'No Politics without Religion, of Secularism and Gandhi', in *Political Hinduism: The Religious Imagination in Public Spheres*, ed. Vinay Lal, pp. 173–210 (New Delhi: Oxford University Press). Also see Ajay Skaria, 'Gandhi's Politics: Liberalism and the Question of the Ashram', *The South Atlantic Quarterly* 101, no. 4 (2002): 955–986.
91. Skaria, 'No Politics without Religion', pp. 173–210.
92. Kaviraj, 'Languages of Secularity', p. 100.
93. Bilgrami, 'Secularism: Its Content and Context', p. 32.
94. Nandy, 'The Politics of Secularism', p. 343.
95. The ideology of the Hindu right in India.
96. Partha Chatterjee, 'Secularism and Tolerance', in *Secularism and Its Critics*, ed. Rajeev Bhargava, pp. 345–379 (New Delhi: Oxford University Press, 2008 [1998]).
97. Kaviraj, 'Languages of Secularity', p. 96.
98. Chatterjee, 'Secularism and Tolerance'.

2

GANDHI'S *ASHRAM* AND POLITICAL THOUGHT

A COUNTER-NARRATIVE OF SECULARITY

In South Africa, my best creation was Phoenix. Without it, there would have been no satyagraha in that country. Without the Ashram here, satyagraha will be impossible in India…. I am going to ask the country not to judge me by either Champaran or Kheda but only by the Ashram. If you find lack of order in this place, and blindness of ignorance, then you will find the same in all my work…. Do not attribute greatness to me for other works of mine; judge me only by the Ashram.[1]

INTRODUCTION

Any scholar embarking on a study of Gandhi's thought must seriously consider Narayan Desai's view (himself a Gandhian and an *ashramite*) that Gandhi's life and thought are intertwined and inseparable, such that the spiritual or religious Gandhi is inseparable from the political one.[2] Desai's opinion that 'Gandhi cannot be properly understood in parts…. He must be studied in totality' reminds us that Gandhi embodied the message of truth and *ahimsa* (non-violence) by the way he lived his life.[3] In his biography on Gandhi, Desai warns us of the ineluctable move to study and thereby create two diametrically opposed Gandhis – the idealist philosopher and the activist politician. Understanding Gandhi's thought thus poses an immense challenge if one wishes to simultaneously examine both the Gandhi that led the Indian masses to freedom from colonial rule and the Gandhi of spinning, fasting, celibacy and silence. As we know, Gandhi's politics brought together the divided elite politics of the Indian National Congress (hereafter, the Congress) and popular uprisings of the masses, particularly the rural peasantry, in the Indian subcontinent. His politics thus simultaneously sought to reach two audiences – the elite and the masses – through two separate registers of 'communication and persuasion'.[4] While Gandhi's writings – speeches, articles, books, interviews, and so on– attended to the elites, to the peasant, words when written appeared 'a taking away of language rather than a giving'.[5] Gandhi therefore resorted to the use of other elements in the complex and wide semiotic register available in rural India, which included 'the symbolism of a whole range of non-discursive and non-modern ways of making meaning – from prayers to silences to dress to food, which for all their non-wordiness represented ideas and persuaded people by techniques that had been deployed for their persuasion for centuries'.[6] Sudipta Kaviraj remarks that while these religious and austerity practices appeared strangely retrograde and perverse to the modernists, the criticism made against these elements of Gandhi's politics missed the point because what was significant about them was not their content but the semiotic form.[7]

This chapter is based on the premise that as Gandhi's politics was inextricably linked to his religious and spiritual values, as well as sociopolitical reform (such as the constructive programme),[8] a closer look at his *ashram* observances and practices can provide us with a nuanced understanding of the relationship he envisaged between religion, society and politics in modern India. His politics, as has been aptly described, was 'religious politics'.[9] By reinventing the traditional hermitage, the *ashram* (Satyagraha/Sabarmati and Sevagram in India) for him became the site where he conducted his tests with 'Truth'[10] and non-violence. One of Gandhi's closest associates, Pyarelal Nayar, observed how much of Gandhi's voluminous writings were devoted to management of *ashrams* than to political campaigns as the former proved to be the toughest testing grounds for his 'experiments with Truth'.[11] Judith Brown maintains that Gandhi's *ashrams* were for him akin to laboratories, where he could attempt to solve in microcosm problems that afflicted India on a much larger scale.[12] The *ashram* then was a 'test-site' and an example, where through his 'experiments', Gandhi sought to (*a*) remedy the defects of Indian society; and (*b*) demonstrate and pursue the nation's public of the centrality of truth and non-violence through exemplary living.

In this chapter, I shall focus on Gandhi's *ashram* observances in order to understand how his religion was related to his politics.[13] Scholars, such as Ajay Skaria, inquiring into Gandhi's conception of religion observe a striking paradox, where, while in the early 1920s and 1930s, Gandhi insists that there can be 'no politics without religion',[14] after India's independence he declares that the Indian state should be secular.[15] Curiously enough, often a simple chronological explanation of this paradox, where Gandhi's formulations about secularism and religion belonged to different periods in his life, is not found satisfactory.[16] Through a close reading of some of Gandhi's works, I shall examine this contradiction in Gandhian thought. The broader question that I seek to answer, in this and the next chapter, is: despite his holistic worldview, which was rooted in a certain religious ethic, how has Gandhian thought and politics influenced and contributed to the discourse of secularity in modern India? It must be noted here that a reading of Gandhi's political thought is done with these questions in mind. As such, my task here is not to provide a systematic philosophical analysis of Gandhi's conception of religion or to provide an exhaustive account of his moral and political thought.[17]

The structure and argument of the chapter is as follows. In the first section, I will discuss Gandhi's conception of the political to argue how his political thought cannot be understood through the language and framework of liberal political thought. In the second section, I will elaborate upon Gandhi's conception of religion and argue that in his thought two distinguishable conceptions of religion are discernible. I refer to these two notions as religion as 'faith' and religion as the 'discovery' of the absolute truth in the practice of ethical living (or, in short, religion as ethical living). In the third section, I will focus on Gandhi's *ashram* observances to discuss the role and relation of religion he envisaged vis-à-vis the state and society. Here, I will argue that Gandhi's strong ethical commitments emanated from his practice of religion, which he understood in terms of ethical living. Since the epistemic basis of religion as ethical living was in the *experience* of living, the practice of religion involved unswerving moral and truthful practice in every aspect of one's life – social, economic and political. In daily conduct, this was realisable through *ahimsa* (non-violence) and in politics through *satyagraha* (literally, insistence on truth).[18] The two – *ahimsa* and *satyagraha* – together brought out the moral dimension in all social and political actions. As Gandhi's moral politics was inextricably linked to and emanated from his construal of religion as ethical living, the political subject (that is, Gandhi's *satyagrahi*) and political action were not autonomous of the ethical. This section thus highlights Gandhi's holistic vision and therefore the counter-narrative of secularity which emerges in Gandhian thought. In order to examine Gandhi's religious politics in detail, in the same section (that is, the third section), I further discuss four of Gandhi's *ashram* vows: (*a*) Satya, or Truth, (*b*) Ahimsa (non-violence), or love, (*c*) Tolerance (equality of all religions), and (*d*) Gandhi's spiritual and ascetic practices. By focusing on these *ashram* observances and practices, I will demonstrate how Gandhi did not just conceive religion in the dual meaning of duty and faith that *dharma* signifies. He understood religion through multiple values that he attached to *ahimsa*, like truth and non-violence, love, compassion and social service. In conclusion, in the fifth section, I maintain that Gandhi's political thought and action provide us with a counter-narrative of secularity along with a non-oppositional alternative to liberal secularism. Unlike most theories of modernisation and secularisation, Gandhi's political philosophy does not seek to privatise or de-politicise religion. His religious politics even negates the functional and institutional differentiation of various spheres like religion, politics and economy. If the core of secularisation theory is the claim that the modern society is characterised by the functional differentiation of the secular spheres from each other and from religious institutions and norms, then Gandhi's *ashram* practices and politics challenge and subvert that modern secularising process.[19] Furthermore, if 'exclusive humanism' is central to a secular social imaginary, then Gandhi's thought and politics are against such a conception of social life.[20] Gandhi provides us, one may say, with a counter-narrative of secularisation and secularity. At the same time, his thought on the religion–state–society relationship evinces a non-oppositional alternative to liberal secularism, which is a 'value-based' doctrine of the state.[21] I conclude that although Gandhi cannot be called a liberal secularist, his ideas are nevertheless in consonance with the goals of liberal secularism, which propagate religious non-discrimination and state impartiality.

WHAT IS THE POLITICAL?

In distinguishing the term 'political' from 'politics', Sheldon Wolin defines the former as 'an expression of the idea that a free society composed of diversities can nonetheless enjoy moments of commonality when, through public deliberations, collective power is used to promote or protect the well being of the collectivity'.[22] Politics, on the other hand, refers to 'the legitimized and public contestation, primarily by organized and unequal social powers, over access to the resources available to the public authorities of the collectivity'.[23] The assumption in Wolin (as in much of democratic theories) is that collective action as the basis of non-coercive social change is always self-evident and accessible, such that there are always already available resources for introducing and sustaining collective public action for social and political transformation. Leigh Jenco, however, asks, 'What happens if we find ourselves in situations where collective or public action is not immediately available, or even widely intelligible?' She diverts our attention to the idea of 'making the political', whereby the insistence is on ordinary individuals who 'must make the political' through effective personal action, like ongoing acts of exemplariness, before social movements or self-aware political communities have materialised.[24] Borrowing Jenco's conception of founding the political by making the political, I wish to suggest that this idea where the political is 'made', as opposed to it being always already available, also provides an answer to another dilemma: what happens when we find ourselves in situations where structures of domination that we seek to resist (and hence structures of subjugation and inferiorisation) also provide the epistemic basis of our understanding of the political? More specific to the context here, how could colonised people of India have methods and means of doing politics that was not dependent on the discourse that British colonial rule had imposed on them?[25] In such a situation, as Gandhi astutely observed in *Hind Swaraj*,[26] only two options seem to be available: either you learn and appropriate the idea of the political from those who dominate – like the constitutional reformism of the Congress – or you completely reject the available means of articulating the political – like the Indian revolutionaries did.[27] While the former represented the elite politics of legally and constitutionally trained, upper-class English-educated Indians (mostly men), the latter found it difficult to rein in the masses due to its complete rejection of the state and its resort to violence as the only means of resisting domination.[28] Thus, both the liberal constitutionalists and the revolutionaries seemed incapable of mass political movement as a means for social and political transformation.

Gandhi's conception of the political and his politics, however, is an intervention and an alternative to the aforementioned options, in which there is lack of force in one (that is, liberal constitutionalism) and excessive use of force in the other (that is, revolutionary politics). Politics for social and political transformation is weak or ineffective in the former because in Gandhi's opinion, 'it is a fact beyond dispute that a petition, without the backing of force, is useless.'[29] For the latter, on the other hand, 'what is gained through fear is retained only while the fear lasts'.[30] Brute force does not see, argues Gandhi, the inviolable connection between means and ends.[31] It was Gandhi who, in his political practice, showed how the choice and enactment of means defined, shaped and changed the character of the ends in politics.[32] In such means-oriented politics, the nature of the political and the method of doing politics depended on the particular relationship and fissures that existed between people: with equals, friendship (*mitrata*); with subordinates, service (*seva*); and with antagonists, *satyagraha* (the political tool of conducting *ahimsa*).[33] Moreover, the means and methods of doing *satyagraha* against the antagonist required personal qualities, like the 'force of love',[34] 'personal suffering',[35] 'sacrifice of self'[36] and 'immeasurable pity'.[37] Apart from noticing the protean nature of Gandhi's politics, what is striking in his politics is that there is a conversion of the personal and particular relationship to the political and universal. The founding of the political then necessarily emerges from the personal and the particular, thereby making the public–private distinction in liberal politics incomprehensible and indeed impossible.

Faisal Devji makes a provoking argument that violence was central to Gandhi's moral politics. He argues that the point of Gandhi's moral politics was to invite violence and, in doing so, 'convert it by the force of suffering'.[38] The key to *satyagraha*, as Gandhi had noted several times, was suffering (*tapasya*).[39] Unlike the violence of killing, where individuals are unequal in their ability to kill, all are equally capable of dying. Self-suffering and sacrifice in politics therefore demonstrated their universal quality.[40] Such Gandhian acts of moral politics became crucial to the anti-colonial struggle because they demonstrated individual acts of exemplariness, where the *satyagrahi*s (Gandhi's non-violent activists)[41] as moral exemplars would provide leadership to the masses in their fight against colonial injustice. One of the ways through which Gandhi sought to convert personal virtues into public values was through *ashram* observances and practices.

Another feature of Gandhian moral politics is the assertion that rights 'correspond' with and are dependent on the duties of man,[42] such that 'the very performance of a duty secures us our right'.[43] Ramin Jahanbegloo argues that the core of Gandhi's theory of politics is to show that the true subject of the political is the citizen and not the state, because 'the political subject embraces moral duty and frees himself or herself from ultimate obedience to existing political powers, thereby inverting our common idea of who is sovereign'.[44] In other words, Gandhi retrieves sovereignty from the state and attributes it a quality vested in individuals or the civil society.[45] Hence, Gandhi declares, 'If a ruler shirks his duties while the people do theirs then the people become the ruler.'[46] And in his typical style of inverting commonly held notions, Gandhi continues, '... in truth a sovereign is only the first servant of the people. It is the duty of the servant to surrender all to the master and then live on what is left over'.[47] Furthermore, unlike rights, which can be guaranteed only by the state, such that they are never really in possession of those who bear them, duties belong to the individuals and cannot be stripped from them.[48]

In this radical construal of the political, the notion of the political subject (and also the notion of the self) is crucial to understand Gandhi's politics and its relationship to the state. In *Hind Swaraj*, he said:

> Passive resistance cannot proceed a step without fearlessness. Those alone can follow the path of passive resistance who are free from fear, whether as to their possession, false honors, their relatives, the government, bodily injury, death.[49]

Fearlessness, included in the *ashram* vows, is an important component of Gandhi's politics and his notion of the political subject. Since Gandhi retrieves sovereignty from the state and attributes it to the civil society, it is the civil society which is sovereign and not the state (as may be the case in canonical liberal tradition). As such, civil disobedience against the state in Gandhian politics is a *civil* and not a criminal matter.[50] The Gandhian *satyagrahi*, under certain conditions, is required to disobey the state and its laws.

> Passive resistance is a method of securing rights by personal suffering; it is the reverse of resistance by arms.... For instance, the Government

of the day has passed a law which is applicable to me. I do not like it.... If I do not obey the law and accept the penalty for its breach, I use soul-force. It involves sacrifice of self.[51]

Furthermore, through his politics (that is, *satyagraha*), Gandhi is not only looking for the transformation of an unjust political system into a more just one, he is seeking to transform the political subject itself in her engagement with the state. Gandhi's *ashram* observances and practices demonstrate his attempts at bringing together ethics, politics and religion, while simultaneously seeking to transform the 'self' into a Gandhian political subject, that is, a *satyagrahi*.

WHAT IS RELIGION?

Gandhi sometimes compared his practice of religion to the pedagogy of science. Another religious nationalist, Mohammad Iqbal saw the aim of religion being same as that of science. In his lecture 'Is Religion Possible?' Iqbal described religious life in a linear movement of three periods: from 'Faith' to 'Thought' to 'Discovery'.[52] In religion as faith, 'religious life appears as a form of discipline which the individual or a whole people must accept as an unconditional command without any rational understanding of the ultimate meaning and purpose of that command'.[53] After this period of unquestioning submission follows a period of rational understanding of religion as thought. In this period, 'religious life seeks its foundation in a kind of metaphysics – a logically consistent view of the world with God as a part of that view'.[54] In the final period of religion as discovery, 'metaphysics is displaced by psychology, and religious life develops the ambition to come into direct contact with the ultimate Reality'.[55] Iqbal stressed that it was this 'higher religion' as discovery which was 'essentially experience and recognized the necessity of experience as its foundation long before science learnt to do so'.[56] Like Iqbal, Gandhi too can be said to have understood religion in terms of faith and discovery. Taking inspiration from Iqbal's tripartite conceptual division and taxonomy of religion, I wish to argue that in Gandhi's thought religion may be described as a *discovery* of the 'absolute truth' through the *experience* of ethical living. In construing religion in terms of a discovery, Gandhi drew an analogy between science and religion:

Now I think that the word 'saint' should be ruled out of present life. It is too sacred a word to be lightly applied to anybody, much less to one like myself who claims only to be a humble searcher after truth, knows his limitations, makes mistakes, never hesitates to admit them when he makes them, and frankly confesses that he, like a scientist, is making experiments about some of 'the eternal verities' of life, but cannot even claim to be a scientist because he can show no tangible proof of scientific accuracy in his methods or such tangible results of his experiments as modern science demands.[57]

After maintaining how his method of searching for truth was akin to a scientific method, Gandhi went on to define religion:

Let me explain what I mean by religion. It is not the Hindu religion, which I certainly prize above all other religions, but the religion which transcends Hinduism, which changes one's very nature, which binds one indissolubly to the truth within and which ever *purifies*. (Emphasis added)[58]

As we shall see later in this chapter, for Gandhi religion involved a daily purification of experience. This practice of purification involved observance of various vows (*vrata*), of which truth was the primary vow.[59] Gandhi, however, did not, to my knowledge, terminologically classify and categorise religion like Iqbal did. However, reading through Gandhi's works one can delineate, at least, two conceptions of religion, which may be compared to Iqbal's typology of faith and discovery. What I wish to suggest is that in Gandhi's thought two conceptions of religion are discernible: first, religion as 'faith' (or religious faith), where there is an unquestioning abidance to an unconditional command without any rational understanding of the ultimate meaning and purpose of that command.[60] The second is, religion as 'discovery' in the experience of ethical living, or, in short, religion as ethical living.[61] This analytical distinction between religion as faith and discovery helps explain Gandhi's practice of public reason-giving and his contradictory claim of being a sceptic about reason's justificatory power. Criticisms against Gandhi that point towards his lack of rationality and scientific mode of knowledge are, in my view, directed against his practice of religion as faith. So, when Rabindranath Tagore criticised Gandhi's 'unscientific view' over his pronouncement that the devastating earthquakes in Bihar in 1934 were a 'divine chastisement' for the sin of untouchability, Tagore was questioning Gandhi's blind *religious faith*, where reason seemed to have no place.[62]

Religion as ethical living was, to borrow Akeel Bilgrami's words, 'universalizable' through exemplary action.[63] Religion as faith, on the other hand, was far more personal in nature. It was embodied, instinctual, even non-reflexive and a personal quest. Its importance in relation to society and politics lay in experiment and in the moral-psychological effect it produced in a political world marked by inherent tendencies towards conflict, domination and violence. This is why Karuna Mantena characterises Gandhi's religious politics as 'dispositional politics of nonviolence'.[64] Moreover, as opposed to reason, which was fallible, religious faith was infallible for Gandhi.[65] Such an understanding of religion and its importance in politics also lay in Gandhi's belief that politics required not merely persuasion by means of reflective argument but also a conversion of the self and the other.[66] He objected to the reduction of mind's capacity to reasoning: '… man does not govern himself by logic. He is a complex being; therefore, a multiplicity of considerations act upon him and move him to do or to refrain from doing things.'[67]

GANDHI'S *ASHRAM* OBSERVANCES AND HIS RELIGIOUS POLITICS

Gandhi claimed that he was not a 'visionary' but a 'practical idealist'[68] who sought to 'spiritualize' politics.[69] In 1915 he set up the Satyagraha *ashram* in Kocharab, Ahmedabad, Gujarat,[70] to 'remedy … defects in our national life from the religious, economic and political standpoint'.[71] The *ashram* became the site where he attempted to give his moral idealism a definite shape through *ashram* vows and work. Gandhi did not understand the *ashram* in a traditional and conventional way, in terms of a spiritual retreat from the material world where religious austerities are performed.[72] Rather, the *ashram* was called *udyog mandir* (temple of industry), which was established in order to be able to conduct experiments with truth and non-violence, and to be able to study and record the effects of the experiments on both the person and community with a view to prepare men and women for national service in ways that were not in conflict with the welfare of other nations of the world.[73]

Writing on the ashram life, Gandhi said:

> I feel that an ashram was a necessary [sic] of life for me. As soon as I had a house of my own, my house was an ashram in this sense, for my life as a householder was not one of enjoyment but of duty discharged from day to day.[74]

The *ashram* thus also stood as a site of duty or *karmabhumi*.[75] Unlike the abstract citizen, who is bestowed with rights in the liberal state, the Gandhian *ashramite*, through personal example, demonstrated to the nation's people how one becomes worthy of rights by following one's duties. At the same time, the observance of *ashramic* vows (*vrat*) by the *ashramite* demonstrated values of self-control, self-denial and sacrifice, which are crucial to Gandhian politics, that is, *satyagraha*. Explaining as to why vows are important, Gandhi says:

> A vow is a purely religious act which cannot be taken in a fit of passion. It can be taken only with a mind purified and composed, and with God as witness.... Acts which are not possible by ordinary self-denial become possible with the aid of vows which require extraordinary self-denial.... But the object of taking the vow is speedily to bring about by the power of self denial a state of things which can only be expected to come in the fullness of time.[76]

Gandhi's *ashram* observances – vows of truth and *ahimsa*, spinning of *charkha* (spinning wheel), practice of *brahmacharya* (celibacy or chastity), fasts, prayers, and so on – were as much a part of his politics as of his religion. In Ashram Observance in Action, writing on the vows and work at the Satyagraha *ashram*, Gandhi begins by stating, 'Ashram here means a community of men of religion.'[77] Then, after stipulating a set of eleven *ashram* observances, Gandhi remarks towards the end of his book, 'Last of all, when you have observed these rules, think that then, and not till then, you may come to politics and dabble in them to your heart's content, and certainly you will then never go wrong. Politics, divorced of religion, has absolutely no meaning.'[78]

What is the relationship between Gandhi's *ashram* observances and his politics? How and why does an individual who has observed these *ashramic* vows become eligible to engage in politics? In other words, what is the relationship among religion, morality, the political subject and politics in Gandhian thought? One of the ways in which Gandhi understood religion was in terms of ethical living. Religion as ethical living meant that it was to be practised in every aspect of one's everyday living. The *ashram* then was not only a site for Gandhi's pilot-tests in his experiments with truth and non-violence; it was also an example of his holistic vision of ethical living, which permeated all aspects of one's life – social, economic and political. The 'exemplary performances' at the *ashram* made it 'the model and exemplar' of Gandhi's imagined society.[79] Bilgrami argues that the distinctiveness of Gandhi's understanding of Hinduism was a certain nested relationship it offered between personal life and the public life of service to one's fellow human beings. That is, while his religion could inspire the daily practices of his life, it also allowed him to view those practices as essentially continuous with his anti-colonial political actions through which he mobilised the Indian masses towards total freedom from colonial rule.[80]

According to Skaria, the *ashram* vows (*vrat*) were modelled on the Jain and Hindu traditions of the major vows (*mahavrat*). Five of these were the conventional *mahavrat*, or the cardinal vows of truth (*satya*), non-violence (*ahimsa*), celibacy (*brahmacharya*),[81] non-stealing (*asteya*) and non-possession (*aparigraha*).[82] Apart from these observances, the *ashram* inmates also had to follow the following six vows: control of palate, physical labour, *swadeshi*,[83] fearlessness, removal of untouchability and tolerance.[84] Veeravalli has argued that all these vows brought together the personal and the political in a way that the practice of any one of them at the complete exclusion of any other would be impossible. She further maintains that while the first five vows are necessary principles which must govern the relation between the mind and the world, the other six are specific to the self-discipline required of the body and the body-politic. These latter vows constitute the sites of experiment which would put to test one's mastery over the five cardinal vows in time or in history.[85] Let us now examine some of these *ashramic* observances in detail to understand how Gandhi related these to the body-politic and politics on the one hand and to the body and the political subject (*satyagrahi*) on the other, thereby denying the private–religious and the public–political distinction and separation in political liberalism.[86]

SATYA (TRUTH)

In both his writings on the *ashram*, Gandhi lists 'Truth' as the first *ashram* vow.[87] Satyagraha *ashram*, he states, 'owes its very existence to the pursuit and the attempted practice of Truth'.[88] By reversing his previous formulation of God ('God is Truth'), Gandhi defines truth as follows:

> The word Satya (Truth) is derived from Sat, which means 'being'. Nothing is or exists in reality except Truth. That is why Sat or Truth is perhaps the most important name of God. In fact it is more correct to say that Truth is God, than to say that God is Truth.[89]

To this, he also adds:

> … without ahimsa it is not possible to seek and find Truth. Ahimsa and Truth are so intertwined that it is practically impossible to disentangle and separate them. They are like the two sides of a coin…. Who can say, which is the obverse, and which is the reverse? Nevertheless Ahimsa is the means; Truth is the end. Means to be means must always be within our reach, and so ahimsa is our supreme duty. If we take care of the means, we are bound to reach the end sooner or later…. Whatever difficulties we encounter, whatever apparent reverses we sustain, we may not give up the quest for Truth which alone is, being God Himself.[90]

Gandhi defined God through his conceptions of 'Truth' and *ahimsa*. He understood truth, or *satya*, as a synonym for God or 'being', and religion for him meant the search for this truth which is absolute. This search for the absolute truth was possible only through the means of *ahimsa*, or non-violence. Without practising non-violence one could not, according to Gandhi, attain absolute truth or realise God. Thus, one could only find the absolute truth in the practice and experience of living a non-violent truthful life, which as the means to God is always within one's reach. Thus, both his conceptions of truth and *ahimsa* require a practical engagement with the world, such that they are realisable for anyone in their daily practice.[91] But before I elaborate on this quotidian and practical aspect of Gandhi's *ahimsa*, let me examine Gandhi's conception of truth further as it challenges a dominant understanding of truth emerging from the legacies of Enlightenment.

Gandhi was a deeply religious man who called himself a *sanatani* (an orthodox Hindu)[92] and yet disregarded many tenets of canonical Hinduism. He said, 'If I were asked to define the Hindu creed, I should simply say: search after *truth* through *non-violent means*. A man may not believe even in God and still call himself a Hindu. Hinduism is a relentless pursuit after truth.'[93] In a correspondence in the journal *Young India*,[94] Gandhi was asked how a *sudra*[95] can be said to belong to Hinduism when the reading, reciting and even the hearing of scriptures were denied to him by canonical Hinduism. Because Gandhi considered reciting the Vedas as obligatory for a *sanatani* Hindu, the correspondent inquired: 'Either one who is born a sudra cannot be a sanatana Hindu in your sense, or else a sanatana Hindu must be something very different from what you define one to be.'[96] To this Gandhi responded:

> I am not a literalist. Therefore, I try to understand the spirit of the various scriptures of the world. I apply the test of Truth and Ahimsa laid down by these very scriptures for interpretation. I reject what is inconsistent with that test, and I appropriate all that is consistent with it.[97]

We see here that for Gandhi truth and non-violence were the two underlying commitments, to be found in *all* great religious books, which provided the criteria for a test for how to detect the spirit that informs the narratives and normative injunctions present in sacred books.[98] This methodological proposal where one focuses on the spirit of the religious text rather than on the letter shows that for Gandhi a *sanatani* did not mean someone who commended strict adherence to textual doctrines in religious books.[99] Rather he argued:

> My belief in the Hindu scriptures does not require me to accept every word and every verse as divinely inspired. Nor do I claim to have any first-hand knowledge of these wonderful books. But I do claim to *know* and *feel* the truths of the essential teaching of the scriptures. I decline

to be bound by any interpretation, however learned it may be, if it is repugnant to reason or moral sense. I do most emphatically repudiate the claim (if they advance any such) of the present Shankaracharyas and shastris to give a correct interpretation of the Hindu scriptures. (Emphasis added)[100]

Thus, both his claim to be a *sanatani* Hindu and a right interpretation of holy scriptures are not based on accepting the sacral status or scholarly knowledge of these scriptures but rather on a claim to have grasped Hinduism's 'true spirit'.[101] While Gandhi did not understand religious truth as strict adherence to scriptural doctrines, neither did he think that the truth contained in religious books is accessible to and understandable by an esoteric few. By repudiating the sole authority of religious scholars (*shankaracharya*s and *shastri*s) in interpreting sacred Hindu texts, by claiming to 'feel' the truths of religious scriptures and by making reason and moral sense the basis of interpretation, Gandhi is keen to allow the greatest possible freedom for each person to access the wisdom of sacred texts.[102] Through such a description of how each person must ratify the scriptures for himself, in theory Gandhi democratises access to sacred Hindu texts to not just the lower castes and the *sudra*s of the Hindu community but people of all faiths. Bilgrami has argued that when Gandhi uses words like 'reason' and 'moral sense' to describe how one should understand the message and the normative injunctions contained in sacred texts, he meant something more instinctive and conceptually far removed from what these words meant in the liberal tradition of philosophers such as Jeremy Bentham, James and J. S. Mill, T. B. Macaulay and John Morley.[103] Reason, for Gandhi (as I will argue later in the chapter), is not opposed to emotions as it can be the case with reason in some strands of thoughts which emerged in the Enlightenment tradition.

Bhikhu Parekh notes that for the orthodox, the Hindu tradition was a binding structure of beliefs deriving its authority from its ancient lineage and/or the *dharmashastra*s.[104] Only men who were of righteous conduct and well-versed in the *shastra*s were granted the right to reform the tradition. Parekh says that Gandhi satisfied the first condition but not the second. Gandhi was thus challenging the orthodox Hindu concept of tradition and seeking to replace it with an alternative view of his own. I have already argued that Gandhi saw religion or Hinduism in terms of a scientific inquiry whose authority lay not by virtue of being a tradition but in *experimental validation*. Because Gandhi had sincerely tried to live by the central values of his tradition, he could claim to understand it better than the *pandits* (Hindu priests)[105] and disregard their interpretations and protests.[106] Thus, experimental validation and experience were the key methods through which one could practise religion as ethical living and through that process discover truth. That is why, I claimed earlier in this chapter, Gandhi equated his practice of religion with the method of science.

It is important to note here that Gandhi understood and applied the conception of truth in a way which, as Partha Chatterjee argues, was utterly inconsistent with the dominant thematic of post-Enlightenment thought. Chatterjee remarks:

> To Gandhi, then, truth did not lie in history, nor did science have any privileged access to it. Truth was moral: unified, unchanging and transcendental.... It could be only found in the *experience of one's life*, by the unflinching *practice of moral living*. It could never be correctly expressed within the terms of rational theoretical discourse. (Emphasis added)[107]

Chatterjee rightly suggests that in Gandhi's thought there is no attempt to historically examine the authenticity of scriptural texts or examine the historicity of the great characters of sacred epics, like the Gita and the Mahabharata. Such exercises were quite irrelevant to the determination of truth. Gandhi did not see the Bhagavad Gita, for instance, as a historical narrative; rather, for him it was a heuristic device for the determination of truth in the present as a description of right action or conduct. In rendering his translation of the Gita, Gandhi contends, '... the Gita says: No one has attained his goal without action.'[108] Disagreeing with the common Hindu belief that the path to salvation is through renunciation of worldly pursuits, he says:

> In my opinion the author of the Gita has dispelled this delusion. He has drawn no line of demarcation between salvation and worldly pursuits. On the contrary he has shown that *religion must rule even our worldly pursuits*. I have felt that the Gita teaches us that *what cannot be followed out in day-to-day practice cannot be called religion*. (Emphasis added)[109]

This action-oriented interpretation of sacred texts ensured that when one came across conflicting interpretations of the scriptures, they could not be resolved theoretically, because 'scriptures cannot transcend reason or truth'.[110] Scriptures, as heuristic devices, are 'intended to purify reason and illuminate truth'.[111] Chatterjee therefore rightly argues that for Gandhi only the living practice of one's faith could show whether or not one's interpretation was correct.[112] Thus, for Gandhi the realisation of truth through belief and practice of religion required a practical engagement with the world such that they were dependent on the everyday and quotidian. That is why Skaria describes Gandhi's religion as 'immanent religion'.[113]

Anuradha Veeravalli has suggested that Gandhi's 'theory', 'method' and 'experiment', including his vocabulary, are specific to its discourse, which opposes and contradicts the presuppositions and views of mainstream *post*-Enlightenment epistemology and politics.[114] She has convincingly argued that truth for Gandhi did not mean objective verifiability but a 'theory' based on 'correspondence of the mind and world'.[115] So far we have observed that Gandhi's understanding and practice of religion hinge on experience and experimental validation to claim its truth.[116] Gandhian thought and practice attack, argues Veeravalli, one of the most fundamental, epistemological and metaphysical presuppositions of post-Enlightenment thought and practice: the Cartesian dualism of mind and the world (and the mind and the body).[117] She reminds us that the Cartesian thesis is not merely that the mind and the world are distinct, such that one is constituted by thought and the other by matter, but that they are *separate*. This dualism of the mind and the world also has the consequence of separating fact and value, or realism and idealism, and therefore science and ethics or politics. Veeravalli argues that what follows from this dualism is a discounting and erasure of an independent metaphysical and epistemological status for the body and, with it, for pain, suffering and labour as signs of the mediation of mind and the world.[118] Gandhi, on the other hand, sought to *embody* his search for truth manifested in his 'biomorality' of fasting, *brahmacharya* (celibacy), vegetarianism, nature cure, and so on.[119] Religion, for Gandhi, was thus embodied religion. Such biomoral practices also demonstrated how he conceived morality in a way in which truth and biology were equally implicated. It may be argued that as a challenge and an alternative to the Cartesian dualism, Gandhi's *ashram* observances and bodily practices evince non-dualism, as they become sites of experiment and experience, and thereby demonstrate his alternative 'science of non-violence', 'science of satyagraha'.[120] Unlike the separation or dualism of the subject and the object as a standard of objectivity set by modern science, for Gandhi, one who experiments and experiences is not merely an observer but also a 'witness', such that in it lies its 'objective subjectivity' and 'subjective objectivity'.[121] That is why, I think, it is possible for Gandhi to make statements like 'feel truth' and 'practice truth'. And that is also why I argue in this chapter that the political Gandhi of *ahimsa* and *satyagraha* cannot be separated from the spiritual Gandhi of spinning, fasting, celibacy and silence.

Gandhi maintained that in the pursuit of truth or God, what may appear as truth to one may appear as untruth to another. And even then, there was nothing wrong in following one's truth because 'what appear to be different truths are like the countless and apparently different leaves of the same tree'.[122] To these seemingly contradictory views on truth, affirming subjectivist ethics in the former and universal ethics in the latter, Gandhi asserted:

> [F]or me, truth is the sovereign principle which includes numerous other principles. This truth is not only truthfulness in word, but truthfulness in thought also, and not only relative truth of our conception, but the Absolute Truth, the Eternal Principle, that is God. There are innumerable definitions of God, because His manifestations are innumerable.... But I worship God as Truth only. I have not yet found Him, but I am seeking after Him.... But as long as I have not realized this Absolute Truth, so long must I hold by the relative truth as I have conceived it. That relative truth must, meanwhile, be my beacon, my shield and buckler.[123]

In a letter to Mirabehn in 1933, Gandhi wrote, 'Truth is what everyone for the moment feels it to be.'[124] It was, in this sense, a personal quest. A few days before, in another letter to her, Gandhi explained:

> We know the fundamental truth we want to reach, we also know the way. The details we do not know, we shall never know them all, because we are but very humble instruments among millions of such, moving consciously or unconsciously towards the divine event. We shall reach

the Absolute Truth, if we faithfully and steadfastly work out the relative truth as each one of us knows it.[125]

In these quotes we can see that there is no attempt in Gandhi to convert, assimilate, subjugate or reject the particular religious and moral ethic that emerges from one's search for truth into a universal ethic. However, to argue from here that Gandhi was a moral anarchist or a relativist is to turn a blind eye to the epistemological basis of Gandhi's notion of truth.[126] Bilgrami convincingly argues that although Gandhi's religious and moral convictions are marked by unabashed subjectivism, as truth for Gandhi is an experiential notion and not a cognitive notion based on universal propositions (like Immanuel Kant's categorical imperative), they are nevertheless 'universalizable'.[127] Truth, argues Bilgrami, carries the conviction it does for those who experience it, and not for others. Gandhi's truth as a subjective experiential notion is universalisable because his *satyagrahis* represented the ideal of an individual's life as their actions were self-consciously conceived as exemplary. Bilgrami argues that through the notion of exemplary action, there is a conceptual transition from individual choice in the realm of religion to a public and universal relevance of one's choices. Gandhi transforms the very idea of religion from its doctrinal and textual form to its experiential yet universal form.[128] Thus, Bilgrami remarks, 'Gandhi's entire life was a religious life because he was utterly driven to universalize the personal convictions that he describes so well in his interpretative ideas about the sacred books of Hinduism.'[129] As the realisation of absolute truth, which is universal, was based on unswerving moral and truthful practice, one could proceed to find it only in the experience of ethical living. Moreover, while ethical living could be realised through duty or *dharma*, the *satyagrahi ashramite* was simultaneously the embodiment of truthful practice and exemplary action. Thus, Gandhi says, 'If we do our duty, others also will do theirs some day. We have a saying to the effect: If we ourselves are good, the whole world will be good.'[130] And since Gandhi's truth is an experiential notion, it follows that one learns from experience, puts one's beliefs to the test, accepts the consequences and revises those beliefs if they are found wanting.[131]

Bilgrami also reminds us that Gandhi's insistence on truth as subjective is not based on our lack of certainty about truth, which is J. S. Mill's argument of an unattainable truth.[132] He remarks that there is 'no Millian diffidence in one's belief' in Gandhi's notion of truth.[133] That is, Gandhi's reason for upholding subjectivist ethics is not based on the argument that we must be diffident about our present opinions because our past opinions have sometimes been wrong. Bilgrami goes on to argue that as the Kantian model of universalism (that is, the categorical imperative) implies forms of moral criticism and judgement of actions of others, which have the potential to generate psychological attitudes like hostility and resentment, they constitute interpersonal violence for Gandhi.[134] But the ethical demand in exemplary action only requires non-compulsory force of the example. Bilgrami notes that unlike the (Kantian) tradition of moral thinking, which says, 'When one chooses for oneself, one chooses for everyone', Gandhi would have proposed something like this: 'When one chooses for oneself, one sets an example to everyone.'[135] Thus Gandhi says, '… there is compulsion and compulsion. We call self-imposed compulsion self-restraint.'[136] Here I would like to further suggest that while truth was an experiential notion for Gandhi, it was, at all times, guided and tethered by a conception of universal moral duties. A list of such moral duties, I suggest, is to be found in Gandhi's *ashramic* vows.[137]

AHIMSA (NON-VIOLENCE), OR 'LOVE'

After truth, Gandhi listed *ahimsa* (non-violence) as the next important ashram vow and entitled it as 'love'.[138] Contrasting the passive spirituality in Indian traditions to his active conception of *ahimsa*, Gandhi pointed out:

> Our non-violence is an unworldly thing. We see its utmost limit in refraining somehow from destroying bugs, mosquitoes and fleas, or from killing birds and animals. We do not care if these creatures suffer, nor even if we partly contribute to their suffering. On the contrary, we think it a heinous sin if anyone releases or helps in releasing a creature that suffers … this is not non-violence. Non-violence means an ocean of compassion.[139]

Parekh points out that Gandhi defined and distinguished *ahimsa* in two senses. In its narrow, literal, negative or passive sense, it meant refraining from causing harm and destruction to living beings. In its broad, positive and active sense, it meant promoting their well-being. Parekh argues that in both senses, *ahimsa* for Gandhi was grounded in compassion or love, as he considered *ahimsa* the same as love: it was 'active love'.[140] Love here meant identification with and service to *all* living beings.[141] The essence of Gandhi's non-violence involved the 'element of conscious compassion', which meant the wish not to cause harm or destruction.[142] Furthermore, while compassion leads to avoidance of harm, it must also include a positive desire to help others. *Himsa* (violence), on the other hand, meant inflicting harm or destruction upon another living being out of ill will or selfishness. Parekh suggests that by distinguishing between self-interest and selfishness, Gandhi considerably broadened the definition of *ahimsa*. While self-interest consisted in securing those conditions without which no man could live a fully human life, selfishness meant putting oneself above others and pursuing one's interest at the expense of others. As such, harm caused to others in the course of pursuing one's legitimate or just self-interest was not *himsa*.[143] Hence, by arguing that non-violence excludes selfish motive, Gandhi even gave the criterion for non-violent killing.[144] Thus, as a philosophical and religious concept, Gandhi's *ahimsa* meant compassion and love involving passionate identification with all living beings (and therefore not just human beings), taking worldly suffering seriously and entailing 'active social service'.[145] I argue in the next chapter that this understanding of *ahimsa* as active social service, which Gandhi emphasised through his constructive programme, was central to his politics.

But *ahimsa*, as we know, was also a political concept par excellence for Gandhi, conducted through innovative political tools like *satyagraha* – its forms include civil disobedience, non-cooperation, boycott, *hartal* (strike), and so on. Gandhi considered his theory of *ahimsa* as the 'perfect instrument' for practising and propagating non-violence in social and political life. Therefore, he declared that even if his technique of *ahimsa* failed, it was the individual's fault: 'If I fail here, it won't be any proof that the theory is wrong. It will simply mean that my *sadhana* [dedication] has been imperfect, that there is some fault somewhere in my technique.'[146] The site for his practice of *ahimsa*, as has been argued, was the Indian subcontinent. Of *ahimsa*, as a political concept, Chatterjee notes:

> In its application to politics, ahimsa was also about 'intense political activity' by large masses of people. But it was not so much about resistance as about the *modalities* of resistance, about organizational

principles, rules of conduct, strategies and tactics. Ahimsa was the necessary complement to the concept of satyagraha which both limited it and at the same time, made it something more than 'purely and simply civil disobedience'. Ahimsa was the rule for concretizing the 'truth' of satyagraha. (Original emphasis)[147]

Chatterjee argues that the concept of *ahimsa* was at once both ethical and epistemological because it was defined within a moral and epistemic practice that was 'wholly experimental'.[148] It was the moral framework for solving every practical problem of the organised political movement. At the same time, it also supplied Gandhi with 'a theory of politics', thereby becoming the ideology of India's national political movement.[149] In this way, Chatterjee secularises Gandhi's religious or ethical politics. Similarly, although Bilgrami has suggested that there was a certain 'integrity' to Gandhi's ideas, in the sense that his thought was highly integrated, he also adds that Gandhi's 'ideas about very specific political strategies in specific contexts flowed from ideas that were very remote from politics. They flowed from the most abstract epistemological and methodological commitments'.[150] I would, however, like to suggest that the 'integrity' that Bilgrami finds in Gandhi's thought neither flowed from 'abstract epistemological' commitments nor were his ideas 'wholly experimental', as Chatterjee suggests. Rather, Gandhi's moral and ethical commitments were guided by and tethered to *ashramic* duties. In other words, his moral and epistemic practice of *ahimsa* found definite expression in his conception of religion as discovery of the absolute truth, which was practised and simultaneously experienced in everyday ethical living. Thus, for Gandhi, the *ashramic* observances and practice of *ahimsa* could not be severed from the political practice of *ahimsa* as *satyagraha*. Understood in this manner, *ahimsa* could not simply be a personal virtue for an individual; it was 'spiritual and political conduct both for the individual and the community'.[151] As the leader of a secular nationalist movement, Nehru was aware of Gandhi's religious basis of *ahimsa*, and therefore he stressed that non-violence could be adopted by him and the Congress as a policy measure only.[152]

TOLERANCE OR EQUALITY OF ALL RELIGIONS

Although tolerance and equality of all religions cohere in Gandhi's list of *ashram* vows, he did not consider the idea of equality of all religions being satisfactorily reflected in the notion of tolerance. Elsewhere, he also said that even the phrase 'respect for all religions' did not capture his understanding of religious tolerance.[153] Criticising the word 'tolerance', he said:

> I do not like the word tolerance, but could not think of a better one. Tolerance may imply a gratuitous assumption of the inferiority of other faiths to one's own, whereas ahimsa teaches us to entertain the same respect for the religious faiths of others as we accord to our own, thus admitting the imperfection of the latter.[154]

Indeed, the idea of tolerance and its practice can be understood in multiple ways. It may value diversity and accommodate differences. But it can also refer to an indifference to, or a mild disapproval of, the practices of others, where the strategy is to distance oneself from others. It can also mean a repugnance of others but still a toleration of their practices. Finally, tolerance can also mean a deep hostility that does not erupt into conflict.[155] For Gandhi, equality of all religions required an acceptance of absolute or unassimilable difference, where tolerance would mean the possibility of acceptance of the 'most orthodox' of religious faith. As such, communal unity through a recognition of absolute difference meant, 'whatever his religion maybe, to represent in his own person Hindu, Muslim, Christian, Zoroastrian, Jew, etc'.[156] Gandhi says:

> ... the true beauty of Hindu–Mohammedan unity lies in each remaining true to his own religion and yet being true to each other. For, we are thinking of Hindus and Mohammedans even of the most orthodox type being able to regard one another as natural friends instead of regarding one another as natural enemies as they have done hitherto.[157]

Here, I would like to suggest that there is a conceptual distance between Gandhi's idea of equality of all religions expressed in the phrase *sarva dharma samabhava* and its expression in the statist version of secularism. The legitimating vocabulary of dominant (Western) conceptions of secularism, which advocate state neutrality, is based on a notion of formal equality.[158] The statist version of secularism in India, however, also seeks substantive equality among all religions, expressed in the idea of *sarva dharma samabhava*. As such, often a justification for the practice of secularism in India is attributed neither to state's equidistance to religion nor to mutual indifference. Rather, secularism is associated with tolerance and is justified on the basis of India's long tradition of peaceful co-existence of diverse communities.[159] In these arguments, not only is the value and practice of tolerance already present in the Indian subcontinent; religious difference can be subsumed in notions such as syncretic traditions and composite cultures. Or, as is frequently found in the Hindu right argument, tolerance is equated with the generosity of Hindu traditions.[160] Although Gandhi also invoked India's shared and pluralist cultures, I suggest, he sought equality of all religions somewhere else. As opposed to the statist conception of tolerance, which is justified by the presence of a tradition of tolerance in India's past, Gandhi sought to *forge* tolerance in society through associational activities, like his constructive programme of social reform, and associational politics, demonstrated in movements like the Non-cooperation–Khilafat alliance of 1919–1922. It is in these forms of 'associationalism', in the sphere of society and politics, where Gandhi saw the political possibility of equality among communities without subsuming difference and diversity to it.[161]

Tolerance in the mainstream nationalist discourse has been largely understood through equality of all religions and respect for all religions – that is, in the nationalist justification of *sarva dharma samabhava*. During the Constituent Assembly Debates, where independent India's constitution took shape, this justificatory argument was again invoked by several members of the assembly for a secular state.[162] Tolerance, in these arguments, is inbuilt in India's cultural past, such that the subcontinent's history is located in a secular historiography of India's composite culture, which is a history about the assimilation and integration of diverse races, ethnicities, religions, languages and cultures. As we shall see in the later chapters on Nehru, such a secular historiography, which highlights India's tradition of tolerance in cultural synthesis, was one of the bases for his secular nationalism and, after independence, also a justification for a secular state. Gandhi, when seen through such a secular historiography, comes out as an odd figure. Like the nationalist movement, Gandhi also called for *sarva dharma samabhava*, and indeed tolerance figures out as one of the *ashram* vows. But his perfunctory narrative of India's history can be easily located within a communal historiography,[163] emphasising, as it does, on separate and distinct identities.[164] For scholars like Parekh, who wrongly identify Gandhi's conception of tolerance with 'synthesis' and 'assimilation' of different cultures, the only reconciliation left is to argue that 'Gandhi's assessment of Muslim rule was less hostile than that of many of his predecessors'.[165]

Gandhi says:

> Time was when Hindus thought Muslims were natural enemies of Hindus. But, as is the case with Hinduism, ultimately it comes to terms with the enemy and makes friends with it. The process has not been completed.[166]

In his assumptions about Indian history and society, it may be argued that Gandhi shared more in common with conservative British colonialists like Sir Arthur Lyall and Sir Herbert Risley, who questioned if India could ever be a nation,[167] as well as the communal political groups, which emerged during the twentieth century to protect their political interests in Britain's 'divide and rule' policy. My suggestion is that Gandhi's idea of tolerance and equality of all religions should be understood from this common ground he shared with conservative British colonialists and communal political organisations. Ravinder Kumar argues that because Gandhi saw India as a loose constellation of castes, communities and religious groups, he was successful in mobilising masses for political action. Kumar contends, 'It was precisely because Gandhi held such a view of society that he was able to generate such widespread support for his political movements, and that he was also able to superimpose over existing loyalties loyalty to the concept of the political nation.'[168] Similarly, Devji finds historical precedents to Gandhi's politics in the Indian Mutiny of 1857, where the mutineers refused to subordinate their caste and religious distinctions to an undifferentiated notion of being Indian. Devji argues that it was exactly 'a faith in these distinctions' that marked Gandhi's politics as well.[169]

When asked about how he could envisage Hindu–Muslim unity when these communities neither dined together nor married each other, Gandhi replied:

> In my opinion the idea that interdining or intermarrying is necessary for national growth is a superstition borrowed from the West. Eating is a process just as vital as the other sanitary necessities of life. And if mankind had not, much to its harm, made of eating a fetish and

indulgence, we would have performed the operation of eating in private even as one performs the other necessary functions of life in private.... But inter-dining and intermarriage have never been a bar to disunion, quarrels and worse. The Pandavas and the Kauravas flew at one another's throats without compunction although they inter-dined and intermarried.[170] The bitterness between the English and the Germans has not yet died out. The fact is that intermarriage and inter-dining are not necessary factors in friendship and unity though they are often emblems thereof. But insistence on either the one or the other can easily become and is today a bar to Hindu–Mohammedan unity.[171]

National unity promoted through a common nationality, which was based on equality of rights embodied in the abstract citizen, was unimportant to Gandhi. How did he, then, envisage a united nation despite his assumption that social loyalties in India were moulded by pre-modern social identities like caste and not modern ones like class? Gandhi's solution did not rely on constitutional changes enforced by the state like a uniform civil code or on legislation on religious freedom.[172] Unlike Nehru, he also did not seek justification for tolerance on already available sources of toleration found in syncretism. Forms of syncretism may be influenced by cosmopolitanism and universal values, or they may emerge among elite cultures, such as the Ganga–Jamuni *tehzeeb* (Ganga–Yamuna culture) among the Nawabs[173] of Lucknow.[174] Such syncretism may be unable to locate, question and challenge existing local hierarchies and power structures. Furthermore, critical studies on syncretism have pointed out to its ambiguous nature, questioning the assumption that syncretism indicates tolerance.[175] Chakrabarti and Sitharaman, for instance, criticise 'liberal secular understanding' of syncretism, where it is considered 'progressive and liberating' by definition and treated as powerful resource to combat communalism. They point out how communalism has gone or can go alongside syncretic religious practices.[176]

Both in the *ashram* and in his constructive programme of village reconstruction and sociopolitical reform of society, Gandhi asked people from various backgrounds to work together on social issues that, in his view, inhibited nation's self-rule. The constructive programme was Gandhi's solution towards *poorna swaraj* (complete independence). In his manual on the constructive programme, Gandhi provided an illustrative but not exhaustive list of such activities, including communal unity, geared towards social and moral reform of society. These activities included, but were not limited to, removal of untouchability, prohibition, *khadi* (handspun and hand-woven cloth), village sanitation, basic education, adult education, upliftment of women and *adivasis* (tribals), economic equality, labour union, and so on.[177] It was through these sociopolitical activities listed in the constructive programme, which as its goal sought society's social and moral reform, that tolerance would develop among various communities. In other words, societal tolerance would be a *by-product* of Gandhi's practice of *ahimsa* that, as we saw already, involved active social service. Gandhi's emphasis on social (and moral) reform as the basis for tolerance in society was based on his faith in religion's internal reform and therefore in its historical quality of evolution. If modernist leaders like B. R. Ambedkar and Nehru sought revolutionary and transformative change through the postcolonial constitution and the modern state for the systemic inequalities that beset Indian society, Gandhi envisaged gradual reform, where the onus for change in society shifted from the state to the community.[178]

GANDHI'S SPIRITUAL OR ASCETIC 'BIOMORAL' PRACTICES

That Gandhi construed religion not as otherworldly but in relation to society and polity is also evident in the spiritual and 'biomoral' practices of prayer, spinning, fasting, celibacy, silence, and so on, observed by him and his fellow *ashramites*.[179] Embodied experience is not just a matter of deliberate, intentional willed action, but also a matter of routines, habits, practices, skills and intended but non-deliberative action.[180] As opposed to traditional and conventional Hindu spiritual and austerity practices, which may be other-worldly and require solitary retreat, in Gandhi's *ashram*, spirituality was given a materialist content, in the sense that it was made this-worldly. Gandhi included a broad range of activities within the ambit of spiritual exercises, like serving Dalits,[181] spinning of *charkha* (spinning wheel) and cleaning of *ashram* latrines. Since religious faith for Gandhi was embodied and instinctive, requiring absolute submission of the devout, it was essentially a personal affair. At the same time, such individual acts of faith expressed in spinning, fasting, praying, celibacy, and so on had political significance. They cultivated values and attitudes such as patience, self-knowledge, self-discipline and sacrifice, which were essential to the dispositional politics of the Gandhian *satyagrahi*. Since the political subject needed to cultivate values such as patience, self-discipline and sacrifice to be a *satyagrahi*, she needed to be *trained* in *satyagraha*. The *ashram* was one such site for training. So, while Gandhi's acts of religious faith were isolated individual acts, they were not 'individualised' because of the effects they were assumed to produce on the *satyagrahi* and, through her politics, on the larger sociopolitical community.

In his book, *Gandhi's Body: Sex, Diet and the Politics of Nationalism*, Joseph Alter criticises studies on Gandhi for relegating Gandhi's insistence, obsession and public advocacy on questions of health and spiritual practices to a personal spiritual project, or psychoanalytical and symbolic significance, with only derivative political value. In such studies, Gandhi's extreme experiments, Alter remarks, 'can be read only as profound asceticism, unique biography, or modern political farce'.[182] Studies on Gandhi, dealing with his celibacy and sexuality, silence and spinning of *charkha*, dietetics and health, have further consolidated the dichotomy between the spiritual and political Gandhi. Alter has argued that Gandhi's politics was deeply implicated in his concern for health and spiritual or austerity practices. Gandhi 'embodied moral reform' and also argued that reform's embodiment of public health was 'inherently political, spiritual and moral'.[183] Indeed, it may be argued that in the ligature in *swaraj*, it is the *swa*, or the self, that predominated Gandhi's idea as opposed to *raj*, or rule or sovereignty. *Swaraj* meant 'rule by the self', but more crucially for Gandhi it also meant 'rule over oneself'. He ingeniously used the dominant theme of Indic religions on the government of the self, especially sensual desires, to construe a political conception of *swaraj* as self-restraint. According to Kaviraj, in Gandhi's political thought, there was a distinction and inverse relation between internal and external government. If the individual could govern, restrain and control himself, especially his material desires, he would find contentment and require less external control from the state.[184] Thus, in Gandhi's political philosophy one cannot separate the body from the body-politic.

Of *swaraj*, Gandhi observed:

> It is easier to conquer the entire world than to subdue the enemies in our body. And, therefore, for the man who succeeds in this conquest,

the former will be easy enough. The self-government which you, I and all others have to attain is in fact this…. The point of it all is that you can serve the country only with this body.[185]

Gandhi's spiritual practices, like *ahimsa*, *brahmacharya*, fasting and silence, were more than just ascetic vows; for him, they had functional value for sociopolitical activism, which was to be utilised for his propagation of non-violent political action against British colonial rule in India. Scholars like Joseph Alter and Veena Howard therefore divert attention to the relationship between Gandhi's sociopolitical actions, his somatic concerns and his spiritual and austerity practices.[186] Here, again the *ashram* became a test-site, where some of Gandhi's biomoral experiments, like the public health measures (for example, dietary reform and nature cure) and spiritual practices (for example, spinning of *charkha* and *brahmacharya*) were implemented. It must be noted that Gandhi's biomoral reform was variously understood and appropriated by the masses, such that it influenced popular consciousness in complex ways. Shahid Amin, for instance, has shown how in the district of Gorakhpur the popularly accepted notions of dietary taboos associated with the 'Mahatma' influenced many lower- and middle-caste *panchayat*s (village councils) to impose novel dietary taboos, such as giving up meat and fish, as a part of the widespread movement of self-assertion. Amin notes that during his visit to Gorakhpur in 1922, Gandhi did not press his audience to forsake fish and meat: 'He only wished the nationalist public to abstain from intoxicants, both liquor and *ganja* [cannabis]. But his speech at the district town and the perorations at all the railway stations, including Chauri Chaura, generated considerable discussion on the virtues of nationalist vegetarianism.'[187]

So far I have argued that the basis of Gandhi's religious politics lay in experience and experimentation. His application of spiritual and biomoral practices to politics, I further maintain, must be seen as an exercise to transform the political subject into a Gandhian *satyagrahi*. Through such practices, the *satyagrahi* is able to cultivate attitudes of detached action, fearlessness, patience, self-discipline, self-suffering and, even ultimately, sacrifice of the self. The centrality of biomoral activities in training the *satyagrahi* demonstrates Gandhi's awareness of the force of affect, like pride and egotism, in political conflicts over reason and rationality. Thus, the spiritual and biomoral *ashramic* practices were important aids to cultivate moral-psychological attitudes important for Gandhi's dispositional politics of non-violence.[188] Devji suggests that the moral practices of spinning and celibacy were non-instrumental yet material activities of everyday life, which were meant neither to just produce homespun cloth in the first instance nor to endow the body with some unusual power in the second. Gandhi was interested in them precisely due to their nature of disengaged action.[189] So, for instance, when Nehru was imprisoned for the first time in 1921, and jail was daunting for him both physically and psychologically, because he was brought up in comfort and prison was assumed to be a place for criminals, Gandhi advised him to take up manual labour and spinning:[190]

> Somehow or the other the jail atmosphere does not allow you to have all the bearings in your mind. I would therefore like you to *dismiss the outer world from your view altogether and ignore its existence.* I know this is a most difficult task, but if you take up some serious study and some serious manual work you can do it. Above all ... don't you be disgusted with the spinning-wheel ... we shall never have the slightest cause of regret that we have pinned our faith to the spinning-wheel or that we have spun so much good yarn per day in the name of the motherland. (Emphasis added)[191]

Only by practising moral activities, like spinning and manual work, a *satyagrahi* leader is 'produced', who would then lead the masses in *satyagraha*. Thus, Gandhi says:

> There is no doubt that it is difficult to produce a satyagrahi leader. Our experience is that a satyagrahi needs many more virtues like self-control, fearlessness etc. than are requisite for one who believes in armed action.[192]

Gandhi usually translated *tapasya* as both self-suffering and self-discipline. Mantena argues that for Gandhi *tapasya* as self-suffering and self-discipline was the distinguishing feature of all modes of non-violent action and key to their effectiveness. Moreover, this disposition towards sacrifice which is implied in suffering also allowed for self-correction and self-examination – that is, 'a disciplined humility that was performed and cultivated through detached action'.[193] Over several days of public reading of his interpretation of the Bhagavad Gita at the Sabarmati *ashram*, Gandhi observed:

> Following the death of non-violence, we discovered the value of spinning-wheel, as also of brahmacharya. Beyond the river Sabarmati is bhogabhumi [site of enjoyment], while this is karmabhumi [site of action].[194]

Gandhi saw the *ashram* as *karmabhumi*, or the site of action, as opposed to the world outside the *ashram*. He linked non-violence to the spinning wheel and *brahmacharya* because when non-violence as a political tool seemed to fail, its redemption lay in these latter ascetic practices. They were aids to internally avert moral erosion and the temptation to violence. It was through these spiritual activities that one cultivated attitudes of self-constraint and self-discipline, which were necessary attributes for a *satyagrahi* to engage in non-violent and moral politics. Understood this way, Gandhi's peace works among Muslims in Noakhali during the 1946 riots (which was marked by violence against women in the form of abductions, rapes and forced conversions) and his *brahmacharya* experiments with his grandniece, Manu, during the same time may be seen as intrinsically linked. Gandhi's resort to these actions, which seemed morally outrageous to even his closest co-workers, demonstrates his conviction about the intrinsic unity of thought and action. Thus, Gandhi's ascetic, spiritual and biomoral practices cannot be simply described as of derivative political significance. By separating the religious Gandhi from the political one, one fails to see the holistic conception of Gandhian thought, where the public and the private, the religious, moral, and the political, the mind and the body, and ultimately the mind and the world are not separate.

CONCLUSION: THE COUNTER-NARRATIVE OF SECULARITY

For long, theories of modernisation and secularisation have postulated the privatisation and decline of religion.[195] Along with religion's decline in modern societies, Rawlsian and Habermasian type of liberal politics are generally seen as the right or the desired kind of politics for secular liberal democracies.[196] It is only with the resurgence of religion in the public domain that there has been a rethinking of the proper place of religion in society, where the solution to societal conflicts does not require hiving off religion to the private sphere.[197] While contemporary scholars of liberalism and secularism have questioned and redefined public–private distinction and separation of religion and politics, keeping in mind the modern societal condition of pluralism and deep diversity, these features continue to be essential for liberalism and secularism. In this chapter, I have argued that while Gandhian thought and political practice disregard the separation of religion and politics and the public–private distinction, it nevertheless propagates a politics whose goals are in consonance with the values that liberal secularism seeks to protect. I have further argued that Gandhi's *ashram* observances and politics challenge and subvert the modern secularisation process understood as functional differentiation of various spheres of the social, political, economic, scientific, and so on. His politics is deeply non-liberal, non-secular and even considered unmodern.[198] It exalts personal virtues like obedience and sacrifice, conditions rights on the performance of duties and infuses religion in politics. His religious politics, one may say, provides a counter-narrative of secularity. And yet, despite his rejection of the modern liberal political imaginary, it may be argued that Gandhi's political thought evinces a non-oppositional alternative to liberal secularism, where his religious morality and politics are nevertheless in consonance with the goals of liberal secularism. In contemporary India, we see that the language of secularism is being increasingly appropriated by those who clearly stand against values which secularism seeks to protect. At the same time, we also see religious majoritarianism challenging liberal rights and equality guaranteed in the constitution. Given this predicament, it may be fruitful to look at varieties and possibilities of political thought and politics that although situate themselves outside the language and structural demands of liberalism and secularism, still promote politics in consonance with values cherished by both liberalism and secularism.

NOTES

1. M. K. Gandhi, 'Address to Ashram Inmates', 17 February 1919, in *The Collected Works of Mahatma Gandhi* (henceforth, *CWMG*), 98 volumes, vol. 17, p. 287 (New Delhi: Government of India), https://www.

gandhiashramsevagram.org/gandhi-literature/collected-works-of-mahatma-gandhi-volume-1-to-98.php (accessed on 14 March 2021). For ease of access as well as to get a sense of the time period in which Gandhi was writing, I have provided the date and the year alongside the volume number.
2. Narayan Desai, raised and educated at Gandhi's *ashram*s (Sabarmati and Sevagram), was the son of Gandhi's personal secretary, Mahadev Desai. He wrote a four-volume biography of Gandhi in Gujarati, *Maru Jivan Ej Mari Vani* (My Life Is My Message), which has been translated in English by Tridip Suhrud.
3. Narayan Desai, *My Life Is My Message: Satyagraha (1915–1930)*, vol. 2, trans. Tridip Suhrud (New Delhi: Orient Blackswan, 2009), pp. xi–xii.
4. Sudipta Kaviraj, *Imaginary Institutions of India: Politics and Ideas* (New York: Columbia University Press, 2010), p. 113.
5. Ibid., p. 114.
6. Ibid.
7. Ibid.
8. M. K. Gandhi, *Constructive Programme: Its Meaning and Place* (Ahmedabad: Navajivan Trust, 1945 [1941]).
9. Ajay Skaria, 'Gandhi's Politics: Liberalism and the Question of the Ashram', *The South Atlantic Quarterly* 101, no. 4 (2002): 955–986; Ajay Skaria, *Unconditional Equality: Gandhi's Religion of Resistance* (Minneapolis: University of Minnesota Press, 2016).
10. 'Truth' capitalised indicates Gandhi's notion of absolute truth.
11. Dennis Dalton, *Mahatma Gandhi: Nonviolent Power in Action* (New York: Columbia University Press, 2012 [1993]), p. xvi. Also see Tridip Suhrud, 'The Story of Antaryami', *Social Scientist* 46, no. 11–12 (2018): 37–60.
12. Judith M. Brown, 'Gandhi as a Nationalist Leader, 1915–1948', in *The Cambridge Companion to Gandhi*, ed. Judith M. Brown and Anthony Parel, pp. 51–70 (New York: Cambridge University Press, 2011), p. 55.
13. Two of Gandhi's writings – *From Yeravda Mandir* (1932) and *Ashram Observance in Action* (1955) – are especially relevant to this chapter. Gandhi wrote *From Yeravda Mandir* (*Mangal Prabhat*) in Guajarati as weekly letters to the Satyagraha Ashram during his incarceration in the Yeravda prison in 1930. It was translated into English by Valji Govindji Desai and published in 1932. According to Tridip Suhrud, Gandhi wrote the last chapter in this work on *swadeshi* after his release from prison as he felt that he could not do justice to the politics of *swadeshi*

without encroaching upon his limits as a prisoner. See Tridip Suhrud, 'Gandhi's Key Writings: In Search of Unity', in *The Cambridge Companion to Gandhi*, ed. Judith M. Brown and Anthony Parel, pp. 71–92 (New York: Cambridge University Press, 2011), p. 90, note 38. Gandhi started writing *Ashram Observance in Action* (*Satyagraha Ashramno Itihas*) in Yeravda Central Prison on 5 April 1932. It was written intermittently and was never completed. It was published after his death in May 1948. Its English translation by Valji Govindji Desai was published in 1955.

14. M. K. Gandhi, 'May God Help', 26 November 1924, *CWMG*, vol. 29, p. 374. In the 98 volumes of the *CWMG*, the word 'secularism' only appears thrice, and except for a newspaper report in 1946, there is no mention of 'secularism' by Gandhi himself. For Gandhi's insistence on the close relationship between religion and politics, see M. K. Gandhi, *An Autobiography or The Story of My Experiments with Truth*, trans. Mahadev Desai (Ahmedabad: Navajivan Trust, 1940). Also see M. K. Gandhi, 'Letter to W.J. Wybergh', 10 May 1910, *CWMG*, vol.11, pp. 39–40; 'Some Questions', 30 January 1921, *CWMG*, vol. 22, p. 284; 'My Mission', 3 April 1924, *CWMG*, vol. 27, p. 156; M. K. Gandhi, 'Arya Samajists Again', 19 July 1924, *CWMG*, vol. 28, p. 178.

15. From the 1940s onwards, Gandhi insists on separating religion and politics. For instance, see M. K. Gandhi, 'Unseemly if True', 9 August 1942, *CWMG*, vol. 83, p. 207; M. K. Gandhi, 'Talk with a Christian Missionary', 22 September 1946, *CWMG*, vol. 92, p. 190; M. K. Gandhi, 'Speech at Prayer Meeting', 31 August 1947, *CWMG*, vol. 96, p. 267. Also see Ajay Skaria, 'No Politics without Religion, of Secularism and Gandhi', in *Political Hinduism: The Religious Imagination in Public Spheres*, ed. Vinay Lal, pp. 173–210 (New Delhi: Oxford University Press); Skaria, 'Gandhi's Politics'.

16. For a counterview, see Akeel Bilgrami, 'Secularism: Its Content and Context', in *Secularism, Identity, and Enchantment*, pp. 3–57 (Cambridge, MA: Harvard University Press, 2014). According to Bilgrami, Gandhi's espousal of political secularism emerged due to the increasing influence of majoritarian nationalism in the later period of the Indian national movement. In such a reading, Gandhi's affirmation of religious politics and political secularism belong in different contextual backgrounds, such that to present Gandhi as a 'proto-secularist' in early twentieth century would be a misreading of Gandhi's thought.

17. For a philosophical analysis of Gandhi's conception of religion, see Margaret Chatterjee, *Gandhi's Religious Thought* (Indiana: University of

Notre Dame Press, 1983). For a historical account of Gandhi's politics, see Judith M. Brown, *Gandhi's Rise to Power: Indian Politics 1915–1922* (London: Cambridge University Press, 1972); and Judith M. Brown, *Gandhi and Civil Disobedience: The Mahatma in Indian Politics 1928–1934* (Cambridge: Cambridge University Press, 2008 [1977]). For Gandhi's political philosophy, see Raghavan Iyer, *The Moral and Political Thought of Mahatma Gandhi* (New York: Oxford University Press, 1973); Bhikhu C. Parekh, *Colonialism, Tradition, and Reform: An Analysis of Gandhi's Political Discourse* (New Delhi: SAGE Publications, 1989); Faisal Devji, *Impossible Indian: Gandhi and the Temptation of Violence* (Cambridge, MA: Harvard University Press, 2012); Anuradha Veeravalli, *Gandhi in Political Theory* (Surrey: Ashgate Publishing, 2014); Ajay Skaria, *Unconditional Equality: Gandhi's Religion of Resistance* (Minneapolis: University of Minnesota Press, 2016); and Aishwary Kumar, *Radical Equality: Ambedkar, Gandhi and the Risk of Democracy* (Stanford: Stanford University Press, 2015). For Gandhi's politics in South Africa, see Ashwin Desai and Goolam Vahed, *The South African Gandhi: Stretcher-Bearer of Empire* (Stanford: Stanford University Press, 2016).
18. Gandhi's re-conceptualisation of passive resistance.
19. José Casanova, *Public Religions in the Modern World* (Chicago: University of Chicago Press, 1994). Also see José Casanova, 'Public Religions Revisited', in *Religion: Beyond the Concept*, ed. Hent de Vries, pp. 101–119 (New York: Fordham University Press, 2008). I have discussed Casanova's secularisation thesis in Chapter 1.
20. Charles Taylor, *A Secular Age* (Cambridge, MA: Harvard University Press, 2007), p. 19. I have discussed Taylor's conception of secularity in detail in Chapter 1.
21. Rajeev Bhargava, 'Political Secularism', in *The Oxford Handbook of Political Theory*, ed. John S. Dryzek, Bonnie Honig and Anne Phillips, pp. 636–655 (Oxford: Oxford University Press, 2006), p. 642. Bhargava and Taylor have argued that secularism is not simply a doctrine of separation of church and state because liberal secularism also includes a commitment to substantive liberal values. I have discussed the conception of secularism in Chapter 1.
22. Sheldon Wolin, 'Fugitive Democracy', in *Democracy and Difference: Contesting the Boundaries of the Political*, ed. Seyla Benhabib, pp. 31–45 (New Jersey: Princeton University Press), p. 31.
23. Ibid.

24. Leigh Jenco, *Making the Political* (Stanford: Stanford University Press, 2010).
25. For a theoretical discussion on how the language of liberal imperialism was utilised by the British empire to justify colonial rule, see Uday Singh Mehta, *Liberalism and Empire: A Study in Nineteenth Century British Liberal Thought* (Chicago: University of Chicago Press, 1999).
26. See the chapter titled 'Brute Force' in *Hind Swaraj*. M. K. Gandhi, 'Indian Home Rule or Hind Swaraj', trans. M. K. Gandhi, in *Hind Swaraj and Other Writings*, ed. Anthony J. Parel, pp. 1–125 (New York: Cambridge University Press, 2009 [1997]), pp. 79–87. Also see M. K. Gandhi, 'Hind Swaraj', 11–18 December 1909, *CWMG* (revised edition, 1939), vol. 10, pp. 245–315.
27. The fact that the moderates of the Congress have been derided as 'inauthentic mimic men' and 'mendicant office seekers' is telling of how ineffectual their politics was conceived to be in bringing social and political transformation. Furthermore, the vast masses were unconnected to this form of constitutional reformism. By 1919, constitutionalism of the Congress had proved ineffective in winning major concessions from the British Raj, and the sporadic, isolated instances of armed resistance had been crushed. That Gandhi's first nation-wide mass mobilisation in 1919 took the British administration 'by surprise' demonstrates the break from earlier politics. See Sugata Bose and Ayesha Jalal, *Modern South Asia: History, Culture, Political Economy* (New Delhi: Routledge, 2004).
28. In a letter to Dinshaw Wacha (moderate Congress leader), Gandhi wrote, '... the growing generation will not be satisfied with petitions etc.... Satyagraha is the only way, it seems to me, to stop terrorism.' Quoted in Sumit Sarkar, *Modern India 1885–1947* (New Delhi: Macmillan India, 2002 [1983]), p. 189.
29. Gandhi, 'Hind Swaraj', p. 84.
30. Ibid., p. 79.
31. Ibid., p. 81. Karuna Mantena contends, '... it was Gandhi who, more than any thinker, took the problem of means and their consequences as the central and defining problem of political life'. Karuna Mantena, 'Gandhi and the Means–Ends Question in Politics', Unpublished Paper (2012). https://karunamantena.files.wordpress.com/2011/04/mantena-gandhimeansends.pdf (accessed on 16 March 2021).
32. Mantena, 'Gandhi and the Means–Ends Question'.

33. Skaria, 'Gandhi's Politics', p. 976. *Satyagraha* literally means 'the insistence on truth', which Gandhi translated as 'truth-force' or 'soul-force'. For a critical engagement with Gandhi's *satyagraha*, see Aishwary Kumar, 'Spirits of Satyagraha: A History of Force', in *Radical Equality*, pp. 59–107.
34. For instance, Gandhi, 'Hind Swaraj', pp. 84, 85 and 89.
35. Gandhi, 'Hind Swaraj', p. 90. Also see M. K. Gandhi, 'Congress Report on the Punjab Disorders: Chapter IV, Satyagraha', 25 March 1920, *CWMG*, vol. 20, pp. 39–45.
36. Gandhi, 'Congress Report', p. 41. Also see Gandhi, 'Hind Swaraj'.
37. Gandhi, 'Hind Swaraj', p. 87.
38. Devji, *Impossible Indian*, p. 7.
39. 'The suffering that has to be undergone in *satyagraha* is *tapasya* in its purest form'. See M. K. Gandhi, 'Satyagraha, Not Passive Resistance', about 2 September 1917, *CWMG*, vol. 16, p. 13. For further elaboration on why Gandhi rejected the phrase 'passive resistance' and instead coined the neologism *satyagraha*, see M. K. Gandhi, 'Chapter XII: The Advent of Satyagraha', Satyagraha in South Africa, 26 April 1928, *CWMG*, vol. 34, p. 93. The *CWMG* version is reproduced from M. K. Gandhi, *Satyagraha in South Africa*, trans. Valji Govindji Desai, ed. Shriman Narayan (Ahmedabad: Navajivan Trust, 1968 [1928]).
40. Devji, *Impossible Indian*.
41. Gandhi described them as 'seekers of truth'.
42. Gandhi, 'Hind Swaraj', pp. 81–82.
43. Gandhi says:

> The Constituent Assembly is discussing the rights of the citizen. That is to say they are deliberating on what the fundamental rights should be. As a matter of fact, the proper question is not what the rights of a citizen are, but rather what constitutes the duties of a citizen. Fundamental rights can only be those rights the exercise of which is not only in the interest of the citizen but that of the whole world. Today everyone wants to know what his rights are, but if a man learns to discharge his duties right from childhood and studies the sacred books of his faith he automatically exercises his rights too.... I learnt my duties on my mother's lap.... Thus if from childhood we learn what our dharma is and try to follow it our rights look after themselves. I could live only on condition that I drank the milk that my mother gave me. If I had shirked the obligation to drink milk I would have forfeited my right to live. The beauty of it is that *the very*

performance of a duty secures us our right. Rights cannot be divorced from duties. This is how satyagraha was born, for I was always striving to decide what my duty was.' (Emphasis added)

See M. K. Gandhi, 'Speech at a Prayer Meeting', 28 June 1947, *CWMG*, vol. 95, p. 353. Also see M. K. Gandhi, 'Letter to Julian Huxley', 25 May 1947, *CWMG*, vol. 95, p. 137; Richard Sorabji, *Gandhi and the Stoics: Modern Experiments on Ancient Values* (Chicago: University of Chicago Press, 2012); and Devji, *Impossible Indian*.

44. Ramin Jahanbegloo, *The Gandhian Moment* (Cambridge, MA: Harvard University Press, 2013), p. 5.
45. For an argument about sovereignty being vested in the individual in Gandhi's political thought, see Ronald J. Terchek, *Gandhi: Struggling for Autonomy* (New York: Rowman and Littlefield, 1998); and Devji, *Impossible Indian*. Partha Chatterjee has famously argued that in Gandhi's political ideal of Ramarajya, there is an 'undivided concept of popular sovereignty', where the community is self-regulating and political power is dissolved into the collective moral will. Partha Chatterjee, *Nationalist Thought and the Colonial World: A Derivative Discourse* (London: Zed Books, 1993 [1986]), pp. 90–93. Anuradha Veeravalli draws attention to a clear separation between the state and civil society in Gandhi's thought. She also argues for a 'theory of substantive sovereignty' of the masses of the nation and the individual in Gandhi's thought. Veeravalli, *Gandhi in Political Theory*, p. 50.
46. M. K. Gandhi, 'Speech at a Prayer Meeting', 28 June 1947, *CWMG*, vol. 95, p. 354.
47. Ibid.
48. Devji makes this point in *Impossible Indian*.
49. Gandhi, 'Hind Swaraj', p. 98. Gandhi goes on to say, 'These observances are not to be abandoned in the belief that they are difficult.... These qualities are worth having, even for those who do not wish to serve the country.' Ibid. Thus, for Gandhi, 'qualities' such as fearlessness must be generally cultivated by an individual.
50. Anuradha Veeravalli, 'Sovereignty: Individual, Civil Society and the State', in *Gandhi in Political Theory*, pp. 49–74. There she argues that canonical liberal tradition does not provide a theoretical ground for dissent against the state.
51. Gandhi, 'Hind Swaraj', p. 90.
52. Mohammad Iqbal, *The Reconstruction of Religious Thought in Islam* (Oxford: Oxford University Press, 1934).

53. Ibid., 171.
54. Ibid.
55. Ibid.
56. Ibid., p. 172.
57. M. K. Gandhi, 'Neither a Saint Nor a Politician', 12 May 1920, *CWMG*, vol. 20, p. 304.
58. Ibid.
59. Skaria, 'No Politics without Religion', p. 196; Suhrud, 'Antaryami'.
60. The use of the term 'religion' as 'faith' here is in the sense Mohammed Iqbal defined it. It does not refer to Ashis Nandy's distinction between religion as faith and ideology. For Nandy's distinction between faith and ideology, see Ashis Nandy, 'The Politics of Secularism and the Recovery of Religious Toleration', in *Secularism and its Critics*, ed. Rajeev Bhargava, pp. 321–344 (New Delhi: Oxford University Press, 2008 [1998]). For a similar characterisation of Gandhi's religious faith as mine, see Suhrud, 'Antaryami'.
61. I have framed Gandhi's idea of religion as ethical living by borrowing Iqbal's typology in order to provide it a conceptual rigour and also distinguish it from right-wing Hindu interpretations. As is well-known, Hinduism as a 'way of living' is a much-abused phrase used to legitimise the Hindutva ideology. For instance, see Supreme Court judgments, *Manohar Joshi v. N. B. Patil*, AIR (1996) 796, and *Dr. Ramesh Yeshwant Prabhoo v. Prabhakar K. Kunte*, AIR (1996) SC 1113. For a discussion of these cases (Hindutva case), see Shylashri Shankar, 'Secularity and Hinduism's Imaginaries in India', in *A Secular Age beyond the West: Religion, Law and the State in Asia, the Middle East and North Africa*, ed. Mirjam Künkler, John Madeley and Shylashri Shankar, pp. 128–151 (New York: Cambridge University Press, 2018).
62. Calling it an unscientific view, Tagore wrote: 'For we can never imagine any civilised ruler of men making indiscriminate examples of casual victims, including children and members of the untouchable community, in order to impress others dwelling at a safe distance who possibly deserve severe condemnation…. We, who are immensely grateful to Mahatmaji for inducing … freedom from fear and feebleness in the minds of his countrymen, feel profoundly hurt when any words from his mouth may emphasise the elements of unreason in those very minds – unreason, which is a fundamental source of all the blind powers that drive us against freedom and self-respect.' See Rabindranath Tagore,

'The Bihar Earthquake', in *The Mahatma and the Poet: Letters and Debates between Gandhi and Tagore 1915–1941*, ed. Sabyasachi Bhattacharya, pp. 157–158 (New Delhi: National Book Trust, 1997).

63. Akeel Bilgrami, 'Gandhi, the Philosopher', in *Secularism, Identity, and Enchantment*, pp. 101–121 (Cambridge, MA: Harvard University Press, 2014), p. 109.
64. Karuna Mantena, 'Another Realism: The Politics of Gandhian Nonviolence', *American Political Science Review* 106, no. 2 (2012): 455–470, at p. 461.
65. See Sorabji, *Gandhi and the Stoics*, pp. 12–14. Also see Suhrud, 'Antaryami'.
66. See Robert Sparling, 'M.K. Gandhi: Reconciling Agonism and Deliberative Democracy', *Representation* 45, no. 4: 391–403. Sparling makes an argument about the limitations of deliberative democracy as reasoned argument and Gandhi's insistence on the political practice of cultivation of virtue and spirit of reciprocity as a possible solution to the impasse of deliberative democracy. I, however, disagree with Sparling's analysis of Gandhi's politics as a 'celebration of Habermasian public sphere'. Susanne H. Rudolph and Lloyd I. Rudolph, for instance, contrast the Habermasian public sphere and the European variant of civil society to Gandhi's *ashram* and his associational politics, and argue for an 'Indian variant' of civil society and public sphere. See Susanne H. Rudolph and Lloyd I. Rudolph, 'The Coffee House and the Ashram: Gandhi, Civil Society and Public Spheres', Working Paper no. 15, South Asia Institute, Department of Political Science, Heidelberg University, 2003.
67. M. K. Gandhi, 'Cow Protection', 11 November 1926, *CWMG*, vol. 37, p. 6.
68. M. K. Gandhi, 'The Doctrine of the Sword', 11 August 1920, *CWMG*, vol. 21, p. 134.
69. M. K. Gandhi, 'Speech at Mirzapur Park, Calcutta', 23 January 1921, *CWMG*, vol. 22, p. 250.
70. The *ashram* was later relocated and renamed as Sabarmati Ashram.
71. Gandhi, *Ashram Observance*, p. 6.
72. Mark Thomson, *Gandhi and His Ashrams* (Mumbai: Popular Prakashan, 1993).
73. Veeravalli, *Gandhi in Political Theory*.
74. Gandhi, *Ashram Observance*, p. 3.
75. 'Following the death of non-violence, we discovered the value of the spinning-wheel, as also of *brahmacharya* [celibacy]. Beyond the river

75. (Sabarmati) is *bhogabhumi* [the site of passivity], while this is *karmabhumi* [the site of action]'. Gandhi quoted in Devji, *Impossible Indian*, p. 98.
76. M. K. Gandhi, 'The Vow of Hindu–Muslim Unity', 8 April 1919, *CWMG*, vol. 17, p. 400.
77. Gandhi, *Ashram Observance*, p. 3.
78. Ibid., p. 81.
79. Rudolph and Rudolph, 'The Coffee House and the Ashram', pp. 7 and 10.
80. Akeel Bilgrami, 'Gandhi's Religion and Its Relation to His Politics', in *The Cambridge Companion to Gandhi*, ed. Judith M. Brown and Anthony J. Parel, pp. 93–116 (New York: Cambridge University Press, 2011), p. 95.
81. Gandhi took to celibacy at the age of 37 in 1906. For him *brahmacharya* did not simply mean sexual control. '... Brahmacharya means the control in thought, word and action, of all the senses at all times and in all places'. M. K. Gandhi, 'Bramhacharya', 25 May 1924, *CWMG*, vol. 28, pp. 22–23. For an explanation on the importance of *brahmacharya* in Gandhi's political thought and practice, see Veeravalli, *Gandhi in Political Theory*, pp. 119–140.
82. Skaria, 'No Politics without Religion', p. 196. Also see 'Speech at a Prayer Meeting', 4 April 1947, *CWMG*, vol. 94, p. 234.
83. *Swadeshi* roughly translates to 'of one's own country' (literally, self's territory). It is an insistence on the use of goods made in one's country.
84. Gandhi, *Ashram Observance*; Gandhi, *From Yeravda Mandir*.
85. Veeravalli, *Gandhi in Political Theory*, p. 114.
86. For debates on the public–private distinction and its importance in liberalism, see Gurpreet Mahajan and Helmut Reifeld, *The Public and the Private: Issues of Democratic Citizenship* (New Delhi: SAGE Publications, 2003).
87. Capitalised 'Truth' denotes Gandhi's conception of a universal truth.
88. Gandhi, *Yeravda Mandir*, p. 4.
89. Ibid. Also see M. K. Gandhi, 'Letter to Prabhudas Gandhi', 2 December 1929, *CWMG*, vol. 48, p. 48.
90. Gandhi, *Yeravda Mandir*, p. 8. Also see M. K. Gandhi, 'A Message', 13 March 1927, *CWMG*, vol. 38, p. 198.
91. 'Ahimsa which to me is the chief glory of Hinduism has been sought to be explained away by our people as being meant for sanyasis only. I do not share that view. I have held that it is *the way of life* and India has to show it to the world' M. K. Gandhi, 'A Talk', 20 November 1946, *CWMG*, vol. 93, p. 43 (emphasis added).

92. *Sanatana*, which translates to 'perennial', refers to the primordial tradition of truth of Hinduism which can manifest itself in different forms in different ages, and does not conform to any dogmatic version of Hinduism. Veeravalli, *Gandhi in Political Theory*, p. 18, note 10. According to Gandhi, *sanatana* specifically meant four things: (*a*) belief in the ancient Hindu scriptures like the Vedas, the Upanishads, the Puranas, and in *avatars* and re-birth; (*b*) belief in the *varnashrama dharma* (here, he adds the qualification that this belief is 'strictly Vedic', based on four-fold division, which is inherent to human nature and based on birth); (*c*) a commitment to cow protection (here, again, Gandhi clarifies that such a commitment was much larger than what was popularly understood); (*d*) idol worship was not a sin. See M. K. Gandhi, 'Hinduism', 6 October 1921, *CWMG*, vol. 24, pp. 370–371.
93. M. K. Gandhi, 'What Is Hinduism?' 24 April 1924, *CWMG*, vol. 27, p. 292 (emphasis added).
94. *Young India* was a weekly journal published in English by M. K. Gandhi from 1919 to 1931. According to Joseph Alter, the title of the journal connotes an imagined celibate nation. Joseph Alter, *Gandhi's Body: Sex, Diet, and the Politics of Nationalism* (Philadelphia: University of Pennsylvania Press, 2000).
95. The ex-untouchables who are designated the lowest ritual status in the Hindu caste system.
96. M. K. Gandhi, 'Sanatana Hindu', 27 August 1925, *CWMG*, vol. 32, p. 335.
97. Ibid.
98. Bilgrami, 'Gandhi's Religion and Its Relation to His Politics'.
99. For instance, while talking about *yajna*, or sacrifice, as an *ashram* vow, Gandhi argues that from the point of view of *ahimsa*, sacrificing lower animals to service humanity cannot be called *yajna*, although animal sacrifice finds legitimacy in the Vedas. This is so because, in Gandhi's opinion, 'such sacrifice cannot stand the fundamental tests of Truth and non-violence'. Gandhi, *Yeravda Mandir*, p. 32.
100. M. K. Gandhi, 'Hinduism', 6 October 1921, *CWMG*, vol. 24, p. 371.
101. M. K. Gandhi, 'Speech at a Public Meeting, Madras', 8 April 1921, *CWMG*, vol. 23, p. 19.
102. Bilgrami, 'Gandhi's Religion and Its Relation to His Politics'.
103. Ibid.
104. *Shastra* is a general term which refers to a large body of Hindu scriptures.

105. *Pandit* here means a Hindu scholar, who typically is also a practising priest (and therefore a high-caste Brahmin), learned in Hindu philosophy and religion. It does not refer to the general use of the term as a 'wise man' or an expert in a particular field.
106. Parekh, *Colonialism, Tradition, and Reform*.
107. Chatterjee, *Nationalist Thought*, p. 97.
108. Ibid., p. 131. Written by Mahadev Desai, *The Gita According to Gandhi* is a translation of Gandhi's *Anasaktiyoga*, which was written in Gujarati. In the foreword to the English translation, Gandhi said: 'I have, therefore, contended myself with showing the genesis of Mahadev Desai's effort. In so far as the translation part of the volume is concerned, I can vouch for its accuracy. He [Desai] carried out the meaning of the original translation'. Mahadev Desai, *The Gospel of Selfless Action or The Gita According to Gandhi* (Ahmedabad: Navajivan Trust, 1946), p. 127.
109. Desai, *The Gospel of Selfless Action*, pp. 128–129.
110. M. K. Gandhi, 'The Sin of Untouchability', 19 January 1921, *CWMG*, vol. 22, p. 225.
111. Ibid. Gandhi continues, 'I am not going to burn a spotless horse because the Vedas are reported to have advised, tolerated, or sanctioned the sacrifice. For me the Vedas are divine and unwritten. "The letter killeth". It is the spirit that giveth the light. And the spirit of the Vedas is purity, truth, innocence, chastity, humility, simplicity, forgiveness, godliness, and all that makes a man or woman noble and brave.'
112. Chatterjee, *Nationalist Thought*, p. 95.
113. Skaria, *Unconditional Equality*, p. ix.
114. Veeravalli, *Gandhi in Political Theory*. A more generic argument, which posits Gandhian thought against the entire Enlightenment tradition has been made by Thomas Pantham. See Thomas Pantham, 'Gandhi, Nehru, Modernity', in *Crisis and Change in Contemporary India*, ed. Upendra Baxi and Bhikhu Parekh, pp. 98–121 (New Delhi: SAGE Publications, 1995). Unlike Pantham, in this chapter I am not positing Gandhian thought against the entire Enlightenment tradition but rather against a dominant mode of thinking that emerged *post*-Enlightenment, in Cartesian dualism.
115. Veeravalli, *Gandhi in Political Theory*, p. 34.
116. Gandhi says, 'I have been practicing with scientific precision non-violence and its possibilities for an unbroken period of over fifty years. I have applied it in every walk of life, domestic, institutional, economic

and political'. Quoted from Veeravalli, *Gandhi in Political Theory*, p. 3. Gandhi also says, 'Ahimsa is definitely an attribute of society. To convince people of this truth is at once my effort and my experiment'. Quoted from Veeravalli, *Gandhi in Political Theory*, p. 23.

117. It is beyond the scope of this chapter to discuss the conception of fact and value in René Descartes. For a critical engagement with Cartesian dualism, see Hubert Dreyfus and Charles Taylor, *Retrieving Realism* (Cambridge, MA: Harvard University Press, 2015).

118. Veeravalli, 'Presuppositions of War and Peace: The Mind, the World and the Law of Non-Violence', in *Gandhi in Political Theory*, pp. 23–47. The Cartesian dualism, according to Veeravalli, also posits a separation of the private sphere from the public sphere which creates an inherent contradiction between the person as individual and as citizen. Ibid.

119. Alter, *Gandhi's Body*.

120. For instance, M. K. Gandhi, 'Notes', 12 January 1922, *CWMG*, vol. 25, p. 405; M. K. Gandhi, 'What Should Kathiawar Do?' 18 May 1924, *CWMG*, vol. 27, p. 439; M. K. Gandhi, 'Never to Be Forgotten', 31 August 1924, *CWMG*, vol. 29, p. 75; M. K. Gandhi, 'On Trial', 20 November 1924, *CWMG*, vol. 29, p. 352.

121. Veeravalli, *Gandhi in Political Theory*, p. viii. Also see Amrit Srinivasan, 'The Subject in Fieldwork: Malinowski and Gandhi', *Economic and Political Weekly* 28, no. 50 (1993): 2745–2752.

122. Gandhi, *From Yeravda Mandir*, p. 5.

123. Gandhi, *An Autobiography*, p. 18.

124. Gandhi quoted in Chatterjee, *Nationalist Thought*, p. 102.

125. Ibid.

126. While writing on the importance of *ashram* vows, Gandhi notes that a vow can be taken only 'on points of universally recognized principles'. Gandhi, *From Yeravda Mandir*, p. 30.

127. Bilgrami, 'Gandhi, the Philosopher'; Bilgrami, 'Gandhi's Religion and Its Relation to His Politics'. 'Bilgrami differentiates between 'universality' and 'universalisable'. He says that the former is the idea that a moral value applies to all persons. Universalisability, on the other hand, suggests that if someone in particular holds a moral value, he must think that it applies to all others who find themselves in similar situations. See Bilgrami, 'Gandhi, the Philosopher', pp. 109–110. For a similar argument, see Uday Mehta's 'Patience, Inwardness and Self-knowledge in Gandhi's Hind Swaraj', *Public Culture* 23, no. 2 (2011): 417–429.

128. Bilgrami, 'Gandhi's Religion and Its Relation to His Politics'.
129. Ibid., p. 97.
130. Gandhi quoted in Bilgrami, 'Gandhi, the Philosopher', p. 112.
131. Chatterjee, *Nationalist Thought*, p. 102.
132. Such an understanding of truth forms the basis for Mill's idea of tolerance.
133. Bilgrami, 'Gandhi, the Philosopher', p. 112.
134. Ibid., p. 113.
135. Ibid., p. 112.
136. M. K. Gandhi, 'Tyranny of Words', 14 October 1926, *CWMG*, vol. 36, p. 401.
137. Gandhi's notion of *svadharma*, or personal duty, however, complicates and, at times, also contradicts the notion of universal duties. For Gandhi's idea of *svadharma* and a criticism of universal duties, see Sorabji, *Gandhi and the Stoics*, pp. 123–142.
138. Gandhi, *From Yeravda Mandir*, p. 6. Also see M. K. Gandhi, 'Satyagraha, Not Passive Resistance', around 2 September 1917, *CWMG*, vol. 16, p. 10.
139. Gandhi quoted in Parekh, *Colonialism, Tradition, and Reform*, p. 115.
140. Ibid., pp. 112–113.
141. It is important to note here that Gandhi uses the phrase 'living beings' as opposed to 'human beings' to describe his conception of *ahimsa*. For a detailed discussion on Gandhi's philosophy of equality of all beings, see Skaria, *Unconditional Equality*.
142. Parekh, *Colonialism, Tradition, and Reform*, p. 113.
143. Ibid., pp. 117–119.
144. See Sorabji, *Gandhi and the Stoics*, pp. 85–86. Indeed, for Gandhi, to practise non-violence, one must have the capacity to kill. So, while Gandhi's non-violence required submission, it was not a 'weapon of the weak'. See M. K. Gandhi, 'Satyagraha, Not Passive Resistance', around 2 September 1917, *CWMG*, vol. 16, p.10. Sorabji notes that while Gandhi followed Tolstoy's conception of non-violence as an attitude of good will and compassion, he occasionally slipped into talking about violence as a 'behavioral conception'. That is, unlike the former attitudinal sense of non-violence, the latter required one to refrain from killing animals even accidentally. However, Sorabji, I think, rightly asserts that despite this slippage, Gandhi officially endorsed nonviolence in the attitudinal sense only. Ibid., p. 82.

145. Parekh, *Colonialism, Tradition and Reform*, p. 114.
146. M. K. Gandhi, *The Way to Communal Harmony*, ed. U. R. Rao (Ahmedabad: Navajivan Trust, 1963), p. 167; also see p. 171.
147. Chatterjee, *Nationalist Thought*, p. 107.
148. Ibid.
149. Ibid.
150. Bilgrami, 'Gandhi, the Philosopher', p. 102.
151. M. K. Gandhi, 'Interview to Francis G. Hickman', 17 September 1940, *CWMG*, vol. 79, p. 236. At the height of communal violence in the mid-1920s, Gandhi, however, did propose 'limited non-violence' for the society at large understood as restraint from committing physical violence. See M. K. Gandhi, 'Hindu–Muslim Tension: Its Cause and Cure', 29 May 1924, *CWMG*, vol 28, p. 47.
152. Jawaharlal Nehru, *Toward Freedom: The Autobiography of Jawaharlal Nehru* (New York: The John Day Company, 1941), p. 82. I discuss this point further in Chapter 4.
153. M. K. Gandhi, 'Letter to Narayan Das', 23 September 1930, *CWMG*, vol. 50, p. 78.
154. Gandhi, *From Yeravda Mandir*, p. 24.
155. Kaviraj makes a point about conceiving tolerance through a conception of 'long continuum' between two extremes of respecting and valuing diversity on one hand, and deep hostility that does not erupt into conflict, on the other hand. See Sudipta Kaviraj, 'Disenchantment Deferred', in *Beyond the Secular West*, ed. Akeel Bilgrami, pp. 135–187 (New York: Columbia University Press, 2016). Also see the debate on tolerance among Wendy Brown, Jan Dobbernack, Glen Newey, Andrew F. March, Lars Tønder, and Rainer Forst, in 'What is Important in Theorizing Tolerance Today', *Contemporary Political Theory*, 14, no. 2 (2015): 1–38.
156. Gandhi, *Constructive Programme*, p. 5. Consider this statement by Gandhi: 'I hope that nobody will bring up here the history of the attempts by Guru Nanak and Kabir [to] unite Hindus and Muslims; for the effort today is not for uniting the religions, but for uniting hearts, despite the differences of religion. The efforts of Guru Nanak and others were towards uniting the two by showing the basic unity of all religions. The attempt today is for cultivation of tolerance. Its aim is to see that the orthodox Hindu remains what he is and yet respects an orthodox Muslim and sincerely wishes him prosperity. This attempt is altogether new but it springs from an ideal

which is at the very root of Hinduism.' M. K. Gandhi, 'Some Questions', 30 January 1921, *CWMG*, vol. 22, p. 289.
157. M. K. Gandhi, 'Hindu–Mohammedan Unity', 25 February 1920, *CWMG*, vol. 19, p. 419.
158. For instance, see Jocelyn Maclure and Charles Taylor, 'Moral Pluralism, Neutrality and Secularism', and 'Principles of Secularism', in *Secularism and Freedom of Conscience*, ed. Jocelyn Maclure and Charles Taylor, trans. Jane Marie Todd, pp. 9–18 and pp. 19–26 (Cambridge, MA: Harvard University Press, 2011).
159. Shefali Jha, 'Secularism in the Constituent Assembly Debates, 1946–1950', *Economic and Political Weekly* 37, no. 30 (2002): 3175–3180; Gurpreet Mahajan, 'Secularism as Religious Non-Discrimination: The Universal and the Particular in the Indian Context', *India Review* 1, no. 1 (2002): 33–51.
160. That is why scholars like Gurpreet Mahajan and Rajeev Bhargava criticise secularism defined as indigenous tradition of tolerance. For a very good critique of tolerance as a secularist ideal, see C. S. Adcock, *The Limits of Tolerance: Indian Secularism and the Politics of Religious Freedom* (New York: Oxford University Press, 2014).
161. I discuss Gandhi's associational activities and politics in detail in the next chapter. There, I argue that Gandhi sought common action and political unity through three interrelated and supplementary forms of associationalism: first, associational politics that seeks to forge political friendship and 'alliance' with community leaders; second, associational activities that require rendering social service, or *seva*, to the community; third, associational living which asserts that the historical fact of centuries of living together creates bonds of fellowship that must be recognised in friendship and brotherhood, and service to the community.
162. Jha, 'Secularism in the Constituent Assembly Debates'.
163. For the difference between secular and communal historiography, see Neeladri Bhattacharya, 'Predicaments of Secular Histories', *Public Culture* 20, no. 1 (2008): 57–73. Irfan Habib has labelled R. C. Majumdar's history-writing as communal. While for Habib such history-writing clearly has a pejorative meaning and leads to division in society, Gandhi's thought and practice, it must be noted, does not lead to a justification or propagation of communalism. This, however, does not discount the fact that the public use of communal history and tales can

sow seeds of dissention and division in society. For further discussion on nationalist and communal historiography in Habib's writings, see Rajeev Bhargava, 'History, Nation and Community: Reflections on Nationalist Historiography of India and Pakistan', *Economic and Political Weekly* 35, no. 4 (2000): 193–200. Also see Rakesh Batabyal, 'In Search of Secular Template: History Writing in India in the First Decade of the Republic', *Studies in People's History* 3, no. 2 (2016): 216–228.

164. For instance, consider this statement by Gandhi: 'Though the majority of the Mussalmans of India and the Hindus belong to the same "stock", the religious environment has made them different. I believe and I have noticed too that thought transforms man's features as well as character. The Sikhs are the most recent illustration of the fact. The Mussalman, being generally in a minority, has as a class developed into a bully. Moreover, being heir to fresh traditions, he exhibits the virility of a comparatively new system of life. Though, in my opinion, non-violence has a predominant place in the Koran, the thirteen hundred years of imperialistic expansion has made the Mussalmans fighters as a body. They are therefore aggressive. Bullying is the natural excrescence of an aggressive spirit. The Hindu has an ages-old civilization. He is essentially non-violent. His civilization has passed through the experiences that the two recent ones are still passing through.... The Hindus as a *body* are, therefore, not equipped for fighting. But not having retained their spiritual training, they have forgotten the use of an effective substitute for arms and, not knowing their use nor having an aptitude for them, they have become docile to the point of timidity or cowardice.' See M. K. Gandhi, 'What May Hindus Do?', 19 June 1924, *CWMG*, vol. 28, p. 183.
165. Parekh, *Colonialism, Tradition, and Reform*, p. 76.
166. Gandhi, *The Way to Communal Harmony*, p. 294.
167. Ravinder Kumar, 'Class, Community or Nation? Gandhi's Quest for a Popular Consensus in India', *Modern Asian Studies*, 3, no. 4 (1969): 357–376.
168. Ibid., p. 360.
169. Devji, *Impossible Indian*, p. 19.
170. The Pandavas, sons of King Pandu, and the Kauravas, sons of King Dhritarashtra, fought against each other the epic battle described in the Mahabharata, although they were cousins.
171. M. K. Gandhi, 'Hindu–Mohammedan Unity', 25 February 1920, *CWMG*, vol. 19, pp. 417–418.

172. Veeravalli, *Gandhi in Political Theory*.
173. Muslim governing elite of the Mughal empire.
174. 'Ganga–Jamuni *tehzeeb*', literally 'the Ganga–Yamuna culture', refers to the rich cultural life of Northern India, where the Nawabs liberally adopted secular Hindu mores and folkways, thereby contributing to Hindu–Muslim cultural synthesis. Such a cultural life also influenced Nehru's celebration of India's composite culture. However, there can be other types of syncretism, which are neither cosmopolitan nor elite. For instance, see Uberoi's description of frontier culture. J. P. S. Uberoi, 'The Structural Concept of the Asian Frontier', in *History and Society: Essays in Honour of Niharranjan Ray*, ed. Debiprasad Chattopadhyaya, pp. 67–76 (Calcutta: K. P. Bagchi and Company, 1978).
175. Anindita Chakrabarti and Sudha Sitharaman, 'Introduction: Anthropology of Islam in Contemporary India', in *Religion and Secularities: Reconfiguring Islam in Contemporary* India, ed. Anindita Chakrabarti and Sudha Sitharaman, pp. 1–29 (Hyderabad: Orient Blackswan, 2020); Sudha Sitharaman, 'Limits of Syncretism: Bababudhan Dargah in South India as a Paradigm for Overlapping Religious Affiliations and Co-existence', in *Rituale als Ausdruck von Kulturkontakt: 'Synkretismus' zwischen Negation und Neudefinition*, Studies in Oriental Religions, vol. 67, ed. A. Pries, L. Martzolff, R. Langer and C. Ambos, pp. 70–109 (Wiesbaden: Harrassowitz Verlag, 2013); Javeed Alam, 'The Composite Culture and its Historiography', in *South Asia: Journal of South Asian Studies* 22, no. 1 (1999): 29–37; Peter van der Veer, 'Syncretism, Multiculturalism, and the Discourse of Tolerance', in *Syncretism/Antisyncretism: The Politics of Religious Synthesis*, ed. Charles Stewart and Rosalind Shaw, pp. 185–199 (London and New York: Routledge, 1994).
176. Chakrabarti and Sitharaman, *Religion and Secularities*, pp. 6–7.
177. Gandhi, *Constructive Programme*.
178. For a detailed argument on India's transformational constitutionalism, which relies on a strong state and bureaucracy, see Sandipto Dasgupta, 'Legalizing the Revolution', PhD dissertation, Columbia University, New York, 2014. For an argument about revolutionary change in Ambedkar's thought, see Kumar, *Radical Equality*.
179. Alter, *Gandhi's Body*.
180. Rasmus Thybo Jensen and Dermot Moran (eds.), 'Editor's Introduction', in *The Phenomenology of Embodied Subjectivity*, pp. vii–xxxiii (New York: Springer, 2013).

181. 'Dalit' (literally meaning 'broken people' in Marathi) is a term used to designate those people who were deemed 'untouchables' in the Hindu caste system.
182. Alter, *Gandhi's Body*, p. 5.
183. Ibid., p. 7.
184. Sudipta Kaviraj, *Trajectories of the Indian State: Politics and Ideas* (Ranikhet: Permanent Black, 2012).
185. Gandhi, quoted from Alter, *Gandhi's Body*, p. 3.
186. Alter, *Gandhi's Body*; Veena Howard, *Gandhi's Ascetic Activism: Renunciation and Social Action* (Albany: State University of New York Press, 2013).
187. Shahid Amin, *Event, Metaphor, Memory: Chauri Chaura 1922–1992* (California: University of California Press, 1995), p. 86.
188. Mantena, 'Another Realism'. Mantena argues that cultivation of values like humility and fearlessness to avoid the slide into the egotism, hubris and cowardice are central to Gandhi's dispositional politics of non-violence.
189. Devji, *Impossible Indian*, p. 100.
190. Gandhi's eccentric practices are usually singled out to demonstrate the stark divide between him and avowedly modern rational politicians like Nehru. But Nehru did not just adopt the sartorial Gandhian simplicity of handmade Indian clothes and the 'Gandhian cap'. While in jail, Nehru spun regularly, often between two to four hours daily, and as a good member of the Gandhian movement, he kept a record of this. See Judith Brown, *Nehru: A Political Life* (New Delhi: Oxford University Press, 2004).
191. M. K. Gandhi, 'Letter to Jawaharlal Nehru', 19 February 1922, in *Together They Fought: Gandhi–Nehru Correspondence 1921–1948*, ed. Uma Iyengar and Lalitha Zackariah, pp. 3–6 (New Delhi: Oxford University Press, 2011), p. 5.
192. M. K. Gandhi, 'Satyagraha, Not Passive Resistance', about 2 September 1917, *CWMG*, vol. 16, p. 14.
193. Mantena, 'Another Realism', p. 463.
194. Quoted in Devji, *Impossible Indian*, p. 98. Devji translates *bhogabhumi* as 'site of passivity' instead of the literal translation as a 'site of enjoyment'.
195. See Chapter 1 in this book for further discussion.
196. Here, I have in mind John Rawls's idea of overlapping consensus and Jürgen Habermas's theorisation of public sphere and 'constitutional patriotism'.

197. And hence Habermas's neologism 'post-secular'. See Jürgen Habermas et al., *An Awareness of What Is Missing: Faith and Reason in a Post-Secular Age*, trans. Ciaran Cronin (Cambridge: Polity Press, 2010).
198. Gandhi's political philosophy is considered unmodern because it does not seek to eliminate pre-modern social formations, like caste, or, as he preferred to understand it, as *varnashram dharma*. As opposed to modern leaders like Nehru and Ambedkar who sought to overcome pre-modern social practices through the force of law and the state, Gandhi sought to *reform* pre-modern ideas and practices in light of changing conditions of modernity. I discuss this point a bit more in Chapter 4 on Nehru, where I argue how the term modern and modernity as such was construed differently by Gandhi and Nehru.

3
GANDHI'S ASSOCIATIONALISM
A NON-STATE ALTERNATIVE TO LIBERAL SECULARISM?

INTRODUCTION

Notions such as *ahimsa* (non-violence), truth as an experiential notion, *dharma* (faith and/or duty), exemplary action, self-discipline and sacrifice (*tapasya*) are some of the recurring motifs in Gandhi's conception of religion. As seen in the previous chapter, Gandhi transforms these religious-moral ideas and ideals into political conceptions and employs them in the political practice of *ahimsa* and *satyagraha* (the political tool of *ahimsa*, literally insistence on truth).[1] Gandhi's inclusion of religion in the public-political sphere shows that he was not simply engaging in an exercise in the semantics of religious experimentation. That is why it was asserted in the previous chapter that Gandhi's religious and moral thought and his political action are inseparable, such that the spiritual Gandhi cannot be understood without the political one. In this chapter, I will look at how, after his return to the Indian subcontinent from South Africa in 1915, Gandhi practised and propagated his religious politics in relation to India's national politics and the freedom movement, and thereby examine the role and relationship he sought among religion, state and society. In order to do so, I shall retrace some of the major sociopolitical events and issues in Indian politics, where Gandhi used his religious-moral politics and showed how, as a 'practical idealist', he put the idealism that animated his religious politics into political practice.[2] By focusing on Gandhi's political action, this chapter assesses his ideas in terms of its efficacy on society and politics.

In this chapter, I will shed light on Gandhi's religious politics with the help of three broad themes: unity between religions, unity within religion and religious tolerance. The outline of the chapter is as follows: I begin the first section of the chapter by distinguishing Gandhi's religious politics from other types of exclusionary politics, like communal politics in India, where religion is also central to political action. Gandhi's religious politics is demonstrative of, what I shall call in the following pages, religion *in* politics, which, in seeking unity in difference and justice for all, emerges as an inclusive political ideal and practice. By contrast, forms of ethnonationalist politics, such as communalism, are divisive and exclusionary, and the use of religion there, I argue, is usually demonstrative of politics *of* religion.[3] In the second section, I argue that Gandhi sought common action and political unity via three interrelated and supplementary forms of, what I call, 'associationalism'. First is associational politics, which seeks to forge political friendship and alliance with community leaders. Second comes associational activities that require rendering social service, or *seva*, to the community. Third is associational living, which asserts that the historical fact of centuries of living together creates bonds of fellowship that must be recognised in friendship and brotherhood, and service to the community. I argue that through these three types of associationalism, Gandhi sought to conduct his moral politics of *ahimsa*. In the third section of the chapter, I discuss the theme of unity between religions and focus on Hindu–Muslim unity. Under this theme, I discuss the following political issues and events: (*a*) the Non-cooperation and Khilafat movements, 1919–1922, (*b*) separate electorates for Muslims and the demand for Pakistan, and (*c*) the 1947 partition of India. In this section, I put forward my analysis of Gandhi's resolution of difference and unity. I argue that his politics, which appealed to moral notions of friendship and neighbourliness, sought unity among different communities based on caste, religion, language, and so on through associational activities in the sociopolitical field that created the possibility of forging bonds of fellowship and solidarity between them. In Gandhi's politics there is an emphasis on building political alliances with local community leaders and also a simultaneous focus on the importance of social reform through the constructive programme. In the fourth section of the chapter, I discuss the theme of unity within religion and focus on caste and untouchability. Here, I argue that in terms of seeking equality of *all* beings, Gandhi's reinterpretation of the tenets of Hinduism may be seen as radical in theory. However, when translated in the sociopolitical realm, this reinterpretation remained rather weak due to its inability to effectively challenge the discriminatory caste system and the practice of untouchability. In the fifth section, under the theme of religious tolerance, I discuss Gandhi's idea of tolerance with the help of examples like cow protection and music before mosques. Here, I argue that in propagating religious tolerance, Gandhi conceived of both independence of religion from state interference and religion's interdependence on society and politics. In the sixth and the concluding section, based on the observation that Gandhi simultaneously sought independence of religion from state and religion's interdependence on society and politics, I draw implications of such politics for contemporary debates on secularism in India. I note that if for the defenders of secularism, separation of state and religion is an essential feature of political secularism, for the critics, religion's independence from modern state power is crucial to ensure non-homogenisation of religious and cultural life. I suggest that Gandhi's associationalism, which simultaneously demonstrates religion's independence from state and its interdependence on society and politics, may provide resources to engage in contemporary debates between liberal secularists and post-colonial critics. In conclusion, I argue that Gandhi's political thought provides resources to engage with contemporary debates on secularity in a novel manner.

RELIGION *IN* POLITICS

In liberal democracies, political commonality and consensus among different and diverse groups based on religion, ethnicity, culture, language, and so on are sought through public deliberation based on contestation, representation and negotiation of 'difference' in the public sphere.[4] Here, collective power of public deliberation is used to promote or protect the well-being of the citizens, which are the rights and liberties guaranteed in the constitution. Different and divergent private interests in the civil society are transmitted to the political apparatus, where a commitment to public reason and deliberative form of democracy seeks to ensure that diverse political interests are justly represented and political consensus or compromise is reached. Here, the state is central to the political life of the citizen as it is the site where difference gets articulated as common and competing political interests. In liberal politics, 'the historical legacy of liberalism – respect for the rule of law, for individual rights, for value pluralism, for constitutional guarantees – must be upheld one way or another'.⁵ Gandhi's moral politics of *ahimsa* at once challenges this 'historical legacy of liberalism' but at the same time sanctifies its commitment to values of equality, difference and unity. Gandhi's moral politics decentres the state from political action by making the political subject central to social and political action. Under certain conditions, his religious politics can demand from the political subject to resist the law through civil disobedience and non-cooperation.⁶ His politics focuses on moral suasion as opposed to political consensus through public deliberation and seeks permanent friendship and brotherhood as opposed to political negotiation and compromise. Gandhi's politics, in other words, cannot be understood through the framework and language of liberal politics.

Faisal Devji, for instance, has argued that Gandhi's politics cannot be construed within the language of liberalism where the elaboration of social order is based upon the freedom of ownership and contract. He suggests that it is this kind of freedom based upon ownership and contractual relations that makes contending interests possible in a liberal regime: 'it is the freedom of ownership that determines the actions of men by the status, property or labor they might possess, exchange and acquire, all within the framework of contractual relations that makes interests what they are'.⁷ Devji notes that the relationship of friendship as 'disinterested choice',⁸ which marks Gandhi's politics, on the other hand, differs from that of interest as it cannot be defined by contract and ownership. Moreover, the centrality of exemplary action in Gandhi's politics makes the courage of 'convictions of conscience'⁹ of a single individual (that is, the *satyagrahi*)¹⁰ crucial for non-coercive social and political change as opposed to the force of deliberation in collective power. His politics sought the well-being of the nation, but this well-being, as seen in the previous chapter, seemed unconcerned with the rights and liberties of people of the nation.¹¹ Rather, his politics focused on the duties of the political subject and service rendered to the nation that emanated from the moral ideals of a *satyagrahi*. And I have argued in the previous chapter that Gandhi's *ashram* observances provide a list of such moral ideals and duties for the *satyagrahi* to follow, which will train her in the moral politics of *ahimsa*.

In his politics, Gandhi emphasises duties over rights and thereby denies the importance of the liberal priority of 'right' over 'good'.¹² Furthermore, it may be argued that one of the most illiberal aspects of Gandhi's politics is his mixing of religion and politics. But while Gandhi introduced religion in politics, it was never utilised by him as a means towards political unification of the nation. That is, political unity based on a notion of common homogeneous religion (like those found in the works of religious extremists like V. D. Savarkar, or in the politics of the Hindu Mahasabha [Grand Assembly of Hindus] and the Muslim League [hereafter, the League]) does not fill the vacuum of common and competing political interest of liberalism that is created by such moral politics. Gandhi categorically refused to make common religion as the basis of political unification.[13] By introducing religion into politics, that is, in his attempt to moralise politics, he sought to convert religious-moral tropes of duty, friendship and brotherhood, and self-suffering and sacrifice (*tapasya*) into political categories. His attempt was to deploy these religious-moral tropes, which could be easily comprehended by the vast illiterate masses, for his mass movement against British colonial rule. At the same time, his invocation of religious-moral language sought to further the cause of equality and justice for all. Thus, despite the seeming illiberalism of infusing religion into politics, Gandhi's politics cannot be labelled as exclusionary or divisive. It was, in this sense, not against 'value-based' secularism.[14] As such, his moral and religious politics may be seen as an alternative to the conventional interest-based liberal politics of the British colonial government and the Indian National Congress (hereafter, the Congress). His was an inclusive religious politics because unlike politics of religion, seen in ethno-nationalist and communal politics, Gandhi never invoked the language of common religion to further the political interest of a particular community. Moreover, unlike politics of religion, religious identity was not equated with cultural identity or with national identity. That is why I wish to suggest that Gandhi's practice of religious politics demonstrates the subtle but important difference between religion used for utilitarian and political ends – that is, the politics *of* religion (like, communalism) and religion *in* politics. For the latter moral ideals, such as *ahimsa* (non-violence) and truth that Gandhi considered common to all religions, are crucial to conduct politics. For communalism or politics of religion, on the other hand, commonality of interest based on a notion of a homogeneous and shared religion is essential for collective political action.[15]

This argument about religion in politics as inclusive politics does not contradict the claim made in the previous chapter that Gandhi assumed that social loyalties in India were moulded by caste and community which lent themselves to political mobilisation. As noted by the historian Ravinder Kumar, for mass mobilisation Gandhi relied on local leaders to provide support to a larger national cause.[16] What motivated the masses was often varied and different, but the national cause included all groups. As we shall see in the section on Non-cooperation and Khilafat movements, Gandhi conceived of a federated idea of national politics, where different communities fought for a common national cause but related to that cause in their own particular and local way. He saw it as the duty of the local leaders of such groups to ensure that politics was conducted in a disciplined and non-violent manner. That is why Gandhi, as the national leader and propagator of non-violence, ironically, saw his *satyagrahi*s in terms of a disciplined army and himself as the 'general' or 'dictator'.[17] As a national and mass leader, Gandhi's success or failure indeed lay in uniting or aligning particular local political interests with the larger national cause.

POLITICAL UNITY IN FORMS OF ASSOCIATIONALISM

If Gandhi did not seek political unity based on the notion of common homogeneous religion (politics of religion), and if, as argued, his politics is not based on common and competing political interest of liberalism, then what is the basis for commonality and political unity in his religious politics?[18] Gandhi sought common action and political unity through, what I call, forms of 'associationalism' that ranges from interpersonal relations and intercommunal engagements in sociopolitical life to rendering service (*seva*) to the community.[19] It is a bottom-up approach to politics, where sociopolitical relations are cultivated by appealing to the community leader and the community, and moral and affective resources of social life replace state-centric interest-based politics. Some of these forms of associationalism that I shall elaborate upon have been variously described by scholars as 'neighbourliness' and as 'friendship and brotherhood'.[20] My argument is that there are, at least, three distinguishable yet supplementary forms of associationalism, which are at work in Gandhi's politics, that as its aim seek to win the 'hearts and minds' of the nation's people.[21] The three interrelated and supplementary forms of associationalism may be identified as follows: first, *associational politics* sought to forge political friendship and alliance with community leaders.

The aim of this form of associationalism was to understand the 'mind' of the leaders, who within their community were considered to be the 'purest and most patriotic representatives'.[22] Gandhi's use of words like 'alliance' or 'representatives' in his associational politics should not be conceptually confused with the meanings that are attributed to them in liberal politics and democratic theory. For instance, Gandhi said, 'Political pacts we know have been and can be, but personal friendship with individuals cannot be prevented. Such friendships, selfless and genuine, must be the basis for political pacts.'[23] Second, associationalism forged through service (*seva*) to the community. These *associational activities* include a range of services that sociopolitical leaders must render to the nation's people. Gandhi provided a list of such services in his constructive programme of social reform. Third and last, community and political leaders through exemplary acts of politics of friendship (that is, associational politics) and service to the community (that is, associational activity) should forge commonality because the fact of centuries of living together creates bonds of fellowship that must be recognised in friendship and brotherhood, and service to the community. I call this final aspect of associationalism, *associational living*. In the following pages, I will demonstrate how these three forms of associationalism in political friendship and brotherhood, service to the community and associational living created sociopolitical conditions through which Gandhi sought to conduct his moral politics of *ahimsa*.

UNITY BETWEEN RELIGIONS: COMMUNAL UNITY BETWEEN HINDUS AND MUSLIMS

In this section I will examine Gandhi's religious politics in his engagement with (*a*) the Non-cooperation and the Khilafat movements (1919–1922), (*b*) separate electorates for Muslims and (*c*) the 1947 partition of India.[24] In his practice of religious politics, Gandhi made Hindu–Muslim unity one of the bases of his ideal of *swaraj* (self-rule), a proposition, he said, made as early as 1919.[25] *Swaraj* for him simply did not mean political autonomy but also included communal unity.[26] In Gandhi's opinion, communal unity was an indispensable condition for political independence if it was to be based on the method of non-violence.[27] Unlike many mainstream Indian nationalist leaders,[28] Gandhi's call for *swaraj* was polysemous in nature and did not limit itself to political independence from the British rule.[29]

His nationalist politics was also far apart from the generic nationalist discourse which is usually based on notions of bounded and singular identities, such as common territory, religion, ethnicity, language, culture and the like. Furthermore, although Gandhi propagated a politics of non-violence, when one looks at his involvement in India's nationalist politics, one realises that his was essentially a politics of confrontation. Gandhi did not shun difference; rather, he recognised societal differences based on religion, caste, community, and so on as important in politics. Indeed, he even forsook temporary peace through compromise in politics for his ultimate goal of a society based on the principles of non-violence (*ahimsa*). Hindu–Muslim unity was central to achieve that goal:

> I had realized early enough in South Africa that there was no genuine friendship between the Hindus and the Musalmans. I never missed a single opportunity to remove obstacles in the way of unity. It was not in my nature to placate anyone by adulation, or at the cost of self-respect. But my South African experiences had convinced me that it would be on the question of Hindu–Muslim unity that my Ahimsa would be put to its severest test, and that the question presented the widest field for my experiments in Ahimsa. The conviction is still there.[30]

Moreover, Gandhi did not seek unity among different communities by simply insisting on India's shared cultural past. According to him, apparent differences may be perceived as permanent, but that does not preclude the possibility to *forge* unity in the future. In other words, unity is not pre-given, the way it is assumed in notions of common religion or shared culture. Gandhi insisted on and persisted for a permanent Hindu–Muslim unity as a prerequisite for *swaraj* (self-rule or sovereignty) because he sought a new moral and political relationship between Hindus and Muslims. His search for Hindu–Muslim unity is an example of, what I have called, associational politics. Such politics has been variously described as 'neighbourliness' and 'friendship'. Both Ajay Skaria and Faisal Devji have noted that Gandhi's politics of neighbourliness and friendship does not seek to efface or subsume difference as it may be the case with abstract and universal rights of citizenship.[31] Although in Gandhi's politics, difference is construed in terms of absolute or unassimilable difference between Hindus and Muslims, there is also a simultaneous attempt to build unity through solidarity. Devji further notes that for Gandhi friendship involves suffering for a friend which is neither because of compassion nor due to some common privation. Rather, it consists in a deliberate choice of an experience whose independence both invites and sustains friendship.[32] Although both Skaria and Devji rightly argue that Gandhi's politics of neighbourliness and friendship is based on the moral and religious language of duty and suffering or sacrifice, their analysis of Gandhi's religious politics raises the question: what brings about a social and political situation where there is 'a sharing in the suffering of the neighbour'?[33]

Gandhi sought to forge unity among different communities through two types of associationalism in the sociopolitical field which created bonds of fellowship and solidarity between them. Gandhi's politics of friendship and neighbourliness, I argue, is incomplete without a simultaneous and dual emphasis on associational politics that entails building political 'alliances' with local community leaders and associational activities, such as the constructive programme which sought social reform in society.[34] Through such associationalism in society and politics, Gandhi sought to

> ... discover the Musalman mind. The closer I come to the best of Musalmans, the juster [sic] I am likely to be in my estimate of the Musalmans and their doings. I am striving to become the best cement between the two communities.... But before I can do so, I must prove to the Musalmans that I *love* them as well as I love the Hindus. (Emphasis added)[35]

Love to Gandhi, as seen in the previous chapter, meant rendering active social service to all. Gandhi's belief was that close associational activities, like rendering social service to the community, provided the opportunity to better understand the perceived 'other' because through such close contact one could 'learn their habits, thoughts and aspirations'.[36] This, in turn, created the possibility of fellowship and solidarity to develop among different and diverse groups. Political alliances with local leaders of different communities meant that (*a*) the grievance of a particular community was equally important as the national cause of freedom from colonial rule, and (*b*) they provided opportunity to the national leaders to show fellow-feeling towards various communities. In order to realise such a communal unity, Gandhi instructed all congressmen to 'cultivate personal friendship with persons representing faiths other than his own'.³⁷ His decision to link the Khilafat movement of Indian Muslims to the national movement of non-cooperation against the British is an example of such associational politics, to which I now turn to.

THE NON-COOPERATION AND KHILAFAT MOVEMENTS, 1919–1922

In 1919 the British colonial government sought to permanently impose wartime restrictions of the First World War on civil rights in India.³⁸ It is not without irony that Gandhi's first nationwide call for a non-violent non-cooperation movement against the Rowlatt Act has been described as 'the largest and most violent anti-imperialist movement India witnessed since 1857'.³⁹ During this period, the pro-Khilafat Muslims in India led by the Ali brothers, who wished to preserve the position of the Ottoman *sultan-caliph* as the temporal head of the Islamic world, joined Gandhi's political struggle with the hope to strengthen their challenge against the colonial power.⁴⁰ Sugata Bose and Ayesha Jalal note, 'As the anti-Rowlatt satyagraha merged with the Khilafat movement, attacks on the symbols of British authority – banks, post offices, railway stations and town halls – as well as assaults on British civilians, were followed by brutal repression.'⁴¹ Gandhi launched the Non-cooperation movement based on the grievances of Indian Muslims in the Khilafat movement.⁴² As a result, the two campaigns soon became part of the same anti-colonial struggle. However, both the movements were short-lived and barely lasted two years, and Gandhi's close association with the Ali brothers ended by 1928–1929. In Indian nationalist politics, the period between 1919 and 1922 has been widely described as the heyday of Hindu–Muslim unity, where *Hindu–Musalman ki jai* (Long live Hindu–Muslim unity) became a familiar cry.⁴³ According to Shabnum Tejani, being a nationalist during this period did not require one to subsume smaller affiliations to the greater ideal of the nation. She maintains that the merger of the Khilafat and Non-cooperation movements demonstrated the possibility of a 'federated nationalism' which was built by its communities, where each, whatever its relative size, was a necessary part of the larger nationalist movement.⁴⁴ It has also been argued that the common cause that Gandhi sought between the Khilafat and the Non-cooperation movements demonstrated the international character of his nationalist politics. In Devji's opinion, the Khilafat movement was the first example of Indian nationalism's claim to speak and act within the arena of international politics and represented 'an extraordinary demand that, India's role in world affairs be acknowledged even while she was a colony'.[45]

For Gandhi, this joint movement was a step towards the realisation of true *swaraj*, which did not just mean political autonomy but one which united Indians with one another. Thus, in his reply to why he linked the national struggle with a particular issue relevant to Indian Muslims only, Gandhi said, 'I discovered the weapon of non-cooperation in the form we know while thinking about the Khilafat.'[46] It was part and parcel of his associational politics, where the national goal of political independence included building political alliances with local leaders based on the grievances of those communities. This was Gandhi's politics of friendship. Thus, he wrote to Mohamed Ali, 'We have a common goal and I want to utilize your services to the uttermost, in order to reach that goal. In the proper solution of the Mahomedan question lies the realisation of Swarajya [self-rule].'[47] During the Khilafat agitation, when leaders such as Hasrat Mohani, who represented the more militant section of the *ulama*, proposed that the Congress and the League should strive to attain 'complete independence', Gandhi went on to maintain:

> Let us understand our limitation. Let Hindus and Muslims have absolute, indissoluble unity. Who is here who can say today with confidence, 'Yes, Hindu–Muslim unity has become an indissoluble factor of Indian nationalism?' Who is here who can tell me that the Parsis and the Sikhs and the Christians and the Jews and the untouchables ... will not rise against any such idea?[48]

Gandhi was acutely aware of the political reality that not all grievances and struggle against power and injustice were anti-colonial. In other words, not every political struggle in the subcontinent was for national self-determination. Moreover, unity did not just mean a political consensus among leaders on a larger issue abstracted from social reality. Political unity for Gandhi meant building alliances with local leaders where their issues could then be juxtaposed with the larger national cause.

On 19 April 1919, when General Dyer's troops massacred 379 people who were peacefully demonstrating against the Rowlatt Act at Jallianwala Bagh in Amritsar, Gandhi saw this tragic incident providing a larger national cause of unity against the colonial power. He asserted:

> The Muslims and Hindus of India were not only united over the question of the Khilafat, but also on all political questions relating to their motherland – India.... The blood of Hindus and Muslims mingled in Jallianwala Bagh and other places last year had cemented the Hindu–Moslem unity.[49]

In the Jallianwala Bagh massacre, where 'the blood of Hindus and Muslims mingled', Gandhi saw common suffering and experience of injustice that cut across religious differences as an opportunity to create the possibility of a common political bond of permanent friendship between Hindus and Muslims. He hoped that the mutual suffering and sacrifice of the two religious communities for a just cause would permanently unite them. By helping the Muslim community in 'the hour of their peril',[50] Gandhi hoped to build a new moral relationship of communal unity between Hindus and Muslims, because such unity was based not on political interest and compromise but rather on the fellowship of brotherhood and friendship demonstrated in shared suffering:

> The duty of Hindus at such a time is obvious. If they regard the Muslims as their brethren, they should fully share their suffering. This is the best and the easiest method of promoting unity between Hindus and Muslims. Sharing another's sorrow is the only real sign of brotherly regard.[51]

Gandhi moreover maintained that this political relationship of brotherhood and friendship could not be quid pro quo. Since this relationship of friendship could not be based on reciprocity or compromise, the Hindu community, for instance, could not demand from Muslims that they refrain from cow slaughter in return:

> But I should like to affirm that, if one brother is in trouble, it is the duty of the other to render him all possible help. When Hindus are in trouble, Moslems should help them and, if Moslems are in trouble, Hindus should come to their rescue. We want no return for our assistance and sympathy. If you Moslems are in the right, we shall offer you *unconditional help*. This is a *hereditary privilege* of the Hindus. If the Moslems themselves voluntarily conceded anything it would be welcome, but we would not care to play the role of mercenary soldiers....

> Let me tell my Hindu brothers that I hold the cows as dear as any of you do, but we cannot save the cows by quarrelling with Moslems. You can save the cows only by following my example, by doing your duty. (Emphasis added)[52]

There are three points to be noted in Gandhi's politics of friendship and brotherhood with regard to the Khilafat movement. First, Gandhi prioritises the moral relationship of communal unity between Hindus and Muslims over national self-determination. Second, by invoking notions of friendship and brotherhood in a political context, where unity is not based on mutual compromise, Gandhi called for a 'disinterested unity'.[53] Here, the eventual political unity between Hindus and Muslims would be between equals who respected each other's religion. Gandhi's inclusion of a religious issue into national politics through the cause of Khilafat is illustrative of political examples of, what I have called, religion *in* politics, where the goals of religious politics can be seen in consonance with the 'multi-value' goals of liberal secularism, which seek to protect religious liberty (including the freedom of unbelief), equality of people belonging to different faiths and fraternity understood as equal say and participation in society, as well as harmony and comity between different religions and worldviews.[54] Lastly, a further point needs elaboration here with regard to Gandhi's notion of brotherhood. In the previous quote, Gandhi maintained that Hindus must provide 'unconditional help' to Muslims because this is their 'hereditary privilege'. Here, Gandhi's allusion to fraternal bonds should not be read as the call for universal fraternity and brotherhood of the French Enlightenment variety. In other words, commonality or political unity is not pre-given in Gandhi's invocation of brotherhood. According to Gandhi, in living together for centuries, Hindus inherited a 'privilege' to help Muslims as a result of the common bonds of fellowship which developed through associational living. Unlike his prodigy Nehru, Gandhi's political thought is not marked by any sustained effort in defining who the collective 'we' is in a nation. So, if one asks Gandhi 'why must we suffer for our neighbour?' we will not find the answer in an already existing fraternity. Rather, Gandhi's answer lies in the historical fact of associational living. A somewhat similar answer was given by the early nationalist Bhudev Mukhopadhyay in conceiving *swajatiya* (one's own kind). Sudipta Kaviraj notes that *swajatiyata*, that is, belonging to the same community or the same relevant class, is not an attribute conferred on a people by themselves or by others. 'It is more like an organic sameness imposed on people living for a long time in the same environment, similar to the process of natural adaptation.... It is a quality that comes to subsist in them by virtue of their sharing the same natural and historical world.'[55] Sharing the same nature and same history creates a quality of *samaduhkhasukhata* among them, that is, a commonality of happiness and suffering.[56]

While discussing Gandhi's politics of friendship and brotherhood, Devji has argued that the political language of brotherhood can be problematic because unlike the language of friendship it does not involve choice but rather implies an inherited commonality.[57] Although Gandhi did sometimes lapse into a language of collective identification based on shared culture or land, when he appealed to the notion of brotherhood I see him mostly advancing a point towards the historical fact of living together for centuries.[58] My understanding of Gandhian fraternity in terms of associational living rests on an argument forwarded by Akeel Bilgrami, where he differentiates Gandhian fraternity from 'traditional' or 'standard' form of fraternity that may signify compassion and familial forms of support in human relations. Gandhian fraternity, Bilgrami argues, reflects 'thicker sources of fraternity', where caring for others involves a moral commitment to 'include others in the [moral] truth' that one cares for.[59] It is a form of fraternity with other human beings, because 'one *cares for them* enough to want to *include* them in something that is important in one's life: the moral and political truth ... as one sees it' (original emphasis).[60] Such a thick conception of fraternity in Gandhi's thought shows that by brotherhood he did not simply mean filial and familial relations that can have the effect of effacing difference but a relationship that needs to be *forged* through exemplary action. In political practice the only inheritance that one may speak of here then is that of the historical fact of living together. Thus, in Gandhi's political thought, it is not the nation with its territorial boundary that assumes commonality; rather, it is the *ashram* life, where people belonging to different nationalities, races, religion and cultures develop bonds of fellowship by living and working together.

With regard to the Non-cooperation movement, Gandhi maintains that it

> ... is not anti-English. It is not even anti-Government. Co-operation is to be withdrawn because the people must not be party to a wrong – a

broken pledge – a violation of deep religious sentiment.... And today if I have thrown in my lot with the Mohammedans, a large number of whom bear no friendly feelings towards the British, I have done so frankly as a friend of the British and with the object of gaining justice and of thereby showing the capacity of the British constitution to respond to every honest determination when it is coupled with suffering. I hope by my 'alliance' with the Mahomedans to achieve a threefold end – to *obtain justice* in the face of odds with the *method of satyagraha* and to show its efficacy over all other methods, to secure Mahomedan friendship for the Hindus and thereby internal peace also, and last but not the least to transform ill will into affection for the British and their constitution which in spite of its imperfections has weathered many a storm. (Emphasis added)[61]

Apart from communal unity and non-violence, *swaraj* for Gandhi also meant a right relationship between the ruler and the ruled.[62] His notion of nationalism was, thus, related to an idea of justice where the rulers forfeited their right to rule over their subjects if they did not act in accordance with demands of justice. Devji notes that throughout his South African career, Gandhi claimed rights for his fellow migrants due to them neither as Indians nor as South Africans but rather as citizens of the empire.[63] Both during his South African campaign and the Khilafat movement, Gandhi asked the imperial government to live up to its own ideals of equality and justice for all enshrined in the British constitution. Cooperation with the British was to be withdrawn because, Gandhi said, 'I serve the Empire by refusing to partake in its wrong.'[64] The introduction of the Rowlatt Acts, the Jallianwala Bagh massacre and the British Empire's inability to redress the Khilafat grievances led Gandhi to lose faith in the empire. By 1921, Gandhi had turned disloyal to the empire, declaring himself 'an implacable foe of the Raj'.[65] Thereafter, he refocused his nationalism to include political independence from the British rule as a necessary condition for *swaraj*, or self-rule.

As the president of the Congress in 1923, Mohamed Ali, who was one of the prominent leaders of the Non-cooperation and Khilafat movements, devoted the majority of his first speech to Hindu–Muslim relations. He maintained that there was no contradiction between loyalty to one's faith and one's nation, such that, 'a Muslim need not be a bad Muslim in order to be a good Indian, but ... an Indian Muslim [can], and should, fight for the freedom of Kashi [Benaras] as well as for the freedom of the Ka'ba'.[66] In such a federated conception of nationalism, Gandhi saw it as the work of political leaders of each community to 'compose our differences and keep us under check'.[67] The merger of the two movements demonstrated the commitment of leaders like Gandhi and Mohamed Ali towards Hindu–Muslim unity as a prerequisite for political independence. However, already by 1921, fault lines were visible in the coalition between the Non-cooperators and Khilafatists.[68] For instance, Tejani notes, 'In April 1921, when the campaigns were at their heights, it was already apparent that many Muslims in Sind supported Khilafat but associated Non-cooperation with Hindus.'[69] Nevertheless, she concludes, 'However brief and ambivalent, there was something unique about the period of the Khilafat and Non-cooperation movements. There was a sense of optimism about the possibility of forging a nationalism that could be shared by Hindus and Muslims alike.'[70] By the mid-1920s, with the eventual disintegration of the Khilafat–Non-cooperation alliance, violent conflicts erupted between Hindus and Muslims all over the country. While Gandhi and Mohamed Ali continued to defend their religious politics, Hindu Mahasabha leaders like Lala Lajpat Rai and M. R. Jayakar blamed Gandhi for the rise of communalism by introducing religion into politics. Many in the Congress, like Madan Mohan Malaviya, Lala Lajpat Rai, Mohammad Ali Jinnah[71] and Motilal Nehru had also feared Gandhi's attempts at forging Hindu–Muslim unity, where a religious issue became central to nationalism.[72]

In 1924, in an article titled, 'Hindu-Muslim Tension: Its Cause and Cure', Gandhi wrote about the 'Hindu Indictment' and the 'Muslim Indictment' against him, concluding in the end that he was 'not guilty' of either of the charges:

> I must plead not guilty to both the charges, and add that I am totally unrepentant. Had I been a prophet and foreseen all that has happened, I should have still thrown myself into the Khilafat agitation. In spite of the present strained relations between the two communities, both have gained. The awakening among the masses was a necessary part of the training. It is itself a tremendous gain.[73]

Gandhi was unapologetic and unrepentant for the political turmoil and violence that followed the break-up of alliances between the Khilafat and Non-cooperation leaders because he saw this joint movement as central to his conception of *swaraj* based on Hindu–Muslim unity. Furthermore, to him the principle of non-violence could not be compromised even for the sake of temporary peace, because in the ultimate analysis, that would mean sacrifice of Truth.[74] Thus, Gandhi said, '... a true satyagrahi has no option but to proclaim the truth.... Truth is infinitely of more paramount importance than Hindu–Muslim unity or swaraj.'[75] This priority of truth and non-violence in politics demonstrates the centrality of morality of politics in Gandhian thought. Thus, Devji remarks that Gandhi's morality exists in 'the shadow of politics, whose practices it had perforce to engage'.[76] Gandhi's associational politics, as witnessed in the Non-cooperation–Khilafat movements, sought to include diverse communities into the national whole by politically engaging and including their distinctive interest in the national politics, outside the representative structures of the state machinery.[77] That is, he sought political unity of groups outside the ambit of group-based electoral politics, such as the mechanism of separate electorates, because, as we shall see next, the latter came in the way of Gandhi's moral politics and replaced the community with the state as central to conducting politics.

SEPARATE ELECTORATES AND THE DEMAND FOR PAKISTAN

There is a palpable tension between Gandhi's moral politics and the universal values of rights and equality as expressed in the liberal tradition, given that neither liberal rights nor interest-based politics were a central preoccupation in Gandhi's politics. This tension between the demand for political rights from the state and Gandhian moral politics is prised open over the question of group representation. Gandhi's moral politics, we will see, was unable to reconcile the demand for political equality as expressed in the demand for separate electorates in representative bodies of the state. He did not consider the question of equality between communities through the mechanism of separate electorates because he did not believe that common religion could be a basis for common political interest. As such, he did not consider communal representation by means of separate electorates as the right political method: 'Our goal must be the removal ... of communal or sectional representation. A common electorate must impartially elect its representatives on the sole ground of merit.'[78] As we shall see in the chapters on Nehru, despite major differences between Gandhi and Nehru on how to conduct politics, both of them agreed on the issue of separate electorates, albeit on different grounds. While Nehru rejected separate electorates as a means of political representation because it was not in accordance with secular politics,[79] for Gandhi the rejection of separate electorates was on moral basis. For Gandhi, it was not the state but the community that was central in bringing about change in society. So, if independence was to be won on the basis of principles of non-violence, then unity had to be achieved outside the domain of state power. Such a moral and political unity among distinct and diverse communities meant forging a fellowship through common social and political activity, which I have called 'associationalism' in this chapter. In such a framework, representative and electoral politics that called for separate or communal electorates was necessarily subservient, even counter-productive, to social and moral reform of society.

According to Gandhi, while the minorities could rightfully demand 'full civil rights', they could not be granted separate representation as this would mean 'nothing short of vivisection of a whole nation'.[80] For him, the political implementation of separate electorates had moral implications in that it presupposed 'mutual distrust and conflict of interest' among nation's people.[81] Therefore, such representative politics could only 'perpetuate differences and deepen the distrust'.[82] The implementation of separate electorates stood against his goal of Hindu–Muslim unity and hence against *swaraj* itself. As a goal, *swaraj* could only be achieved from a 'national standpoint'; separate electorates, on the other hand, suggested that 'responsible government will always have to contend against these [communal or sectional] interests which will always be in conflict with the national spirit'.[83]

In the beginning of this chapter, I suggested that Gandhi's politics cannot be understood through the lens of liberalism because unlike liberal politics, his was not an interest-based politics. Instead, I argued that religious and moral tropes of duty, common suffering, friendship and brotherhood were converted into political conceptions that filled the gap of interest as the basis for political unification. Gandhi's firm rejection of separate electorates, and later the two-nation theory as an 'untruth', was based on his belief that politics cannot be based on interest, where the interests of Muslims were seen as separate and distinct from Hindus.[84] As we know, the gradual expansion of representative government in British India through constitutional provisions like the separate electorates shaped Hindus and Muslims as political groups with distinct political interests. Gandhi disapproved the representative mechanism of communal electorates because it transformed apparent religious differences into permanent political differences.

> Here in India we have been pretending to work the parliamentary system under separate electorates which have created artificial incompatibles. Living unity can never come out of these artificial entities being brought together on a common platform. Such legislatures may function. But they can only be a platform for wrangling and sharing the crumbs of power that may fall from rulers whoever they may be.[85]

Separate electorates as 'artificial incompatibilities' denied the possibility of fellow-feeling among different communities. Gandhi's refusal to accept separate electorates as a mechanism of politics should be seen as a refusal to accept a fundamental change that colonial modernity brought in society. Colonial modernity, Kaviraj observes, transformed the structure of identity of communities in pre-modern times from 'fuzzy' to 'enumerated' ones.[86] The population census introduced by the British colonial government created 'majorities' and 'minorities', which, unlike majorities of a democracy that are supposed to be random and temporary, objectified communities into permanent majorities and minorities. Since the fuzzy communities in pre-modern times were not objectified as social groups, there was no clarity in terms of their number and therefore lacked the 'precision' for identifying themselves from others that is seen in modern types of collective action in political life.[87] Modern forms of collective political action thus created hurdles in forging the kind of associationalism that formed the basis of Gandhi's politics.

Thus, we see that on the issue of representative politics what stands out is Gandhi's unwillingness to see the logic of electoral politics that, through descriptive or mirror representation, seeks substantive political equality.[88] Given the developments in theories of group rights,[89] in a liberal democracy today demands for mirror representation based on identity can be seen in consonance with the requirements of substantive equality. For Gandhi, however, the demand for separate electorates went against a politics conceived in moral terms, although his politics also demonstrated simultaneous affirmation of difference, like religion and caste, and political unity. Jinnah, in his 1940 address to the League, pointed out that Gandhi said, 'There was a time when I could say that there was no Muslim whose confidence I did not enjoy. It is my misfortune that it is not so today.' Jinnah rhetorically asked the crowd, 'Why has he [Gandhi] lost the confidence of the Muslims today?'[90] Here, Jinnah was pointing out that Gandhi had failed in his political project that sought equality between communities outside the arena of representative politics. Thus, Jinnah argued that since Gandhi had lost the confidence of the Muslim population, he had also lost the political right to represent Muslims. Indeed, by 1940, Gandhi's influence in national politics had vastly diminished. It was also during this phase of his political life that he started insisting on the separation between religion and politics. As a result of the entrenchment of political differences based on religious identity and Gandhi's inability to effectively influence the Congress, by the 1940s Gandhi had increased his insistence on the separation between religion and politics in order to realise political independence through non-violent means. So far, in this chapter, we have seen that Gandhi sought minimal state intervention in his politics. The state, as a political actor, does not figure centrally in his political thought. His associationalism focused more on the constructive programme of social reform and building political alliances with community leaders. However, in the changed sociopolitical situation, by the 1940s we see a greater emphasis on separating state and religion in Gandhi's speeches.

Gandhi also maintained that the partition of India did not in any way prove the truth of the two-nation theory. He contended that the notion that Hindus and Muslims were two distinct nations could only be so if both the parties in question accepted it. That is, only by 'otherising' the nation's people could India become two separate nations. Insistence on common territory based on common religion did not prove that a nation's identity was based on such commonality. That is why Gandhi referred to the partition as 'vivisection' of the nation.[91] He said:

> Does the readjustment of the geography of India mean two nations? I admit that the division having been agreed upon, unity becomes somewhat difficult. But assuming that the Muslims of India look upon themselves as a nation distinct from the rest, they cannot become so, if the non-Muslims do not respond. The Muslim majority areas may call themselves Pakistan but the rest and the largest part of India need not call itself Hindustan. In contradistinction to Pakistan it will mean

the abode of the Hindus. Do the Hindus feel so? Have the Parsis, the Christians and the Jews born in India, and the Anglo-Indians ... any other home than India?[92]

Since the idea of nation was reflected in *associational living* and not in common religion or territory, Gandhi frequently used the word 'vivisection' when he talked about the partition. Thus, we see the centrality of the idea of a multi-national state in Gandhi's idea of the nation, which, I argued in the introduction to this book, binds the Gandhi–Nehru tradition of secularity. As we know, the events leading up to the partition majorly altered the context in which Indian politics would play out in future. Partition challenged Gandhi's narrative of the nation which emphasised associational living between Hindus and Muslims; the reality now mirrored the Westphalian nation-state. Partitioned India now faced a political reality of a dominant Hindu majority both within the state machinery and outside it. As political differences based on religion entrenched, Gandhi appealed more to a separation of religion from the state, a concern not visible in his politics before the 1940s.

THE PARTITION OF INDIA, 1947

As the partition of the subcontinent drew closer, all efforts to end communal riots seemed to fail. Everyday Gandhi received new reports of carnage and killings of Hindus and Muslims in Punjab, Bihar, Bengal and Delhi. Despite the fact of violence around him, for Gandhi his theory of non-violence as the basis for society and politics and of *swaraj* thereof had not failed. It only meant that he had fallen short in *his* efforts, that his experiments in non-violence were imperfect.[93] Anuradha Veeravalli argues that the situation demanded that Gandhi intensify his efforts at self-purification, and the ultimate and the only method he knew to perfect his non-violence was by testing himself with experiments in *brahmacharya* (celibacy).[94] Thus, towards the end of the 1940s, when communal violence was at its height, Gandhi increased his emphasis on 'biomoral' activities, like fasting and celibacy, in order to reaffirm his theory of non-violence in its application.[95]

Recalling the call for Hindu–Muslim unity during the Non-cooperation movement, in 1946 Gandhi said:

That was the time when Hindus and Muslims for the time forgot all their difference. The Ali Brothers and I used to go all over the country together like blood-brothers. We spoke with one voice and delivered the message of Hindu–Muslim unity and swaraj to the masses.... But the situation has changed today. We have gone wrong somewhere. The hearts of Hindus and Muslims are sundered. The air is poisoned with communal bitternes[s] and rancour. A section of the Muslims has begun to claim that they are a separate nation. This, however, is not the time to go into the reason for it. I confess that it baffles my understanding.[96]

The demand for a separate nation based on religious difference 'baffled' Gandhi because the Westphalian model of the nation-state, where common territory corresponds with commonality of identity, such as race, religion and language, was outside his moral and political imagination. Moreover, it went against both his assumption and faith in unity that is forged through politics of associationalism. So while there was a time 'when Hindus thought that Muslims were natural enemies of Hindus', for Gandhi it was also the case that Hinduism ultimately 'comes to terms with the enemy and makes friends with it'.[97] Partition did not let that process of moral unity through friendship, fellowship and social reform see its completion.

UNITY WITHIN RELIGION: CASTE AND UNTOUCHABILITY

Gandhi called himself a *sanatani* (an orthodox Hindu) and yet, as we saw in the previous chapter, disregarded many aspects of canonical Hinduism. His rejection of several tenets of Hinduism was based on (*a*) his denial to strictly adhere to scriptural doctrines, focusing instead on the 'spirit' rather than the 'letter' of the religious text, and (*b*) his repudiation of the sole authority of religious experts over religious texts. Despite this, to Gandhi's mind he was an orthodox Hindu because he believed in ancient Hindu scriptures, the *varnashrama dharma*,[98] cow protection and, finally, despite his personal disbelief, accepted idol worship.[99] To Gandhi, his belief in and adherence to the aforementioned tenets of Hinduism made him a *sanatani*, but his radical reinterpretation of these religious ideals also made him diverge from canonical Hinduism. So, while Gandhi believed in ancient Hindu scriptures, like the Vedas and the Upanishads, he also added that he did not believe in their exclusive divinity. He also did not think that he was bound by interpretation of these scriptures if they went contrary to 'reason' or 'moral sense'.[100] Second, he often clarified that his belief in the *varna* system was 'strictly Vedic' and not as was understood in the 'popular sense'.[101] According to him, *varnashrama dharma* was inherent in human nature because it was attached to birth. It followed that one could not change his or her *varna* by choice as it was based on heredity. He argued that originally there were only four *varna*s – Brahmins, Kshatriyas, Vaishyas and Sudras – and therefore the division of the *varna* system into innumerable castes was an 'unwarranted liberty'. The four *varna*s, according to him, defined and determined a man's duty and conferred no privileges. It was therefore, in Gandhi's opinion, a non-hierarchical system of division of labour and social organisation. For him, the problem in Hinduism was not this social division of labour but the assumption of hierarchy that was brought in the practice of caste system, and untouchability was the expression of injustice and inequality in the caste system. Third, Gandhi argued that his commitment to cow protection involved a much larger and symbolically important commitment than what was widely understood. The cow was symbolic of equality of *all beings* and its protection meant 'the protection of the whole dumb creation of the God'.[102] Lastly, Gandhi argued that his acceptance of idol worship in Hinduism, despite his personal disbelief in that practice, demonstrated his practice of tolerance. We have already seen in the previous chapter that Gandhi's reinterpretation of Hinduism introduces a radical post-human moralism in that it involves equality of *all* beings. In this chapter, however, we will see that this radical rethinking was rather weak in terms of the effects it produced in the sociopolitical realm due to its inability to effectively challenge the systemic inequalities perpetuated and sanctioned by the caste system.

In defending equality within Hinduism, Gandhi distinguished between two aspects of religion – historical and eternal. He attributed the practice of untouchability to the former and did not consider it to be an integral part of Hinduism. While religion as a historical practice was specific to a society and, in time, its eternal principles of truth and *ahimsa* were valid for all times which guided human action:

> There are two aspects of Hinduism. There is, on the one hand, the historical Hinduism with its untouchability, superstitious worship of stocks and stones, animal sacrifice and so on. On the other, we have the Hinduism of the Gita, the Upanishads and Patanjali's Yoga Sutra which is the acme of ahimsa and oneness of all creation, pure worship of one immanent, formless imperishable God.[103]

We see that in Gandhian thought religious texts simultaneously transcended time and were conditioned by it. So while the values of truth and *ahimsa* contained in them were eternally valid, the practices that these texts recommended had limited validity.[104] Before Gandhi's arrival in Indian politics, social reform was not a priority on the Congress agenda.[105] Several untouchable leaders had claimed that they would prefer the 'inhuman British rule' over the 'tyrannical Brahmin rule' and would want the former to continue until such time as they secured full social and political unity.[106] Gandhi knew that for his non-violent mass nationalism to succeed, he needed Indians to stop cooperating with the colonial government. This required him to win over the pro-government untouchable groups:

> Non-cooperation against the government means cooperation among the governed, and if Hindus do not remove the sin of untouchability there will be no Swaraj whether in one year or in one hundred years.... Swaraj is as unattainable without the removal of the sins of untouchability as it is without Hindu–Muslim unity.[107]

Again, we see here that, like the necessity of Hindu–Muslim unity, unity and equality within Hinduism was another necessary condition for *swaraj* for him. Gandhi envisaged achieving this equality and unity through moral and social reform of Hinduism and the Hindu community. Such an approach was based on his belief that all religions were capable of evolution, visible in the history of internal reform of religions. As we shall see now, this moral ideal and belief in Hinduism's internal reform, and therefore its essential unity, stood in tension with the possibility of substantial political equality that could be achieved through representative mechanisms of the state, like separate electorates.

While Gandhi was interned in Yeravda jail, the then British prime minister Ramsay MacDonald announced the provisional scheme of minority representation, known as the Communal Award. The Macdonald Award of 1931 granted separate electorates to the 'depressed classes',[108] or the untouchables, in the Hindu community and recognised them as a minority community. Protesting against the communal award, Gandhi declared a 'fast unto death' on 20 September 1932. He saw the introduction of separate electorates for the untouchables as a negation of his moral philosophy of unity of Hinduism and its capacity for reform. Veeravalli opines that if partition for Gandhi meant the vivisection of the nation, then separate electorates for the untouchables signalled vivisection of Hinduism. She argues that for Gandhi such a political mechanism would foreclose any possibility of reconciliation between the upper castes and the untouchables, and any room for atonement for the wrongs committed by the upper-caste Hindus. Furthermore, such a move would only perpetuate caste divisions by creating political factions along these lines.[109] Separate electorates, as a basis for equality in society, was dependent on state power rather than on community and social reform. Therefore, it also precluded the possibility of transformation of the hearts and minds of *both* the communities involved in the practice of untouchability: *savarna* Hindus and the untouchables.[110]

But for the leader of untouchables, Ambedkar, the question of separate electorates was not a matter of principle or a moral issue but a mechanism to achieve certain ends through state power:[111] 'As far as we are concerned we have no immediate concern other than securing political power ... and that alone is the solution to our problem.... We want our social status raised in the eyes of the *savarna* Hindus.'[112] Ambedkar was also attacking Gandhi's moral claim that if the untouchables were recognised as a separate community from *savarna* Hindus, then it would be a failure of Hindus to have a properly humane and inclusive religion. Ambedkar opined:

> There is another point of view also. The object of this effort could be that you want the depressed classes to be retained in the Hindu religion, in which case I am inclined to believe that it is not sufficient in the *present awakened state* of the depressed classes.... If I call myself a Hindu I am obliged to accept that by birth I belong to a low caste. Hence I think I must ask the Hindu to show me some sacred authority, which would rule out this feeling of lowliness. If it cannot be I should say goodbye to Hinduism.... I am not going to be satisfied with measures,

which would merely bring some relief.... I don't want to be crushed by your charity. (Emphasis added)[113]

Ambedkar was thus also questioning Gandhi's claim that the untouchables were part of the Hindu community. Unlike Gandhi, he saw inequality inherent to Hinduism, and that is why Ambedkar was not just concerned with the removal of untouchability but the 'annihilation' of the entire caste system.[114] Thus, for low-caste leaders like Ambedkar, Gandhi's distinction between historical and eternal Hinduism was specious. Ambedkar stressed, 'My quarrel with Hindus and Hinduism is not over the imperfections of their social conduct. It is much more fundamental. It is over their ideals.'[115] Furthermore, as the untouchables were now a political group in themselves, in their politically 'awakened state' as depressed classes, it was not possible to retain them within Hinduism with social reform only. As a political group of depressed classes, representative politics required that their political interests be recognised as separate from that of upper-caste Hindus. As such, the depressed classes did not have any reason to accept Hinduism's ideals or its ordering principles over formal and equal rights granted by modern institutions of state power. In such a situation, *seva*, or service, rendered to lower castes by upper-caste Hindus as suggested by Gandhi could only be seen as largess or charity by the lower castes. Thus, for leaders like Ambedkar, who belonged to and represented the untouchable community, social emancipation and equality of, what the colonial government designated as, the depressed classes could only be achieved through their political empowerment. The mechanism of separate electorates was one such means to secure political power.

Thus, we see that the political mechanism of separate electorates for the untouchables challenged the heart of Gandhi's philosophy and belief in Hinduism – its capacity for internal reform and its essential unity. For Gandhi, the mechanism of separate electorates transformed various social divisions into permanent political differences. That is why he sought the eradication of untouchability, not in the capture of state power, but in social and religious reform. Gandhi did not consider the fact that for centuries the untouchables had been so systematically excluded from mainstream Hindu society as to hardly be said to belong to the Hindu community. Veeravalli goes on to argue that Gandhi's refusal to accept separate electorates is demonstrative of his political ideal where he sought to maintain a clear separation between civil society and the state in order to affirm the sovereignty of society in opposition to the general presumption that sovereignty can pertain only to the state. And social reform was located within the purview of civil society rather than in legal affirmation and empowerment and state's enforcement of formal and equal rights to the depressed classes.[116] Also, as argued already, the question of separate electorates (for both Dalits and Muslims) issued a direct challenge to Gandhian politics by creating hurdles in utilising moral and affective resources of social life that are central to his associationalism and replacing them with interest-based politics which could be only conducted through political institutions of the state.

RELIGIOUS TOLERANCE

We have already seen how Gandhi emphasised the importance of social service as the basis for moral and social reform of society. Tolerance, I argued in the previous chapter, would be an outcome of such active social service. In this chapter, we have also seen how Gandhi preferred minimum state intervention and state support on the question of social and political equality of various communities. In this section, with the help of examples, we will further see that Gandhi sought minimum state intervention on the question of religious tolerance as well. All religions, Gandhi believed, had the capacity for evolution. That is why, personally, he was against religious conversion, although he did not disbelieve in the possibility of a 'genuine conversion':

> I came to a conclusion long ago ... that all religions were true and also that all had some error in them.... So we can only pray, if we are Hindus, not that a Christian should become a Hindu, or if we are Musalmans, not that a Hindu or Christian should become a Musalman, nor should we secretly pray that any one should be converted, but our inmost prayer should be that a Hindu should be a better Hindu, a Muslim a better Muslim and a Christian a better Christian. That is the fundamental truth of fellowship.[117]

Gandhi's belief in religion's internal reform was of a piece with his political thought that stressed on moral and social reform rather than on political equality. In other words, the priority of morality in his thought and politics meant that a change of hearts and minds of people was necessary before any consideration of a political pact which enforced tolerance upon people. In India, practices such as cow-slaughter by Muslims and the playing of religious music (*arati*) by Hindus while passing through mosques had been a constant source of consternation between the two communities. Gandhi noted that a political agreement on these issues to ensure peace would be meaningless unless it was preceded by voluntary efforts on the part of quarrelling groups:

> It is clear that we have not even arrived at the stage when a pact is even a possibility. There can be, it is clear to me, no question of bargain about cow-slaughter and music. On either side it must be a voluntary effort and, therefore, can never be the basis of a pact. For political matters, a pact or an understanding is certainly necessary. But, in my opinion, the restoration of friendly feeling is a condition precedent to any effectual pact.[118]

Gandhi sought transformation of the people and thereby a transformation of existing social relations rather than a political compromise, where tolerance is associated with 'a political theory of *modus vivendi*'.[119] Furthermore, we have already seen in our discussion on the Khilafat movement how the demand for cow protection by Hindus in return for their political support to the Muslim cause of Khilafat could not be based on mutuality of compromise as that would be contrary to a relationship based on friendship, that is, associational politics. Gandhi's point was that to make associationalism the basis of society and polity meant that the quarrelling parties must first accept the proposition that religious disputes could not be solved through an appeal to the state. Moreover, his associational politics based on friendship and brotherhood demanded that 'we serve one another without laying down conditions'. Because only then was it possible that 'affection and fraternal love grow amongst us'.[120] Gandhi did not seek the state's mediatory role in order to ensure freedom of religion and peace in society. These two goals can, in fact, work at cross-purposes, and if any one of these becomes a priority of the state over another then, it indeed may be the case that one of the values is sacrificed all together for the other one. But if one considers Gandhi's proposition regarding the role of the state in religious conflict, this dilemma to choose between freedom of religion and peace in society may not arise in the first place.

Let us further examine Gandhi's understanding of religious tolerance with the examples of cow-protection and music before mosque. First, in contrast to the state of nature argument found in the liberal tradition that sees violence, self-interest and self-preservation as the basis of human condition, Gandhi wants us to seriously consider his proposition where non-violence is an attribute of human condition.[121] Liberal theory – like in the contractarian tradition of Thomas Hobbes, Jean-Jacques Rousseau and John Locke – holds that individuals in society are in competition with each other with respect to freedom, property and self-preservation. Gandhi is challenging that assumption and suggesting that human relationships are based on love rather than self-love, non-violence rather than violence, voluntary self-suffering and sacrifice in the service of the other rather than self-preservation.[122] He says, 'I refuse to suspect human nature. It will, is bound to, respond to any noble and friendly action'.[123] Second, Gandhi is of the view that deeply held religious convictions, like cow-protection and religious music, which may be considered essential to religion are non-negotiable under any condition. If the religious practice indeed turns out to be inessential to religion, it will, in his view, wither away on its own, 'the zest being wanting'.[124]

Gandhi's views on religious tolerance are, thus, not pleading for protection of religion by the state; rather, he institutes religion's sovereignty by stating that religious duty is above both obedience to the state and considerations of peace understood as mutual compromise. In calling for religion's independence from the state, Gandhian politics seeks to ensure that religion is uninfluenced by the homogenising tendencies of modern state power. For instance, the state is not called on to determine what practice is 'essential' to a religion to protect the freedom of religion, as is increasingly being done by the Indian judiciary today.[125] At the same time, Gandhi's views on religious tolerance also show religion's interdependence on society and politics, where associational activities like service to the community and associational politics that aim at fellowship and solidarity forged through politics of friendship determine the relationship among religion, society and politics. Such an interdependent relationship is not based on a conception of the political where tolerance is required to protect the freedom and rights of the citizen, which is the case in the liberal tradition. Rather, it is the sphere of ethical, based on religious-moral notions of duty and sacrifice, brotherhood and friendship, and love as fellow-service, which is crucial in envisaging individual's relationship to society and politics.

CONCLUSION: GANDHI'S FAILURE AND SECULARISM'S FUTURE

As late as 1941, Gandhi admitted that his 'non-violent experiment' was 'still in the making', and that he had 'nothing much yet to show by way of demonstration [of its results]'.[126] Sandipto Dasgupta observes that as independence became imminent, the question of how to order a new society and the contrasting role of the 'constructive programme' versus the modern state assumed centrality. The process of constitution-making provided the setting for that debate to play out. At the Constituent Assembly, Dasgupta notes, Gandhi's vision of a polity constituted around decentralised village republics and constructive programme was 'comprehensively rejected'.[127] Unlike India's modernist leaders like Nehru and Ambedkar, Gandhi did not seek revolutionary societal transformation through a modern centralised state. Instead, his politics may be described as a form of conservative politics which sought societal *reform* (not radical transformation) through his politics of associationalism. The basic political unit for such associational politics was not the distant and impersonal state but the village community. A major issue with Gandhian associationalism remains that the social power that is utilised for both mass mobilisation and reform in society is also the centre for hierarchical and oppressive social relations.[128] Gandhian associationalism therefore may not be amenable to a liberal transformative project of individual emancipation from traditional social formations, such as the caste system. However, such politics may contain possible resources for India's imperilled secularism.

In his scathing criticism of secularism in India, Ashis Nandy suggests that instead of aping structures of tolerance from Western theories of statecraft, it may be a fruitful venture to explore the philosophy, the symbolism and the theology of tolerance present in everyday religious faith.[129] By rejecting secularism, which is seen as anti-religion because it hives off religion to the private sphere as a solution to religious intolerance, Nandy directs our attention towards alternatives *to* secularism present in forms of tolerance found internal to religions that leaders like Gandhi invoked to manage religious conflict in India. If in rejecting secularism, Nandy seeks religion's independence from modern statecraft, in his defence of secularism, Nandy's interlocutor, Rajeev Bhargava, argues that as opposed to western models of 'wall of separation', secularism in India is based on a distinctive understanding of political neutrality of the state, which he calls 'principled distance'.[130] He argues that Nandy's criticism of secularism is misplaced because Indian secularism is different from Western conceptions of state secularism that may impose a particular conception of good life on society through an interventionist state. By distinguishing between ethical and political secularism, he points out that it is the latter type which animates India's constitution. Unlike ethical secularism which seeks to protect ultimate ideals like democracy, equality and autonomy, political secularism is a minimalist conception of separation of religion and state based on the principle of political neutrality. The centrality of how this political neutrality is conceived in Bhargava's theory of secularism shows that secularism requires not just a justification of separation, but also how religion and politics must relate to each other after the separation. His appeal is that the idea of separation in secularism need not mean a strict separation of state and religion. It need not mean 'strict non-interference, mutual exclusion or equidistance'.[131] According to him, 'In the strategy of principled distance, the state intervenes or refrains from interfering, depending on which of the two better promotes religious liberty and equality of citizenship.'[132] It may be argued that even in the strongest defence of Indian secularism, as offered by Bhargava, it is nevertheless ultimately the state's discretion to decide how 'principled' this distance between state and religion should be. It seems that even with its minimalist agenda, political secularism does not offer a resolution to the dilemma where the modern secular state, in the name of protecting freedom of or from religion, is capable of altering the very nature of religion. In other words, political secularism does not seem to offer a solution to the homogenising tendencies of modern statecraft. Added to it is the fact that in contemporary India, where Hindu majoritarianism has been very successful in electoral politics, the secular state remains prone to the ruling dispensation's commitment to the values of secularism.

Although Bhargava's theory of political secularism convincingly argues for an Indian variant of secularism, the political reality is that, since several decades, the Hindu right has managed to appropriate the language of secularism to pursue utterly anti-secular ends. That is why Partha Chatterjee maintains that the Hindu right is perfectly at peace with the institutions and procedures of the modern state. Through a secular position, the Hindu right can mobilise on its behalf the will of an interventionist modernising state in order to erase the presence of religious or ethnic particularisms from the domain of law and public life.[133] In such a situation, Chatterjee opines that secularism may not be an appropriate ground to meet the challenge of the Hindu right. What are the possible ways to engage with the modern state, which, in its engagement with religion, threatens homogenisation of religious difference? It must be noted here that, in their critique of secularism, both Chatterjee and Nandy shift the discussion on secularism from the nature and content of Indian secularism to modern statecraft. Although this book does not directly engage with the issue of state intervention, Gandhi's associationalism seems to provides possible resources to redress Nandy and Chatterjee's unease with modern statecraft, given how such politics relies on minimum state intervention for societal change. I have elaborated upon Gandhi's religious politics in terms of a range of associational practices in the field of religion, society and politics. His associational politics, as seen in this chapter, does not seek religion's independence from politics. He is paradoxically and wrongly seen to affirm both religious politics and secularism, because in his political thought and practice, religion and politics are interdependent, but at the same time he insists on religion's independence from state intervention. Given contemporary concerns of a homogenising modern state, it may be fruitful to consider possible ways of including forms of Gandhian associationalism within the framework of liberal secularism and liberal politics more generally.[134]

Gandhi's ideas and politics did not gain popular acceptance in Indian polity and society after independence; its lasting influence on the polity has mostly been symbolic – in the politician's sartorial attire of *khadi*, in the Gandhian cap and in the nationalist rhetoric of non-violence.[135] The discussions in this and the previous chapter attempted to show that those who argue that Gandhian religious politics was opposed to secularism fail to recognise that secular ideals can also be endorsed by forms of conservative politics of reform. Thus, despite its non-liberal epistemology and politics, Gandhian associationalism may be seen as compatible with liberal secularism.

NOTES

1. Gandhi often translated *satyagraha* as 'truth-force' or 'soul-force' and differentiated it from 'passive resistance'.
2. M. K. Gandhi, 'The Doctrine of the Sword', 11 August 1920, in *The Collected Works of Mahatma Gandhi* (henceforth, CWMG), 98 volumes, vol. 21, p. 134, https://www.gandhiashramsevagram.org/gandhi-literature/collected-works-of-mahatma-gandhi-volume-1-to-98.php (accessed on 6 August 2021). To get a sense of the time period in which Gandhi was writing, I have provided the date and the year alongside the volume number.
3. I use the phrase 'politics of religion' with a definitive pejorative connotation and refer to exclusionary ethno-nationalist politics. It must be noted that I do not identify politics of religion with certain forms of identity and caste-based politics in India, which are couched within the language of group rights for socially marginalised communities. Such politics, most famously championed by B. R. Ambedkar, is an example of inclusive representative politics. Thus, forms of inclusive representative politics do not fall within the category of politics of religion because their demands are shaped by concerns of political equality and social justice. For group-based theories of political representation, see Anne Phillips, *The Politics of Presence* (Oxford: Clarendon Press, 1995); and Melissa Williams, *Voice Trust and Memory: Marginalized Groups and the Failings of Liberal Representation* (New Jersey: Princeton University Press, 1998).
4. Seyla Benhabib, 'Introduction: The Democratic Moment and the Problem of Difference', in *Democracy and Difference: Contesting the Boundaries of the Political*, ed. Seyla Benhabib, pp. 3–18 (New Jersey: Princeton University Press, 1996), p. 4.
5. Ibid., p. 9.
6. See the section 'What is the Political?' in Chapter 2. There, I have argued that in Gandhi's political thought it is the individual and not the state which is the central political actor. Scholars like Partha Chatterjee and Anuradha Veeravalli have convincingly argued that in Gandhi's political thought it is the civil society, and not the state, which is sovereign. For a detailed discussion of Gandhi's critique of the modern state, see Karuna Mantena, 'On Gandhi's Critique of the State: Sources, Contexts, Conjectures', *Modern Intellectual History* 9, no. 3 (2012): 535–563. For a

critique of Gandhi's anti-statist vision of decentralised village republics for post-colonial India, see Sandipto Dasgupta, 'Gandhi's Failure: Anti-colonial Movements and Post-colonial Futures', *Perspectives on Politics* 15, no. 3 (2017): 647–662.

7. Faisal Devji, *Impossible Indian: Gandhi and the Temptation of Violence* (Cambridge, MA: Harvard University Press, 2012), pp. 68–69.
8. Ibid., p. 69.
9. Using the phrases 'core or meaning-giving beliefs and commitments' and 'convictions of conscience' interchangeably, Charles Taylor and Jocelyn Maclure define it as follows: 'By the terms "core or meaning-giving beliefs and commitments" we understand the reasons, evaluations, or grounds stemming from the conception of the world or of the good adopted by individuals that allow them to understand the world around them and to give a meaning and direction to their lives. It is in choosing values, hierarchizing or reconciling them, and clarifying the projects based on them that human beings manage to structure their existence, to exercise their judgment, and to conduct their life—in short, to constitute a moral identity for themselves. Core beliefs and commitments, which we will also call 'convictions of conscience', include both deeply held religious and secular beliefs and are distinguished from the legitimate but less fundamental 'preferences' we display as individuals.' Charles Taylor and Jocelyn Maclure, 'Moral Pluralism, Neutrality, and Secularism', in *Secularism and Freedom of Conscience*, trans. Jane Marie Todd, ed. Jocelyn Maclure and Charles Taylor, pp. 9–18 (Cambridge, MA: Harvard University Press, 2011), pp. 12–13.
10. Gandhi's non-violent activists, whom he called 'seekers of truth'.
11. Akeel Bilgrami has argued that ideals of 'liberty' and 'equality' are not the primary focus in Gandhian thought. Rather, in his view, it is a concern for 'unalienated life' that is central to Gandhi's political thought. Akeel Bilgrami, 'Gandhi (and Marx)', in *Secularism, Identity, and Enchantment*, pp. 122–174 (Cambridge, MA: Harvard University Press, 2014), p. 129.
12. For a discussion on Gandhi's emphasis on duties over rights, see the previous chapter. The liberal notion of the priority of right over good was emphasised by John Rawls in his book *A Theory of Justice* (Cambridge, MA: Belknap Press of Harvard University Press, 1971). It was further elaborated by him in *Political Liberalism* (New York: Columbia University Press, 1993). According to Rawls, the priority of right implies that the principles of (political) justice set limits to permissible ways of life, such

that the claims citizens make to pursue ends that transgress those limits have no weight as judged by that political conception.

13. For instance, see M. K. Gandhi, *The Way to Communal Harmony*, ed. U. R. Rao (Ahmedabad: Navajivan Trust, 1963), pp. 294–301.
14. Rajeev Bhargava, 'Indian Secularism: An Alternative Trans-cultural Ideal', in *The Promise of India's Secular Democracy*, pp. 63–105 (New Delhi: Oxford University Press, 2010), p. 77.
15. Such politics of religion, which conjures a homogeneous self, usually requires a homogeneous and threatening 'other' to self-identify itself as a collective group with shared interests and enemies.
16. Ravinder Kumar, 'Class, Community or Nation? Gandhi's Quest for a Popular Consensus in India', *Modern Asian Studies* 3, no. 4 (1969): 357–376.
17. Gandhi quoted in Bhikhu C. Parekh, *Colonialism, Tradition, and Reform: An Analysis of Gandhi's Political Discourse* (New Delhi: SAGE Publications, 1989), p. 136.
18. Gandhi maintained, 'The spinning-wheel, unity between the different communities and removal by Hindus of untouchability were the items on which perhaps all could unite.' M. K. Gandhi, 'Never to be Forgotten', 4 September 1924, *CWMG*, vol. 29, p. 75. According to Veeravalli, Hindu–Muslim unity, rejection of untouchability and adoption of non-exploitative means of livelihood, symbolised by the *charkha* are the 'three indispensable pillars of swaraj' in Gandhi's thought. See Anuradha Veeravalli, *Gandhi in Political Theory* (Surrey: Ashgate Publishing, 2014), p. 19.
19. Susanne H. Rudolph and Lloyd I. Rudolph also talk about 'associational forms' in Gandhi's *ashram* practices that were related to his politics. By conceiving Gandhi's *ashram* as the 'heuristic marker' for the public sphere (as opposed to the coffee house in eighteenth-century Europe), they argue for an 'Indian variant' of the civil society and public sphere. See Susanne H. Rudolph and Lloyd I. Rudolph, 'The Coffee House and the Ashram: Gandhi, Civil Society and Public Spheres', Working Paper no. 15, South Asia Institute, Department of Political Science, Heidelberg University, 2003.
20. For an elaboration of neighbourliness in Gandhi's thought, see Ajay Skaria, 'Gandhi's Politics: Liberalism and the Question of the Ashram', *The South Atlantic Quarterly* 101, no. 4 (2002): 955–986; and Ajay Skaria, *Unconditional Equality: Gandhi's Religion of Resistance* (Minneapolis:

University of Minnesota Press, 2016). Also see Ramin Jahanbegloo, *The Gandhian Moment* (Cambridge, MA: Harvard University Press, 2013). For Gandhi's politics of friendship, see Devji, *Impossible Indian*.
21. Stanley Wolpert, *Gandhi's Passion: The Life and Legacy of Mahatma Gandhi* (New York: Oxford University Press, 2002 [2001]), p. 11.
22. Gandhi, *The Way to Communal Harmony*, p. 5.
23. M. K. Gandhi, 'Foreword', *Constructive Programme: Its Meaning and Place*, pp. iii–iv (Navajivan Trust, 1945 [1941]), p. iii.
24. My aim here is not to provide a detailed account of these events and issues, which by themselves require individual scrutiny. They are used here as illustrative examples of how Gandhi conducted his religious politics in colonial India. There is a vast literature on each of these issues separately. I only mention some of the major and recent studies here. On the Non-cooperation movement, see David Hardiman, *Noncooperation in India: Nonviolent Strategy and Protest, 1920–22* (New York: Oxford University Press, 2021). On the Khilafat movement, see Gail Minault, *The Khilafat Movement: Religious Symbolism and Political Mobilization in India* (Delhi: Oxford University Press, 1982); and M. Naeem Qureshi, *Pan Islam in British Indian Politics: A Study of the Khilafat Movement, 1918–1924* (Leiden: Brill, 1999). For the Khilafat movement in the Muslim world, see Mona Hassan, *Longing for the Lost Caliphate: A Transregional History* (New Jersey: Princeton University Press, 2016). On the question of separate electorates in colonial India, see James Chiriyankandath, '"Democracy" under the Raj: Elections and Separate Representation in British India', *The Journal of Commonwealth and Comparative Politics* 30, no. 1 (1992): 39–64; Farzana Sheikh, *Community and Consensus in Islam: Muslim Representation in Colonial India, 1860–1947* (Cambridge: Cambridge University Press, 1989); and Shabnum Tejani, *Indian Secularism: A Social and Intellectual History 1890–1950* (Ranikhet: Permanent Black, 2007). On communalism in colonial India, see Gyanendra Pandey, *The Construction of Communalism in Colonial North India* (Delhi: Oxford University Press, 1990); Joya Chatterji, *Bengal Divided: Hindu Communalism and Partition 1932–47* (Cambridge: Cambridge University Press, 1995); Bipan Chandra, *Communalism in Modern India* (New Delhi: Vikas Publishing House, 1984).
25. Gandhi, *The Way to Communal Harmony*, p. 136. Joseph Lelyveld has argued that during the 1920s Hindu–Muslim unity got priority over untouchability in Gandhi's struggle for *swaraj*. See Joseph Lelyveld,

'Unapproachability', in *Great Soul: Mahatma Gandhi and His Struggle with India*, pp. 197–226 (New York: Alfred A. Knopf, 2011).

26. For instance, M. K. Gandhi, 'Speech at Meeting in Bulsar', 20 April 1921, *CWMG*, vol. 23, p. 71–72. Also see Edmund Candler, 'Mahatma Gandhi', *The Atlantic*, July 1922, https://www.theatlantic.com/magazine/archive/1922/07/mahatma-gandhi/306373/ (accessed on 12 August 2021).
27. Gandhi, *The Way to Communal Harmony*, p. 136.
28. Nehru conceived *swaraj* solely as political independence from the British rule. See the chapters on Nehru in this book.
29. For a detailed description of Gandhi's conception of *swaraj*, see M. K. Gandhi, 'Indian Home Rule or Hind Swaraj', trans. M. K. Gandhi, in *The Hind Swaraj and Other Writings*, ed. Anthony J. Parel, pp. 1–125 (New York: Cambridge University Press, 2009 [1997]).
30. M. K. Gandhi, *An Autobiography or The Story of my Experiments with Truth*, trans. Mahadev Desai (Ahmedabad: Navajivan Trust, 1940), p. 489.
31. Thus, Skaria argues that Gandhi sought a friendship with Muslims which was simultaneously based on 'absolute difference and full equality'. Skaria, 'Gandhi's Politics', p. 977.
32. Devji, *Impossible Indian*, p. 88.
33. Skaria, 'Gandhi's Politics', p. 979.
34. Gandhi's booklet on the constructive programme was published in 1941. The unrevised version of the constructive programme is available in M. K. Gandhi, *CWMG*, vol. 81, pp. 354–374.
35. Gandhi, *The Way to Communal Harmony*, p. 5.
36. Ibid., p. 3.
37. M. K. Gandhi, *Constructive Programme: Its Meaning and Place* (Navajivan Trust, 1945 [1941]), p. 2.
38. After the Defence of India Act lapsed with the end of the First World War, a committee appointed in December 1917 headed by Justice Rowlatt recommended that the colonial government should have emergency powers to deal with any area officially proclaimed as subversive. The Rowlatt Act of 1919 was an attempt by the colonial government to make wartime restrictions on civil rights permanent, including detention without trial for minor offences, such as the possession of seditious tracts. Gandhi called the Rowlatt law a 'black act' passed by a 'satanic' government. Gandhi quoted in Sugata Bose and Ayesha Jalal, *Modern South Asia: History, Culture, Political Economy* (New York: Routledge, 2004 [1997]), p. 110.

39. Ibid., p. 111.
40. In 1919, in the aftermath of the First World War, Muslims in colonial India were mobilised for the Khilafat movement which sought to pressurise the British government to retain the boundaries of the defeated Ottoman empire as they had existed before the war in 1914, and to preserve the position of the *khalifa* as the temporal head of the Islamic world. Shaukat Ali and his younger brother Mohammad Ali, who were associates of Maulana Abdul Bari of Lucknow's Firangi Mahal theological seminary, along with Mushir Hussain Kidwai, were the three central figures in the Khilafat movement. For more on the Khilafat movement, see Gail Minault, *The Khilafat Movement: Religious Symbolism and Political Mobilization in India* (Delhi: Oxford University Press, 1982); and Qureshi, *Pan Islam in British Indian Politics*.
41. Bose and Jalal, *Modern South Asia*, p. 111.
42. For Gandhi's reasons as to why he decided to link the Non-cooperation movement with the Khilafat issue, see the section in M. K. Gandhi, 'Why I Have Been Working for Khilafat So Seriously', in 'Some Questions', 30 January 1921, *CWMG*, vol. 22, pp. 288–291.
43. Tejani, *Indian Secularism*, p. 145; Hardiman, *Noncooperation in India*.
44. Tejani, *Indian Secularism*, p. 146.
45. Devji, *Impossible Indian*, p. 73.
46. M. K. Gandhi, 'Some Questions', 30 January 1921, *CWMG*, vol. 22, p. 288.
47. M. K. Gandhi, 'Letter to Mahomed Ali', 18 November 1918, *CWMG*, vol. 17, p. 246. Also see Gandhi, *The Way to Communal Harmony*, pp. 8, 14; M. K. Gandhi, 'Speech at Public Meeting, Nellore', 12 April 1921, *CWMG*, vol. 23, pp. 10–15.
48. M. K. Gandhi, 'Speech on Hasrat Mohani's Motion II', 19 January 1921, *CWMG*, vol. 25, p. 354.
49. Quoted from Tejani, *Indian Secularism*, pp. 154–155.
50. M. K. Gandhi, 'Khilafat: Further Questions', 2 June 1920, *CWMG*, vol. 20, p. 383.
51. M. K. Gandhi, 'Fasting and Prayer', 12 October 1919, *CWMG*, vol. 19, 47. Also see M. K. Gandhi, 'Prayer and Fasting', 4 October 1919, *CWMG*, vol. 19, pp. 21–22.
52. M. K. Gandhi, 'Speech at Khilafat Conference, Delhi', 6 December 1919, *CWMG*, vol. 19, p. 138. Also see Gandhi, *An Autobiography*, pp. 527–531.
53. Gandhi, *The Way to Communal Harmony*, p. 9.

54. Charles Taylor, 'The Polysemy of the Secular', *Social Research* 76, no. 4 (2009): 1143–1166. For an argument about secularism as a 'multi-value' doctrine which seeks to protect values like peace, liberty and equality, see Rajeev Bhargava, 'Political Secularism' in *The Oxford Handbook of Political Theory*, ed. John S. Dryzek, Bonnie Honig and Anne Phillips (Oxford: Oxford University Press, 2006). Also see Bhargava, 'Indian Secularism'.
55. Sudipta Kaviraj, 'The Reversal of Orientalism: Bhudev Mukhapadhyay and the Project of Indigenist Social Theory', in *The Imaginary Institution of India: Politics and Ideas*, pp. 254–288 (New York: Columbia University Press, 2010), p. 259.
56. Ibid., p. 260.
57. Devji, *Impossible Indian*, p. 67.
58. According to Devji, brotherhood of the egalitarian or nationalist sort remained to be thought through by Gandhi.
59. Akeel Bilgrami, 'Gandhian Fraternity', *The Immanent Frame: Secularism, Religion and the Public Sphere*, 13 September 2012, https://tif.ssrc.org/2012/09/13/gandhian-fraternity/ (accessed on 19 August 2021).
60. Bilgrami, 'A Different Notion of Fraternity', *The Immanent Frame: Secularism, Religion and the Public Sphere*, 7 September 2012, https://tif.ssrc.org/2012/09/07/a-different-notion-of-fraternity/ (accessed on 19 August 2021).
61. M. K. Gandhi, 'How to Work Non-cooperation', 5 May 1920, *CWMG*, vol 20, pp. 286–288.
62. Judith M. Brown, *Gandhi's Rise to Power: Indian Politics 1915–1922* (London: Cambridge University Press, 1972), p. 194.
63. Devji, *Impossible Indian*, p. 46.
64. Gandhi, 'How to Work Non-Cooperation', pp. 287–288.
65. Parekh, *Colonialism, Tradition, and Reform*, p. 71. 'Two things have inflamed his countrymen—"the Punjab wrongs, and the breach of faith against the Mohammedans". Until Government repaired the breach and repented of the wrong, Gandhi declared a fight to the finish. He pledged himself to preach disaffection openly and systematically until it pleased Government to arrest him'. Candler, 'Mahatma Gandhi'.
66. Quoted in Tejani, *Indian Secularism*, pp. 172–173.
67. Gandhi, *The Way to Communal Harmony*, p. 9.
68. Tejani, *Indian Secularism*; Rakahahari Chatterji, *Gandhi and the Ali Brothers: Biography of a Friendship* (New Delhi: SAGE Publications, 2013).
69. Tejani, *Indian Secularism*, p. 161.

70. Ibid., p. 162.
71. Jinnah resigned from the Congress soon thereafter. For Jinnah's position against conjoining a religious issue with the national movement, see Ayesha Jalal, *The Sole Spokesman: Jinnah, the Muslim League and the Demand for Pakistan* (New York: Cambridge University Press, 1999 [1985]).
72. Tejani, *Indian Secularism*; Mushirul Hasan, 'Islam, Khilafat and Nationalism', in *The Mushirul Hasan Omnibus*, pp. 104–144 (New Delhi: Manohar Publications, 2006).
73. M. K. Gandhi, 'Hindu–Muslim Tension: Its Cause and Cure', 29 May 1924, *CWMG*, vol. 28, pp. 43–44.
74. See Veeravalli, *Gandhi in Political Theory*, p. 138. Truth capitalised here denotes Gandhi's conception of the 'absolute truth'. See Chapter 2 for a detailed discussion on Gandhi's notion of truth.
75. M. K. Gandhi, 'Hindus and Moplahs', 26 January 1922, *CWMG*, vol. 26, pp. 24–25, note 2.
76. Devji, *Impossible Indian*, p. 115.
77. In the chapters on Nehru, we will see that he also sought political equality of various groups outside the representative structures of state machinery, but for very different reasons.
78. Gandhi, *The Way to Communal Harmony*, p. 149.
79. For Nehru's position on separate electorates, see Chapter 5 in this book.
80. Gandhi, *The Way to Communal Harmony*, pp. 150–151.
81. Ibid., p. 152.
82. Ibid.
83. Ibid., pp. 150–151.
84. Ibid., p. 297.
85. Gandhi, *Constructive Programme*, p. 3.
86. Sudipta Kaviraj, 'Religion, Politics and Modernity', in *Crisis and Change in Contemporary India*, ed. Upendra Baxi and Bhikhu Parekh, pp. 295–316 (New Delhi: SAGE Publications, 1995), p. 299.
87. Ibid., p. 299. Scholars, like Bernard S. Cohn and Nicholas B. Dirks, have highlighted the imbrication of colonial knowledge with colonial rule. They have shown how technologies of colonial governmentality, like enumeration and representation, encouraged the view that caste and religious communities were separate, distinct and reified groups. See Bernard S. Cohn, *Colonialism and Its Forms of Knowledge: The British in India* (Princeton: Princeton University Press, 1996); and Nicholas B. Dirks,

Castes of Mind: Colonialism and the Making of Modern India (Princeton: Princeton University Press, 2001).

88. For a comprehensive discussion on the concept of representation, see Hanna Pitkin, *The Concept of Representation* (Berkeley: University of California Press, 1972).
89. On theories of group rights, see Williams, *Voice, Trust and Memory*; Phillips, *Politics of Presence*; and Iris Marion Young, *Justice and the Politics of Difference* (New Jersey: Princeton University Press, 1990).
90. M. A. Jinnah, *Address by Quaid-i-Azam Muhammad Ali Jinnah at Lahore Session of Muslim League, March, 1940* (Islamabad: Directorate of Films and Publishing, Ministry of Information and Broadcasting, Government of Pakistan, Islamabad, 1983), pp. 5–23, http://www.columbia.edu/itc/mealac/pritchett/00islamlinks/txt_jinnah_lahore_1940.html (accessed on 20 August 2021).
91. Gandhi, *The Way to Communal Harmony*, p. 296.
92. Ibid., p. 300.
93. Veeravalli, *Gandhi in Political Theory*, p. 123. Also see the previous chapter for the centrality of experiment in Gandhian non-violence, or *ahimsa*.
94. For a discussion on the relationship between Gandhi's theory of non-violence and the practice of *brahmacharya*, see Veeravalli, *Gandhi in Political Theory*.
95. Joseph Alter has called Gandhi's attempts to embody his search for Truth and non-violence through fasting, *brahmacharya* (celibacy), vegetarianism, nature cure, and so on as 'biomorality'. For a discussion of the same, see the previous chapter. Also see Joseph Alter, *Gandhi's Body: Sex, Diet, and the Politics of Nationalism* (Philadelphia: University of Pennsylvania Press, 2000).
96. M. K. Gandhi, 'Speech at Prayer Meeting, New Delhi', 21 April 1946, *CWMG*, vol. 90, pp. 199–200.
97. Gandhi, *The Way to Communal Harmony*, p. 294.
98. The *varna* system is the hereditary fourfold system of social division of labour in Hinduism. According to the *varna* system, the Brahmins are at the top of the hierarchy and consist of the priests and scholars. Kshatriyas are the warrior class and consist of political rulers and soldiers. Vaishyas are the merchants and traders. Sudras are the lowest in the hierarchy, who perform menial work and usually consist of labourers, peasants, artisans, and so on.
99. M. K. Gandhi, 'Hinduism', 6 October 1924, *CWMG*, vol. 24, pp. 370–371.

100. Ibid., p. 371.
101. Ibid.
102. Gandhi, 'Hinduism', p. 373.
103. M. K. Gandhi, 'A Talk', 8 December 1946, *CWMG*, vol. 93, p. 43.
104. Parekh, *Colonialism, Tradition and Reform*, p. 218.
105. Parekh points out that the Congress started tentatively criticizing untouchability from the early years of the twentieth century and passed an explicit resolution condemning it in 1917. Ibid., p. 213.
106. Ibid., p. 212.
107. Gandhi quoted in Ibid., p. 216.
108. This term was coined by the colonial state for the 'untouchables' or the lowest members in the Hindu caste hierarchy.
109. Veeravalli, *Gandhi in Political Theory*, p. 63.
110. Veeravalli, *Gandhi in Political Theory*. Savarna refers to the first three of the four castes – that is, Brahmins, Kshatriyas, and Vaishyas. Sudras, or the untouchables, are designated the lowest status in the Hindu caste hierarchy.
111. Valerian Rodrigues, 'Ambedkar as a Political Philosopher', *Economic and Political Weekly* 52, no. 15 (2017): 101–107.
112. B. R. Ambedkar, 'Appendix X: Discussion with B.R. Ambedkar', 4 February 1933, *CWMG*, vol. 59, p. 509.
113. Ibid.
114. B. R. Ambedkar, 'Annihilation of Caste: Speech Prepared for the Annual Conference of the Jat-Pat-Todak Mandal of Lahore But Not Delivered, 1936', in *Annihilation of Caste: The Annotated Critical Edition*, ed. S. Anand, pp. 181–356 (London: Verso, 2016 [2014]).
115. B. R. Ambedkar, 'A Reply to the Mahatma: B.R. Ambedkar', in *Annihilation of Caste: The Annotated Critical Edition*, ed. S. Anand, p. 353 (London: Verso, 2016 [2014]).
116. Veeravalli, *Gandhi in Political Theory*, pp. 50–65.
117. Gandhi, *The Way to Communal Harmony*, pp. 56–57. Also see M. K. Gandhi, 'Notes' in 'Shraddhanand Memorial', 6 January 1927, *CWMG*, vol. 38, p. 16.
118. M. K. Gandhi, 'Hindu–Muslim Tension: Its Cause and Cure', 29 May 1925, *CWMG*, vol. 28, pp. 59–60.
119. See John Gray, *Two Faces of Liberalism* (New York: The New Press, 2000).
120. M. K. Gandhi, 'Punjab Letter', 7 December 1919, *CWMG*, vol. 19, p. 151.
121. Veeravalli, *Gandhi in Political Theory*.

122. Ibid., p. 29.
123. M. K. Gandhi, 'Cow Protection', 4 August 1920, *CWMG*, vol. 21, p. 119.
124. M. K. Gandhi, 'That Eternal Question', 22 October 1925, *CWMG*, vol. 33, p. 137.
125. Here, I am referring to the use of the reasoning of 'essential practices test' by Indian courts, where judges engage in religious exegesis to determine whether a particular cultural practice is integral to the conception of religion or not. For a discussion of these court cases, see A. K. Abraham, 'Essential Religious Practices Test and the First Amendment: A Comparative Analysis of the Free Exercise of Religion in India and the United States', in *The Indian Yearbook of Comparative Law 2019*, ed. Mathew John, Vishwas H. Devaiah, Pritam Baruah, Moiz Tundawala and Niraj Kumar, pp. 279–301 (Singapore: Springer, 2021).
126. Gandhi, *Constructive Programme*, p. 15.
127. Dasgupta, 'Gandhi's Failure', p. 648.
128. See Dasgupta, 'Gandhi's Failure' for Ambedkar's critique of Gandhian dependence on traditional social hierarchies for sociopolitical change.
129. Ashis Nandy, 'The Politics of Secularism and the Recovery of Religious Tolerance', in *Secularism and Its Critics*, ed. Rajeev Bhargava, pp. 321–344 (New Delhi: Oxford University Press, 2008 [1998]).
130. Rajeev Bhargava, 'What is Secularism For?' in *Secularism and Its Critics*, ed. Rajeev Bhargava, pp. 486–555 (New Delhi: Oxford University Press, 2008 [1998]), p. 493.
131. Ibid, p. 520.
132. Ibid., p. 515.
133. Partha Chatterjee, 'Secularism and Tolerance', in *Secularism and Its Critics*, ed. Rajeev Bhargava, pp. 345–379 (New Delhi: Oxford University Press, 2008 [1998]).
134. I would like to flag a note of caution here. Since *intra-group* domination (that is, inequality within a religious or caste group or community) is not central to Gandhi's associationalism, an Ambedkarite critique of Gandhian associationalism may be necessary in such politics.
135. *Khadi* refers to handspun and handwoven cloth, which was popularised by Gandhi during the national struggle.

4

WAS NEHRU NEHRUVIAN?

RELIGION, SECULARITY AND NEHRUISM

As far as India is concerned, I can speak with some certainty. We shall proceed on secular and national lines ... in the future, India will be a land, as in the past, of many faiths equally honoured and respected. (Jawaharlal Nehru, An Address at the Aligarh Muslim University, 24 January 1948)

There is an essential unity about it [India] and India is also a country with very remarkable diversity, and the problem in India is to maintain both, not to crush the diversity and obviously not to lessen the unity. (Jawaharlal Nehru, Speech at the 40th Session of the Indian Science Congress, 2 January 1953)

INTRODUCTION

In both his personal and political life, Nehru stands diametrically opposed to Gandhi, stridently Western in his demeanour, outlook and politics. While independence for Gandhi meant the historical opportunity to move out of the forcible imposition of Western modernity on India, for Nehru modernity was a universally desirable condition which was impeded due to British colonial rule. India's nationalist leaders had diverse and often contending ideas of India as a political community, but Nehru's vision of society dominated years after independence – a nationalist leader and the first prime minister of independent India – who, as Sunil Khilnani remarks, was ostensibly the most anglicised of them all.[1] As is well known, in terms of their vision of Indian society in its relation to modernity, Nehru and Gandhi stood on opposite ends. Unlike Gandhi, Nehru, an unapologetic modernist, did not seek to reform pre-modern social formations to changing conditions of modernity. Instead, Nehru's idea of India was based on a belief in modernity as progress which required overcoming pre-modern social formations, not reconfiguring it. If Gandhi desired his ideal of the nation realised in India's village life, Nehru's vision of modern India lay in industrialisation. And yet Gandhi and Nehru shared an intimate and intriguing political relationship, with the latter being Gandhi's protégé and political successor.[2] As the leader of the Indian National Congress (hereafter, the Congress) and the new nation-state, Nehru's modern and secular vision directly influenced independent India's polity and society for seventeen years, initially heading the interim legislature (1947–1952) and thereafter winning three successive general elections (1952, 1957 and 1961).[3] Thus, while Gandhi brought independence to India, it was Nehru who was handed the responsibility to decide what to do with that independence. In Nehru's new sovereign nation-state, 'expertise' and 'scientific temper' were given privileged positions.[4] In the Nehruvian period, the Indian polity and society saw an emphasis on state-led developmentalism and a commitment to values of secularism and scientific temper.[5]

In this chapter, I will focus on Nehru's writings to examine the role and relation of religion he envisaged vis-à-vis the state and society under conditions of modernity. In other words, this chapter examines Nehru's conception of secularity as it emerges from his writings. Such an exercise will shed light on how Nehru's notion of secularity influenced the 'Gandhi–Nehru tradition' and thereby the discourse of secularity in modern and contemporary India. The first section of the chapter begins with a discussion on Nehru's idea of modernity and its relation to society. The discussion in this section focuses on the exchange of letters between Gandhi and Nehru on the role of modernity in society and shows how the two national leaders differed in their idea of India. After arguing how modernity was central to Nehru's conception of both state sovereignty and society, I move on to the second section to elaborate upon his notion of religion in relation to his political thought. Here, I argue that a dominant view of religion that emerges in Nehru's political thought is in terms of its affective dimensions which appeal to emotions and passions. I also argue that, in his political thought, we find a clear distinction between religion and secular based on whether ideas and practices are this-worldly or otherworldly. Based on this observation, I maintain that Nehru distinguishes religion from forms of morality and spirituality that he thought could be practised in non-transcendental, this-worldly form. In the third section, following my analysis of Nehru's idea of religion (discussed in the second section), I examine the relationship that he envisaged between religion and politics in a modern society. In this section, I engage with his views on Gandhi's practice of religious politics and discuss the reasons for his ambivalence towards involving religion in the political sphere. Nehru's ambivalence towards Gandhi's religious politics raises the question as to why he sought to separate religion and politics. I note that Nehru had deep misgivings towards conducting politics that was based on religious faith. For him, it was desirable and feasible to separate religion from politics because such a separation would ensure reasoned politics and keep religion's emotional and irrational appeal away from the political sphere. In the fourth section, I ask: if religion was not the moral basis of politics and society in Nehru's political thought, what sort of morality undergirded his politics? Nehru's attempt was to base his morality on non-religious sources, which he often described as 'scientific temper', a disposition that he thought should encompass one's thinking, behaviour and association with other members in society and politics. Nehru considered his politics as modern and secular because his political action was based on a secular-scientific epistemology which was capable of producing universal conclusions. Furthermore, he linked this idea of scientific temper to what he considered the 'spirit of the age', which he believed was expressed in the modern principles of secular humanism and scientific spirit. He thus saw his morality and politics to be based on such twentieth-century modern principles. In the fifth and the sixth sections of the chapter, I discuss Nehru's notion of secularity and distinguish between his 'nationalist' and 'humanist-universal' narratives of secularity. I argue that these two narratives together give expression to Nehru's idea of secularity that is simultaneously indigenous and universal. In the seventh section, I outline his conception of secularism, as can be deduced from a discussion on Nehruvian secularity in the previous two sections. The eighth section distinguishes Nehruvian secularity from the ideology of Nehruism that emerged in the 1970s and 1980s under the leadership of his daughter Indira Gandhi. The ninth section is a critical appraisal of Nehruvian secularism, which is followed by a conclusion to the chapter.

MODERNITY IN *SWARAJ* AND *SWARAJ* IN MODERNITY

While Gandhi's imagination of the political was radical within the context of colonial rule, it failed to capture independent India's political imagination. Instead, it was the political discourse of Nehru and the Dalit[6] leader Ambedkar that came to dominate the political landscape of independent India. What differentiated Gandhi's political vision from the latter two was its critical approach to Western modernity's vision of the world. In 1945, Gandhi wrote to Nehru:

> I am convinced that if India is to attain true freedom and through India the world also, then sooner or later the fact must be recognised that people will have to live in villages, not in towns, in huts, not in palaces. Crores of people will never be able to live at peace with each other in towns and palaces. They will then have no recourse but to resort to both violence and untruth. I hold that without truth and nonviolence there can be nothing but destruction for humanity. We can realise truth and non-violence only in the simplicity of village life and this simplicity can best be found in the Charkha [spinning-wheel] and all that the Charkha connotes.[7]

Swaraj (self-rule) to Gandhi denoted much more than simply political independence. It meant the realisation of political freedom through non-violent means. Such non-violent measures included a commitment to the constructive programme, which was Gandhi's project of village reconstruction and social and moral reform of society. For Gandhi, the transformation of society based on the premises of non-violence meant reform of traditional social formations, not their removal. This entailed, among other things, a commitment to village reconstruction through activities like the promotion of *khadi*.[8] Gandhi explained to Nehru that an admiration for modernity and modern science did not require disavowal of the pre-modern: 'While I admire modern science, I find that it is the old looked at in the true light of modern science which should be reclothed and refashioned aright.'[9]

In his reply, Nehru said to Gandhi:

> I do not understand why a village should necessarily embody truth and non-violence. A village, normally speaking, is backward intellectually

and culturally and no progress can be made from a backward environment. Narrow-minded people are much more likely to be untruthful and violent.

Again it seems to me inevitable that modern means of transport as well as many other modern developments must continue and be developed. There is no way out of it except to have them. If that is so, inevitably a measure of heavy industry exists. How far will that fit in with a purely village society? ... *If two types of economy exist in the country there should be either conflict between the two or one will overwhelm the other.*

The question of independence and protection from foreign aggression, both political and economic, has also to be considered in this context. *I do not think it is possible for India to be really independent unless she is a technically advanced country.* I am not thinking for the moment in terms of just armies but rather of scientific growth. In the present context of the world *we cannot even advance culturally without a strong background of scientific research in every department.* (Emphasis added)[10]

Unlike Gandhi who seemed critical of a linear and progressive narrative of history as economic development and modernisation, Nehru considered modernity a good in itself. In Nehru's opinion, the ineluctability of modernity meant that it would 'overwhelm' and overtake pre-modern socio-economic formations, like a village economy. Akeel Bilgrami has argued that Gandhi's rather critical stance against Western modernity can be attributed to his belief that India was at the cusp that Europe had been in the early modern period and that Gandhi was anxious about India potentially going down the path of Europe in its passage from early to late modernity.[11] But because Nehru disagreed with Gandhi on this historical assumption, his thought and politics conceived of a genuine realisation of modernity through political independence, because he saw British colonialism standing in the way of India's path to modernity.[12] Moreover, as modernity meant advancement in science and technology, it would also secure India's future political sovereignty, along with socio-economic progress. As Nehru attributed India's economic backwardness to imperialist exploitation, and especially the neglect of industrial development under colonial rule, continued dependence on colonial powers for complex technology and capital goods seemed to him to threaten the real core of sovereignty.[13] Hence, in contrast to Gandhi's politics, where socio-economic reforms in the form of constructive programme found a priority over *purna swaraj*[14] (complete independence), Nehru's politics was marked by the single importance of *swaraj* as political independence from British colonial rule.[15] Thus, it may be argued that Gandhi and Nehru's completely different assumption on the historical construction of India's path to modernity determined their differences about India's future and therefore their political methods and means to achieve that future. Such being Nehru's preference for modernity for India's development, what role and place did religion have in modern society and politics? To examine Nehru's position on religion's relationship to society and politics, we must first understand his conception of religion.

RELIGION IN NEHRU'S POLITICAL THOUGHT

If for Gandhi religion is uncomplicated in terms of its meaning as 'faith' and 'ethical living',[16] for Nehru, religion is a complex idea with multiple meanings, which ranges from expressions of institutional and non-institutional forms of ethical and social orders. In his writings, we find that Nehru grapples to define religion in terms of a 'complex of ideas and images', which includes

> ... ideas and images [...] of rites and ceremonial, of sacred books, of a community of people, of certain dogmas, of morals, reverence, love, fear, hatred, charity, sacrifice, asceticism, fasting, feasting, prayer, ancient history, marriage, death, the next world, of riots and the breaking of heads, and so on.[17]

According to Nehru, religion is imbued with varied and conflicting meanings, and in his writings we find multiple conceptions of religion. However, a dominant view of religion that can be discerned in his thought is that religion almost invariably invokes passions and strong emotional response which makes 'dispassionate consideration impossible'.[18] As we shall see later in this chapter, it is this affective dimension of religion which makes its involvement in politics precarious and undesirable. The point, however, to be noted here is that, in Nehru's view, there are multiple conflicting conceptions of religion, some of which may provide fullness to an individual or community's life, while others may be regressive and may lead to conflicts and stagnation in society. Therefore, a dominant and simplistic view of Nehru that he was 'from the very beginning quite hostile, unsympathetic and intolerant in his comments on religion' is not reflected in his writings or in his politics.[19]

Nehru approves of a 'modern definition' of religion and quotes John Dewey:

> Any activity pursued in behalf [sic] of an ideal end against obstacles, and in spite of threats of personal loss, because of conviction of its general and enduring value, is religious in quality.[20]

Nehru says that if this is what defines religion, then 'surely no one can have the slightest objection to it'.[21] Therefore, before he discusses this modern notion of religion, Nehru approvingly quotes Gandhi's statements regarding religion's inclusion in politics because he sees the latter's notion of religion as an expression of a modern definition of religion. So, for instance, when Gandhi says that 'those who say that religion has nothing to do with politics do not know what religion means',[22] in Nehru's opinion Gandhi is 'using it in a sense – probably moral and ethical more than any other' and therefore – 'different from that of the critics of religion'.[23] Indeed, when Nehru says that such modern definitions would horrify 'men of religion' and 'orthodox of organised religions',[24] we know that Gandhi's practice of religion did draw condemnation from the men of religion. But while Nehru admired what he saw as Gandhi's application of 'an ethical doctrine to large-scale public activity',[25] he always remained sceptical of its religious sources.[26]

In Nehru's autobiography, the first five pages of his chapter on religion are veritably irate, yet in these pages one also sees his attempt to seek inspiration from Gandhi's religious politics. What is striking about these initial pages, written by an avowed secular-modernist, is Nehru's attempt to understand Gandhi's mixing of religion and politics, and not an outright rejection of it. Referring to Gandhi's twenty-one-day anti-untouchability fast in 1933, Nehru writes:

> Again I watched the emotional upheaval of the country during the fast, and I wondered more and more if this was the right method in politics. It seemed to be sheer revivalism, and clear thinking had not a ghost of a chance against it. All India, or most of it, stared reverently

at the Mahatma and expected him to perform miracle after miracle and put an end to untouchability and get Swaraj and so on and did precious little itself! And Gandhiji did not encourage others to think; his insistence was only on purity and sacrifice. I felt that I was drifting further and further away from him mentally, in spite of my strong emotional attachment to him. Often enough he was guided in his political activities by an unerring instinct. He had the flair for action, but *was the way of faith the right way to train a nation?* It might pay for a short while, but in the long run? (Emphasis added)[27]

Throughout his political life Nehru seemed ambivalent of Gandhi's religious politics. Although he viewed Gandhi's religion as something 'moral and ethical',[28] he was doubtful whether the application of such ethical religion to politics was the right method. Being grounded on 'faith', religion's method of approach to life's problems, Nehru noted, was 'certainly not that of science'.[29] Unlike Gandhi, who, as we saw in the previous chapters, equated his practice of religion with the method of science, Nehru saw religion as completely devoid of reason and objective outlook as it relied on 'emotion and intuition'.[30]

Furthermore, Nehru had absolute disdain for and unequivocally rejected what he called 'organized religion':

The spectacle of what is called religion, or at any rate organized religion, in India and elsewhere has filled me with horror, and I have frequently condemned it and wished to make a clean sweep of it. Almost always it seems to stand for blind belief and reaction, dogma and bigotry, superstition and exploitation, and the preservation of vested interests.[31]

Ashis Nandy makes a conceptual distinction between religion as faith and ideology. According to Nandy, as opposed to religion as faith, which is a way of life or a tradition, religion as ideology is a sub-national, national or cross-national identifier of populations, which contests for or protects non-religious, usually political or socio-economic, interests.[32] Nehru is clearly rejecting religion as constructed ideology, which he finds in forms of institutionalised religion. Nehru says that organised religion, that is, religion in its institutionalised form, has given way to preservation of 'vested interest' and 'big business'.[33] He is extremely critical of Britain's 'brand of religion', which, he maintains, has helped serve the purposes of British imperialism 'by blunting their moral susceptibilities where their own interests were concerned'.[34] Nehru is against organised religion because he sees it emptied of moral and ethical values. The Church of England, he notes, has provided a 'moral and Christian covering' to British imperialism and capitalism and justified unjust social practices in the past, like slavery and serfdom.[35]

Nehru is critical of organised religion, but what about his views on non-institutional forms of religion visible in everyday faith? In his opinion,

> ... the usual religious outlook does not concern itself with *this world*. It seems to me to be the enemy of clear thought, for it is based not only on the acceptance without demur of certain fixed and unalterable theories and *dogmas*, but also on *sentiment* and *emotion* and *passion*. It is *far removed from what I consider spirituality* and things of the spirit, and it deliberately or unconsciously shuts its eyes to reality lest reality may not fit in with preconceived notions. It is narrow and intolerant of other opinions and ideas; it is self-centered and egotistic; and it often allows itself to be exploited by self-seekers and opportunists...
>
> ... the *religious outlook* does not help, and even *hinders, the moral and spiritual progress* of a people, if morality and spirituality are to be judged by this world's standards, and not by the hereafter. (Emphasis added)[36]

In this quote, Nehru defines faith in terms of an oppositional dyad between this-world and the other-world, such that there can be no intermixing between these two worldviews.[37] Furthermore, he blames all of religion's defects – 'dogmas', 'sentiment', 'emotion', 'passion' – to its other-worldly character. He argues that even in its non-institutional form, this other-worldly religion may hinder moral and social progress of society. He goes on to add:

> Usually religion becomes an asocial quest for God or the Absolute, and the religious man is concerned far more with his own salvation than with the good of society.... Moral standards have no relation to social needs but are based on a highly metaphysical doctrine of sin. And organized religion invariably becomes a vested interest and thus invariably a reactionary force opposing change and progress.[38]

We see that in Nehru's view, religion, in both its organised or institutional and otherworldly or transcendental form, can become undesirable for societal progress. In both these forms, religion can lack the moral standards that propels society towards social change and progress because its 'asocial' transcendental morality is unrelated to social needs and therefore to conceptions of social justice. Moreover, unlike Gandhi, he draws a distinction between spirituality and religion and between morality and religion. Such a distinction allows him to argue that while spirituality and morality may be connected to the social needs of the people, religion may not. It follows that, for Nehru, both morality and spirituality can be construed and practised independently of religion – in non-transcendental, this-worldly form. If it was not religious morality, what sort of morality was the basis for Nehru's politics? Before we consider that question, let us first delve into the reasons for Nehru's apprehension towards religion's inclusion into politics.

RELIGION AND POLITICS

It must be reminded and stated clearly here that Nehru was not against religion per se, but he did have a disdain for religion's involvement in politics. Despite this, Nehru did not outrightly reject Gandhi's religious politics. His grudging acceptance of Gandhi's religious politics came from a realisation that the latter's 'religious' and 'sentimental' approach to politics garnered mass support for the freedom struggle in a way that the Congress's constitutional politics never could.[39] Nehru also realised that as opposed to the English educated and the *zamindari* classes[40] for whom the goal of political independence also came with the attendant fear of huge socio-economic losses, the vast masses constituting the peasantry and the industrial working classes had 'a great deal to gain and very little to lose' if British rule was abolished.[41] Unlike the urban and upper classes, the rural masses did not have vested interest in the colonial government. Indeed, the rural masses, particularly the peasantry, were the ones who had consistently faced colonial oppression and injustice. Thus, Nehru notes:

> These [the peasantry and the working class] are the people who must form the armies or forces to fight the battle of India's freedom....

Primarily the struggle will rest on them and it is bound to rest on them.... Without the support of the masses or the industrial or the agricultural workers it is inconceivable that India can achieve her freedom.[42]

Partha Chatterjee has argued that in Nehru's view, since the masses did not act according to 'reason', they were susceptible to 'religious passions'.[43] Chatterjee notes that Nehru's modern and scientific approach to society and politics that was based on 'objective economic interests'[44] could not rationally comprehend the subjective beliefs of the masses of peasantry as these were located in the realm of 'unreason', 'passion' and 'spontaneity'.[45] Thus, in order to overthrow colonial rule with the help of mass nationalism, Nehru's secular and scientific approach to politics was inadequate as it could not mobilise the vast illiterate masses for political independence.[46] The fight for *swaraj*, in Nehru's view, required 'nationalism pure and simple, the feeling of the humiliation of India and a fierce desire to be rid of it and to put an end to our continuing degradation'.[47] But nationalism's affect was missing from the Congress's constitutional politics. The latter was based on limited franchise, whereas nationalism could garner the support of the masses to confront foreign rule. And within the Congress, it was only the national leader Gandhi who knew how to draw mass support for a national cause. Thus, for Nehru, Gandhi was 'a symbolic expression of the confused desires of the people'.[48] Moreover, Gandhi

> ... is the greatest peasant, with a peasant's outlook on affairs, and with a peasant's blindness to some aspects of life. But India is peasant India, and so he knows his India well, reacts to her slightest tremors, gauges a situation accurately and almost instinctively, and has a knack of acting at the psychological moment.[49]

Gandhi was, in Nehru's view, a 'magician' who could understand the psychology of the masses and produce 'great results' for the national struggle.[50] It may be argued that Nehru held a rather instrumental view with regard to Gandhi's religious and mass politics. Since for Nehru, the goal of political independence from colonial rule was the most vital issue in the national struggle,[51] Gandhi's mixing of religion and politics to garner mass political support for the anti-colonial struggle seemed somewhat acceptable to him. Therefore, for both Nehru and several members of the Congress, Gandhi's religious politics came with an expiry date – it was to be accepted and accommodated only for India's anti-colonial struggle; they did not see a place for it in politics after India's independence. As has been already argued, Gandhi's religious politics seemed unacceptable to Nehru because it relied on passions and emotions and therefore it was considered irrational. Furthermore, such politics had a 'peasant outlook' based on 'old ways of thought and custom',[52] and hence it was also unmodern. So, while for Gandhi the early 1920s was a high watermark for his religious politics, for Nehru and several members of the Congress this was a disturbing trend in the national struggle.[53]

Commenting on Gandhi's Non-cooperation movement in the 1920s, Nehru says:

> Gandhiji was continually laying stress on the religious and spiritual side of the movement. His religion was not dogmatic, but it did mean a definitely religious outlook on life, and the whole movement was strongly influenced by this and took on a revivalist character so far as the masses were concerned.
>
> I used to be troubled sometimes at the growth of this religious element in our politics, both on the Hindu and the Moslem side. I did not like it at all. Much that Moulvies and Maulanas and Swamis and the like said in their public addresses seemed to me most unfortunate. *Their history and sociology and economics appeared to me all wrong*, and the *religious twist* that was given to everything *prevented all clear thinking*. Even some of Gandhiji's phrases sometimes jarred upon me thus his frequent reference to Rama Raj as a golden age which was to return. But I was powerless to intervene, and I consoled myself with the thought that Gandhiji used the words because they were well known and understood by the masses.
>
> As for Gandhiji himself, he was a very difficult person to understand; sometimes his language was almost incomprehensible to an average modern. But we felt that we knew him quite well enough to realize that he was a great and unique man and a glorious leader, and, having put our faith in him, we gave him an almost blank check, for the time being at least. Often we discussed his fads and peculiarities among ourselves and said, half humorously, that when Swaraj came these fads must not be encouraged. (Emphasis added)[54]

The 'history and sociology and economics' of Gandhi, who introduced religion into politics, seemed 'all wrong' to Nehru because 'the religious outlook' that animated the national movement lacked, what he considered, the 'objective method of science'.[55] Furthermore, for a self-avowed modernist like Nehru, a vision of society based on religious language and religious tropes, such as Gandhi's ideal of Ramrajya,[56] was 'incomprehensible' because such sociopolitical imagination insisted on pre-modern social distinctions of caste and community instead of articulating an imagination of the nation based on the universal language of rights. Its political economy also relied on such pre-modern social formations, instead of modern ones like class, which Nehru considered central to understanding the socio-economic problems of society. Chatterjee therefore rightly argues that for Nehru the metaphysical assumption of Gandhian religious politics which had a 'revivalist character' needed to be separated from its political consequences which had the power to mobilise the masses towards political independence.[57] Moreover, by separating what was politically expedient from the religious, Nehru could also justify Gandhian politics of non-violence as practical politics for national freedom:

> I did not give an absolute allegiance to the doctrine of nonviolence or accept it forever, but it attracted me more and more, and the belief grew upon me that, situated as we were in India and with our background and traditions, it was the right policy for us.... That seemed not only a good ethical doctrine but *sound, practical politics,* for the means that are not good often defeat the end in view and raise new problems and difficulties.... And the *noncooperation movement offered* me what I wanted the *goal* of *national freedom.* (Emphasis added)[58]

Nehru clarified that Gandhian non-violence could be adopted by him and the Congress only as a policy measure and therefore as a means to achieve the goal of national independence and its effectivity judged on that basis: 'for the National Congress as a whole the nonviolent method was not, and could not be, a religion or an unchallengeable creed or dogma'.[59] Nehru separated Gandhi's philosophy from the practice of *ahimsa* (non-violence), and the latter was to be used as a practical tool against colonial rule and not as the epistemological basis of the national struggle.[60] This was so because, in Nehru's view, 'Individuals might make of it a religion or incontrovertible creed. But no political organization, so long as it remained political, could do so.'⁶¹ Thus, we see that Nehru seeks a separation between religion and politics, where the creedal and dogmatic religion whose methods were not based on scientific method of objectivity needed to be separated from practical, secular and scientific politics. Thus, despite grudgingly accepting Gandhi's religious politics, Nehru had deep misgivings about mixing religion and politics.⁶² Therefore, the differentiation between religion *in* politics and politics *of* religion, which was made in the previous chapter with regard to Gandhi's religious politics, would be specious to Nehru.

REASON AND POLITICS

If religion could not be the moral basis of politics, what sort of morality undergirded Nehru's politics? According to Nehru, he relied on something more than just intellect and reason, which may just have 'a tinge of religion in it' and yet 'wholly different from it'.⁶³ Nehru called it 'scientific temper', which, in his view, was a form of objective outlook and critical thinking that went beyond science and its 'domain of positive knowledge'.⁶⁴ According to Sunil Khilnani, Nehru recognised the many-sidedness as well as the limits of reason, and while he perceived the limits of reason, this did not lead him to abandon it. He also notes that reason for Nehru was not merely an instrument to accomplish goals. Nehru's understanding of reason and his reliance on it went beyond its instrumental aspect as 'through reasoning, moral ends and goals were themselves determined, and by reasoning for oneself, one took responsibility for one's commitments and moral beliefs'.⁶⁵ Khilnani argues that Nehru's attempt was to base public life on non-religious morality, which was a 'reasoned morality' that oriented his intellectual and political understanding.⁶⁶ Indeed, as we shall see later in this chapter, Nehru's pragmatism was not driven by unalloyed rationalism, rather his advocacy of scientific temper was incomplete without, what he referred to as, the 'humanism' of the twentieth century.⁶⁷ However, unlike Gandhi, he was far more influenced by the dominant post-Enlightenment discourse, which not only distinguishes fact and value but also separates one from the other.⁶⁸ A consequence of such a separation was that, for Nehru, an approach to politics based on scientific temper meant that it was possible to conduct reasoned politics unaffected by emotions and passions. Such politics was, at the same time, modern and secular politics because political action was based on a secular-scientific epistemology which was capable of producing universal or generalisable conclusions.

In Nehru's opinion, 'scientific temper' should not be restricted to the branch of science alone; it should be a way of life:

> The applications of science are inevitable and unavoidable for all countries and peoples to-day. But something more than its application is necessary. It is the scientific approach, the adventurous and yet critical temper of science, the search for truth and new knowledge, the refusal to accept anything without testing and trial, the capacity to change previous conclusions in the face of new evidence, the reliance on observed fact and not on pre-conceived theory, the hard discipline of the mind—all this is necessary, not merely for the application of science but for life itself and the solution of its many problems. Too many scientists to-day, who swear by science, forget all about it outside their particular spheres. The scientific approach and temper are, or should be, a way of life, a process of thinking, a method of acting and associating with our fellowmen.... Science deals with the domain of positive knowledge but the temper which it should produce goes beyond that domain.[69]

Nehru saw scientific temper as a form of disposition that should encompass one's thinking, behaviour and association with other members of society. In expanding the meaning of the term 'scientific temper' which goes beyond the rationalism of empirical facts and 'positive knowledge',[70] Nehru is elaborating a conception of social being based on cognitive reflexivity and non-dogmatic thinking. Thus, Nehru says, 'Now if the critical faculty does not function that means the scientific faculty does not function because science must be critical.'[71] Khilnani points out that Nehru's own understanding of reason was forged in circumstances when reason seemed to be in retreat – in the 1930s and 1940s, as fascism was ravaging Europe and religious chauvinism was splintering India. As such, it was not the 'rational monism' that has been associated with Nehru. Khilnani says, 'Nehru's faith in reason did not lead him to an easy belief that history was on the side of reason: he was without the rationalist's faith that reason's historical triumph was guaranteed.'[72] What Khilnani's defence of Nehru's faith in reason elides here, however, is that for Nehru human reason can and should be separated from another human attribute – emotion in conducting politics. And that is why Nehru had a particular disdain for religion's involvement in politics, because by introducing emotions and affect in politics, religion made it difficult to conduct reasoned politics. We thus find a contradiction in Nehru's thought regarding his support for mass nationalism on the one hand, and reasoned politics, on the other. While 'pure' nationalism, which would bring freedom from colonial rule, was driven by the 'humiliation' felt by the masses, strong emotions and passions had no place in politics.[73]

Khilnani goes on to argue that Nehru recognised the instrumental power of reason in its most materially powerful forms – as 'scientific reason' and as 'social reason'.[74] While scientific reason could alter the natural world for human purposes, reason in its social form could use human institutions – most significantly the state – and remake society. At the same time, both scientific and social reason could be used for better or for worse. Khilnani maintains that the tactical aspect of reason, which could alter both the natural world and human institutions, did not exhaust its resources as reason could also be used as a way of creating an ethics that sustained moral imagination. That is, 'the act of reasoning about history and experience was a way of discovering moral truths: through such testing and questioning, personal identity was shaped, and moral commitments were discovered'.[75] Khilnani's distinction between tactical reason and reason as morality highlights the importance of separating the two while criticising Nehruvian politics. One may rightly criticise the Nehruvian state for its excessive reliance on economics (as Partha Chatterjee does), but in so doing it may be consistent to also argue that what is valuable in Nehruvian thought (and therefore in Nehruvian secularity) is the morality that undergirded reason. This reasoned morality was unique neither to the West, nor to the East, and was reflected in Nehru's commitment to 'scientific humanism'.[76] Indeed, I shall argue later in this chapter that it was this aspect of morality that enabled Nehru to argue for an Indian secularity.

For Nehru, it was precisely because morality was accessible to reason that 'it was possible to bring others over to one's beliefs – by hearing and acknowledging opposing views, and by offering one's interlocutors reasons to believe, by convincing them'.[77] Thus, for Nehru, the scientific approach, that is 'scientific temper', did not just imply post-Enlightenment rationalism, which is solely based on empirical facts and empirically verifiable truths. It encompassed a societal culture, which meant 'the application of the spirit of science to social affairs'.[78] Nehru says:

> What is a scientific approach to life's problems? I suppose it is one of examining everything, of seeking truth by trial and error and by experiment, of never saying that this must be so but trying to understand why it is so and, if one is convinced of it, of accepting it, of having the capacity to change one's notions the moment some other proof is forthcoming, of having an open mind which tries to imbibe the truth wherever it is found. If that is culture, how far is it represented in the modern world and in the nations of today? Obviously, if it was represented more than it is, many of our problems, national and international, would be far easier to solve.[79]

David Arnold suggests that Nehru's interest lay as much in the culture of science as in its material achievements. Nehru's philosophical appeal to science, Arnold argues, enabled him to present his own social ideals and political convictions as being grounded in rationality, which was part of his secular worldview and 'scientific' socialism.[80] Moreover, morality was also accessible to reason in a modern world because:

> The modern mind, that is to say the better type of the modern mind, is practical and pragmatic, ethical and social, altruistic and humanitarian. It is governed by a practical idealism for social betterment. The ideals which move it represent the spirit of the age, the Zeitgist, the Yugadharma.[81]

In Nehru's view, the twentieth century, that is the 'spirit of the age', is defined by the twin ideals of humanism and scientific spirit. And while, he notes, in the past there has been apparent conflict between these two approaches, there has been 'a growing synthesis between humanism and the scientific spirit, resulting in a kind of scientific humanism'.[82] Thus, we see that a secular and scientific humanism undergirded Nehru's conception and application of reason to politics and society. And despite the universal appeal of secular humanism and scientific spirit, one could, in Nehru's opinion, 'add to them or seek to mould them in accordance with our national genius'.[83] Thus, Nehru's reasoned politics was not simply based on rationality; it was a politics based on the twentieth century modern universal principle of scientific humanism as well as on the national characteristic of the nation.

With the rise of communal politics in the 1980s, and the destruction of the Babri Masjid in 1992 which was symbolic of withering Nehruvian secularism, Nehru's success has been described as merely a 'holding process' as it failed to gain ground in independent India.[84] Bilgrami remarks that to describe Nehru's success of a secular-modernist vision of India in terms of a holding process is to describe it as a success of a limited sort. He asks, 'Why is that the Nehruvian vision of a secular India failed to take hold?' Nandy's critique of Nehruvian statecraft and secular ideology maintains that there was something deeply flawed in the vision itself. In his opinion, Nehru's statist ideology along with its modernist tyranny has distorted the pluralist and tolerant traditions of religion as ways of life (Nandy calls it 'religion as faith') into monolithic and constructed religious ideologies (Nandy labels it as 'religion as ideology') that are geared towards political gains.[85] And therefore, for critics of secularism like Nandy, communalism, which itself is a product of modernity, exists because of an internal dialectical relation it has with another product of modernity – secularism. By seeking to separate religion from politics, secularism is seen as an alien imposition by the modern state upon a people and society, where religion is part of everyday life. Such a modern state policy, Nandy argues, pushes religion as faith with its traditional forms of religious tolerance to a corner and the only religious politics that is then allowed by modernity's stranglehold are the ones like Hindu nationalism. While for Nandy the modern state's push for secularisation to realise political secularism has resulted in religious intolerance, for T. N. Madan secularism in India has come under crisis because it is devoid of Western secularisation. In Madan's view, the historical process of secularisation in the West is a condition for state secularism. He contends that when modernisation introduces secularism to non-Western societies like India, where religious traditions are marked by their high degree of religiosity both in the public and private domain, secularism's existence in these societies becomes weak as it is a doctrine which exists only empirically and not ideologically.[86] Thus, for both Nandy and Madan, secularism was doomed to fail in India.[87]

Did secularism fail in India because it was a Western imposition on a society with no concomitant process of secularisation? Has secularism failed in India? Is it inextricably linked to a historical process of secularisation, such that its failure means secularism's doom? In other words, is it the case that because Nehru's vision of Indian society imbued with secular humanism and scientific temper failed to entrench itself in the social fabric of society that Nehruvian secularism, as an ideology of the state, was bound to fail eventually? To assume such an organic relationship between secularism as a doctrine of the state and secularisation as a historical process is to argue that (a) the modular form of secularism is Western in its origin and content, and (b) because secularism is a Western conception both in its form and content, it is culturally inadaptable in a religious country like India. One needs to examine Nehru's conception of secularism in light of aforementioned claims and ask whether it was, as remarked by Bilgrami, merely a holding process unable to entrench itself in Indian society. In what follows, I identify two strands of arguments in Nehru's reflection on the role of religion in state and society under modern conditions. One argument of secularity, I argue, can be located in Nehru's nationalist narrative about its cultural familiarity and suitability for the Indian society; and the other argument, I maintain, relies on the success of secularity in the West and hence its emulation and desirability in India. I will call the first secularity narrative in Nehru's thought 'nationalist', and the second, 'humanist-universal'. I shall argue that both these strands of arguments were brought together by Nehru to construct a narrative of Indian secularity and to also argue that secularity as such is an universalisable ideal.

NEHRU'S NATIONALIST NARRATIVE OF SECULARITY

V. K. Krishna Menon, a politician, diplomat and Nehru's close aide, remarked that Nehru's autobiography should be considered a writing in history because of the 'objectivity' and 'restraint' that pervaded his thought and writing.[88] Notwithstanding this exaggeration, Nehru's writings, in my view, can be seen as part of a particular strand of history writing that was attempting a secular history of the Indian subcontinent. In a critical reflection on secular history writing in India, Neeladri Bhattacharya has noted that the professional history writing that developed in India in the early decades after independence was influenced by the intellectual culture of the time. He says that troubled by memories of the communal carnage and trauma of the partition years – when thousands of Hindus and Muslims killed each other – the intellectuals of this new India struggled to create a secular and democratic public culture. Inspired by the ideals of democratic citizenship, they hoped for a society where individuals would be emancipated from their religious and affective ties and see themselves as secular citizens of a democratic state. As such, historians turned to the past to counter communal representations of history, question communal stereotypes and write a secular national history. The critique of communal prejudice was seen as necessary for developing a history that was scientific and objective. To be authentic, it was believed, this new history had to be both scientific and secular. Bhattacharya has observed that secular historians have sometimes sought to reaffirm the efficacy of secularism, its universal relevance, through the narrative of the past.[89] Nehru's nationalist narrative of secularity, I suggest, is of a piece in the construction of the secular historiography that Bhattacharya has described.[90] In narrating India's pre-colonial history in the ancient and medieval period, Nehru's construction of religious life, to use Sudipta Kaviraj's phrase, may be described as an unexamined nationalist position that deploys arguments of 'composite culture' and 'habitually peaceable existence' between Hindus and Muslims to provide an exaggerated and flattering picture of India's past.[91]

In *The Discovery of India*, Nehru recounts India's past through two great moments in nation's history, which Chatterjee describes as consisting of a long cycle and a short cycle.[92] The long cycle begins with the earliest known historical period, that of the Indus Valley Civilisation, and ends with the first Turko-Afghan invasions of the eleventh century. It was the period which saw the flowering of a great civilisation marked by some astonishing achievements in the field of philosophy, literature, drama, art, science and mathematics. This long cycle, however, comes to a halt because of the growing rigidity and exclusiveness of the Indian social structure, which was chiefly attributed to the caste system in India. For Nehru, this growing rigidity in social life did not mean the death of the glorious Indian civilisation because some vitality still remained. According to Chatterjee, the evidence for this was in the historical continuity of a shorter second cycle of civilizational growth in the period of Islamic empires, which reached its zenith during the reign of the Mughal emperor Akbar. However, as this shorter cycle was a state-sponsored effort with the personality of emperor Akbar playing a crucial role, its overall effect was not deep enough to change the structure of society in a fundamental way. In the following paragraphs, I will argue that it is in these two glorious cycles of Indian civilisation on which Nehru rests his nationalist narrative of secularity for the subcontinent's historical familiarity with, and hence, the possibility of cultural adaptation to the modern secular values of the West. Nehru believed that these two great cycles of Indian civilisation stamped what Indian culture truly is; it is this 'old' India that has shaped the 'new' India in terms of its influence on the people in their thinking and ways of living.[93]

Nehru describes the Indus Valley civilisation in terms of a 'secular civilization' and argues how this was a 'precursor to later cultural periods' in India.[94] Through this narrative he highlights the pre-history of 'new' India's secular, or at least its proto-secular, past:

> The Indus Valley civilization, as We find it, was highly developed and must have taken thousands of years to reach that stage. It was, surprisingly enough, a predominantly *secular civilization*, and the *religious element*, though present, *did not dominate the scene*. It was clearly also the precursor of later cultural periods in India. (Emphasis added)[95]

Nehru further maintains that although this secular ancient civilisation is to be found several thousand years ago, 'their religion is so characteristically Indian as hardly to be distinguished from still living Hinduism'.[96] Nehru says:

> The links joining one period to another are not always evident, and a very great deal has of course happened and innumerable changes have taken place. But there is *always an underlying sense of continuity*, of an unbroken chain which joins modern India to the far distant period of six or seven thousand years ago when the Indus Valley civilization probably began. It is surprising how much there is in Mohenjodaro and Harappa which reminds one of persisting traditions and habits—popular ritual, craftsmanship, even some fashions in dress. (Emphasis added)[97]

In Nehru's nationalist reconstruction, the continuity of this 'predominantly secular civilization' is visible in India's traditions, habits, arts and crafts, and architecture; their archaeological evidence further attests to the fact that modernity and secularity are not essentially occidental traits of the West:

It is interesting to note that at this dawn of India's story, she does not appear as a puling infant, but already grown up in many ways. She is not oblivious of life's ways, lost in dreams of a vague and unrealizable *supernatural world*, but has made considerable *technical progress* in the arts and amenities of life, creating not only things of beauty, but also the *utilitarian* and more *typical emblems of modern civilization*—good baths and drainage systems. (Emphasis added)[98]

In Nehru's historiography, we see that the secular is differentiated from the religious in terms of a binary distinction between the natural and the supernatural world, and an argument is forwarded which demonstrates the dominance of the secular over religious in the ancient civilisation. His construal of the secular in ancient Indian history in terms of a binary between the natural and the supernatural is illustrative of the presentist assumption that pervades the modern notion of the secular.[99] Nehru's conception of the secular is influenced by a dominant Western idea of the secular, where the assumption is that through distinctions, such as the natural and the supernatural, one can clearly discern and differentiate the religious from the secular in terms of knowledge production, sensibilities and behaviours. In light of the developments in critical studies on secularity, one may argue that Nehru's differentiation between the secular and the religious through a binary distinction between the natural and the supernatural fails to comprehend that what we consider secular and religious today may have had a certain porosity in meaning and action in India's ancient civilisation. However, a main point to be noted here is that, for Nehru, the secular is not Western or modern; his thought challenges the easy equivalence of the secular with the modern West.

According to Nehru, apart from showing India's familiarity with, and indeed, in some aspects, its excellence in, what are considered modern secular values of the West, the Indus Valley civilisation's openness to cultural intermixing also illustrates the tradition of tolerance in the subcontinent. He maintains that the migration of the Aryans to the Indian subcontinent resulted in the 'first great cultural synthesis and fusion' between the incoming Aryans and the indigenous Dravidians:[100]

> Out of this *synthesis and fusion* grew the Indian races and the *basic Indian culture*, which had distinctive elements of both. In the ages that followed there came many other races: Iranians, Greeks, Parthians,

Bactrians, Scythians, Huns, Turks (before Islam), early Christians, Jews, Zoroastrians; they came, made a difference, and were absorbed. India was, according to Dodwell, 'infinitely absorbent like the ocean'. It is odd to think of India, with her caste system and exclusiveness, having this astonishing *inclusive capacity* to absorb foreign races and cultures. Perhaps it was due to this that she retained her vitality and rejuvenated herself from time to time. The Moslems, when they came, were also powerfully affected by her. 'The foreigners (Muslim Turks)', says Vincent Smith, 'like their forerunners the Sakas and the Yueh-chi, universally yielded to the wonderful *assimilative power* of Hinduism, and rapidly became Hinduised'. (Emphasis added)[101]

The 'basic' Indian culture, that is, India's national character, is one which can be expressed in terms of syncretic and composite cultures, which, by their very nature of being born out of intermixing, are assimilative and tolerant cultures. Thus, in Nehru's view, inclusiveness and tolerance are built into Indian culture due to the subcontinent's exposure to migration and therefore to religious and cultural diversity several thousand years ago:

> They [Indo-Aryans] produced an astonishing flowering of civilization and culture which, though largely confined to the upper circles, inevitably spread to some extent to the masses. By their *extreme tolerance of other beliefs and other ways than their own*, they avoided the conflicts that have so often torn society asunder, and managed to maintain, as a rule, some kind of equilibrium. (Emphasis added)[102]

As we know, this nationalist narrative of an unbroken and unhindered tradition of tolerance from ancient India to the present is often used by Hindu nationalists to claim the superiority of Hinduism over other religions. Since such tradition of tolerance arguments lack justifications based on liberal values of liberty and equality for all, which are 'constitutively tied' to secularism, this nationalist narrative alone may not be sufficient to counter communalism.[103]

Nehru further argues that during the Mughal era, although tolerance was adopted by the conquerors as a measure of deliberate policy, a gradual process of 'Indianization' began due to the influence of Indian culture and environment. This then led to 'a synthesis of thought and ways of living'.[104] As a result, a 'mixed culture' emerged on whose foundations Akbar built.[105]

Indian culture was thus 'variegated and yet essentially unified culture'.[106] That Nehru did not seek a replication of Western-style modern secularity is most visible in these arguments where he does not see religious diversity as inherently threatening peace in society. British colonialists had emphasised that what held India's immense social diversity together was the colonial power. The history of European nationalism attested to this, as homogeneous cultures based on monolingual and a predominant religious community seemed a precondition for the establishment of successful nation-state. In Nehru's view, however, imposition of a homogenising Western model of the nation-state would go against the grain of Indian culture and therefore disrupt the formation of an inclusive nation-state. That is why Pakistan, for him, came into being 'rather unnaturally'.[107] Nehru notes:

> There is nothing in Indian history to compare with the bitter religious feuds and persecutions that prevailed in Europe. So we did not have to go abroad for ideas of religious and cultural toleration; these were inherent in Indian life.[108]

According to Nehru, it was a mistake to consider India's diversity a disadvantage for the nation-building process. While he did not approve of religion's involvement in politics, he equally did not see religious differences emanating from the fact of India's diversity as being an inherent cause for intolerance in society. If anything, religious diversity and difference, through synthesis of cultures, provided for societal tolerance along with greater cultural and intellectual resources.

Kaviraj's study of religious difference in the Vedic and post-Vedic religious traditions shows how separate religious forms or communities of worship coexisted in the subcontinent, creating a culture of tolerance based on, what he calls, 'competitive diversity'.[109] He argues that religious life in ancient and medieval India followed a trajectory, where diversity of religious beliefs and observances proliferated in the subcontinent without restraint. Nehru's nationalist narrative of secularity can be seen as tapping this pre-history of Indian secularity, where various religious traditions, political power and society devised mechanisms of tolerance for inter and intra-religious difference. Bilgrami contends that it was this lived pluralist tradition of India's past which was reconstructed and represented by Nehru in the political sphere as a form of nationalism that was not only intended to be unlike the European nationalism but intended to prevent the emergence of that form of nationalism in India.[110] In the next chapter, we will see the powerful influence of this pluralist conception of India's past and composite culture on Nehru's nationalist politics. However, it must also be recalled that mainstream nationalist ideology which carried Nehru's imprimatur projected an exaggerated argument about India's composite culture which was 'in the nature of a hopeful abstraction rather than a belief supported by a detailed and serious enquiry into India's cultural past'.[111] Moreover, as we shall see in the next chapter, Nehru quite unreflexively assumed the continuity of religious tolerance exhibited in composite cultures as he did not sufficiently consider its relationship to the modern state and civil society.

NEHRU'S HUMANIST-UNIVERSAL NARRATIVE OF SECULARITY

While Indian society and culture fell into a decline in the fifteenth century, in Europe

> ... the Renaissance had, however, released the mind of Europe from many of its old fetters and destroyed many an idol that it had cherished ... a new spirit of objective inquiry was making itself felt, a spirit which not only challenged old-established authority, but also abstractions and vague speculations.[112]

And with the advent of Enlightenment, Western society developed as science and technology progressed: 'In 1660 the Royal Society of England, which was to advance the cause of science so much, was organised. A hundred years later, in 1760, the flying shuttle was invented, and there followed in quick succession the spinning jenny, the steam engine, and the power loom.'[113] But for Nehru, modernity and science were not essential characteristics of the West:

> Science and technology know no frontiers. Nobody talks or ought to talk about English science, French science, American science, Chinese science.... There ought to be no such thing as Indian science. So also with technology. This great business of looking at these questions in a

narrow nationalist way will ultimately lead to narrowing your science and the narrowing of your technology and your work itself.[114]

In Nehru's view, the universality of science and the progress attributed to Western society meant that the stagnated feudal society in India needed to follow the Western path as this was the normal path that was impeded due to colonial rule. Chatterjee has argued that in Nehru's nationalist reconstruction of colonial rule, historical time is seen as 'episodic', where every civilisation has its periods of growth and decay.[115] He maintains that for Nehru the particular historical conjecture at which India had come under foreign subjugation was one where the European nations were forward-looking and dynamic while Indian society was in a stage of stultification. The subsequent failure of Indian society to match up to the universal historical norm of development was because British colonial rule consistently impeded the growth of the forces of modernity because of which Indian society was unable to develop. As such, what India experienced under colonialism was only a degraded version of modernity. Thus, in Nehru's opinion, as a universal historical norm, modernity was not Western; it was a universal ideal represented in the 'spirit of the age' that required improvisation based on India's 'national genius'.[116] It meant 'to function in line with the highest ideals of the age we live in', which in the modern age was represented in the twin values of humanism and scientific spirit.[117] Thus, we see that, for Nehru, modern, secular and scientific were not synonymous with the West.[118] Modernity and science were separate from the Western, and they were, at the same time, universally applicable. In Nehru's political vision, the new nation-state was to be based on values – secular and modern, humanistic and scientific – as these were the universal values of the twentieth century.

In his politics, Nehru sought to realise these universal values through the framework of the modern state. We have already seen in his nationalist narrative of secularity that Nehru's vision of the political was not influenced by the Western idea of the modern state as the common instrument for a homogeneous nation. This was the common ideal of a multi-national state that brought the divergent Gandhian and Nehruvian traditions together.[119] But, at the same time, Nehru, as we know, was far more attracted to Western liberal political ideas of constitutionalism and citizenship on the one hand and the socio-economic models of European-style social democracy on the other. Taken together, these political and economic ideals provided a sociopolitical picture of India where religion was seen as unimportant in politics. In Nehru's political thought, this took a shape where it was class and not religion that was important to understand the problem of communalism in modern Indian politics. Communal politics showed how 'religious passion' was used to 'hide their barrenness'.[120] Therefore, in Nehru's opinion, the problem of communalism that India faced during the national struggle was essentially an economic problem:

> The want of clear ideals and objectives in our struggle for freedom undoubtedly helped the spread of communalism.... It is ... extraordinary how the bourgeois classes, both among the Hindus and the Moslems, succeeded, in the sacred name of religion, in getting a measure of mass sympathy and support for programs and demands which had absolutely nothing to do with the masses, or even the lower middle class. Every one of the communal demands put forward by any communal group is, in the final analysis, a demand for jobs, and these jobs could only go to a handful of the upper middle class.[121]

In this view then, communalism was an artificial creation of a small section of upper-class Indians, who in seeking political power and privileges for themselves did not wish to address it as a question of economic equality. Nehru was clear that the national struggle needed to be fought on the basis of an economic programme.[122] Moreover, Nehru's philosophical appeal to science, as argued already, enabled him to present his own sociopolitical ideals as being grounded in reason, which was part of his secular and scientific worldview. Chatterjee has argued that for Nehru this appeal to science and scientific method also meant the primacy of the economic sphere in all social questions, which was a 'distinctively modern, or 20th century, way of looking at history and society'.[123] This 'primacy of the sphere of the economic'[124] in Nehru's political thought meant that he did not see 'why political or economic rights should depend on the membership of a religious group or community'.[125] On this view, the right to freedom of religion and one's culture was a constitutionally *given* right, and it was not a difficult matter 'to ensure their continuance'.[126] It was only with the events leading up to the partition and the creation of Pakistan that Nehru realised the danger of inter-religious domination and majoritarian national politics and worked towards safeguarding religious, cultural and educational rights of religious minorities. As such, because the constitution of independent India would guarantee minority rights, the primacy of the economic sphere would continue even after the attainment of national independence:

> Having assured the protection of religion and culture, etc., the major problems that were bound to come up were economic ones which had nothing to do with a person's religion. Class conflicts there might well be, but not religious conflicts, except in so far as religion itself represented some vested interest.[127]

We see that in Nehru's political thought there is a desire to follow the Western path of secularisation, wherein a scientific-humanist approach fused with a leftist economic programme towards society and polity would assure that religious and communal differences would recede from the public-political sphere. Such an enterprise, in Nehru's opinion, needed to be state-led. This strand of Nehruvian nationalism has been heavily criticised for its excessively economistic conception of the idea of development which reduced all other elements in it – social, political, cultural – to the status of corollaries.[128] According to Kaviraj, this political vision also relied too heavily on the instrumentality of the state by equating the principle of public good with the institutional form of state control, thereby suffocating non-state institutions of civil society.[129] What Nehru's vision of secularity envisaged was, with a state-led thrust towards advancement in science and technology, with modernisation and industrialisation, and with a scientific and technical expertise towards the polity and society, religious and communal issues would gradually become unimportant in the political sphere. Had this sociopolitical vision of society, which remained restricted to the Indian elite and intelligentsia, gained momentum, one may conjecture that a thoroughgoing secularised society, where religion became relatively unimportant in the public-political sphere, could have emerged. Such a worldview characterised by a this-worldly understanding of human flourishing based on 'exclusive humanism' was part of the hegemonic view of Western secularity, which contributed in shaping the West's public-political sphere.[130] But in modern India, as Kaviraj has remarked, disenchantment was deferred.[131] Independent India's adoption of a democratic form of government and Nehru's deference towards such a form of political arrangement meant that any imposition of Western-style secularisation became impossible. Thus, not only did Nehru's secular modernist political vision face several challenges during the drafting of the constitution itself,[132] it also had to negotiate with unfavourable democratic outcomes.[133] While India's modernist leaders like Nehru (and also others like Ambedkar) theoretically agreed with and accepted European ideals of secularism and modernity, their political actions and judgements showed quite a different understanding of how these ideals could be made to work in Indian polity and society. Kaviraj remarks that when these modernist leaders went about 'applying' these universal principles or ideals that were generated by early modern European debates, as practical politicians they necessarily had to submit to the logic of present historical conditions.[134] One such historical condition, I argue, was the institutionalisation of democracy alongside the establishment of state secularism in independent India.

NEHRUVIAN SECULARISM: NEHRU AGAINST NEHRUISM

In an insightful article, Rajeev Bhargava has sought to defend 'Nehru against Nehruvians' by arguing that, as opposed to what the critics of Nehruvian secularism claim, Nehru is not against religion.[135] According to him, Nehru's distrust of religion's involvement in politics was only towards institutional forms of religion (Bhargava typifies as 'Religion B') and not non-institutional forms of religion (Bhargava calls it 'Religion A'). He maintains, 'Nehru could not see how politics could be conducted without Religion A and like Gandhi, he would not mix politics with Religion B'.[136] However, to defend Nehru by demonstrating his support towards non-institutional forms of religion is based on a misunderstanding as to why Nehru sought religion's separation from politics. As argued, Nehru's ambivalence towards religion's inclusion in conducting politics emanated from his belief that an appeal to religion involved a strong emotional appeal. He thought that to mix religion with politics, like Gandhi's merger of the Non-cooperation and Khilafat movements in the early 1920s, created the danger in appealing to intemperate emotions and passions that would make conducting reasoned politics difficult. That is why, first, Nehru was extremely ambivalent about Gandhi's introduction of religion in politics. Nehru, I have argued, had an instrumental approach to Gandhi's religious politics, which he saw necessary for mass nationalism. He did not think that after the attainment of independence such politics would be necessary. This was what animated Nehru's political thought. In his political practice, however, religion *did* intervene on issues such as the 'communal question' and the 'minority question'. Moreover, religion became a central issue to be debated in the Constituent Assembly, where India's secular constitution was shaped. When religion did intervene in politics, Nehru preferred constitutional and institutional measures, such as providing expansive cultural rights to minority religious communities rather than, say, granting group rights through representative measures, such as reservation of seats in legislative bodies for minority religious communities (including the depressed classes).[137] In Nehru's political view, such an approach to politics would ensure that religion was not politicised. Thus, Nehru's secular politics does not consider demands of representative politics of group rights based on common religion being concomitant with secular ideals. Second, to argue that Nehru did not find it desirable to include religion into politics does not mean that he wanted an anti-religious secular state. The nationalist narrative of secularity in Nehru's writings makes it amply clear that Nehruvian secularism cannot be equated with French *laïcité*. In fact, Nehru, as I have argued already in this chapter, cherished and valued India's religious and cultural diversity, which he thought needed constitutional protection. By linking this cultural aspect to his political vision, it may be argued that Nehru's influence gave a multicultural inflection to the Indian constitution and by extension to Indian state practices.

From the two narratives that I have outlined in this chapter about Nehru's conception of secularity, we may deduce the following as Nehru's idea of secularism. First, for Nehru, it was not only desirable but also possible to separate religion from politics. A secular state must refrain from religion – be it in its reasoning or in practice. In Nehru's rhetoric of socialism we see this desire for such a separation in Indian politics.[138] However, this ideal was challenged, and its impossibility was demonstrated to Nehru both in the later phase of the Indian national movement (1940s), and especially in the aftermath of the partition and during the nation-building process. It may be argued that this desire to keep politics away from religion was also what weakened Nehruvian secularism after Nehru's death. This secular bias in Nehru's political thought, which separated religion and politics to ensure reasoned politics and de-politicised religion in society, led to a lack of recognition on his part that even secular language and politics can hinder values of secularism.[139] Second, while secularisation of society was desirable for the practice of modern politics in Nehru's vision of a secular state, it was not a necessity; or rather, it could not have been a necessity given the social fabric of Indian society. This process, however, was to be actively taken up by the state machinery to resolve problems that beset Indian society.[140] That is why a scientific and a technocratic state was the way forward. If this was Nehru's vision of society, it was also one where he and Gandhi disagreed the most. Whereas Gandhi's idea of India was a society imbued with religious-ethical values, Nehru's was that of scientific-humanism. From the previous points, we may deduce that in Nehru's idea of secularism we can discern a distinction between, what Bhargava calls, ethical and political secularism:[141]

> Where the great majority of the people in a state belong to one religion, this fact alone may colour, to some extent, the cultural climate of that state. But nevertheless the state, as a state can remain independent of any particular religion.[142]

In Nehru's view, the English society was 'more advanced', because there they underwent a secularisation process: 'the state and the people there largely function in a secular way'.[143] At the same time, the Indian constitution was 'more advanced' than the English because it does not have a state religion.[144] While the value of secular-scientific humanism was desirable for the advancement of society, Nehru was aware that it could only be imposed on Indian society by disregarding the demands of democracy. Therefore, a third attribute of Nehru's secularism would be its respect for and commitment to the values of democracy and democratic politics. This commitment to democracy, I will argue in the next section, was unimportant for the Nehruism of the 1970s and the idea of secularity it propagated.[145] Nehru's commitment to secularism was not autonomous from the values of democracy; they were interdependent. He accepted that his strong advocacy of democratic politics sometimes also meant that his ideal of modern secularity as a society based on secular and scientific-humanist values would have to settle for compromises when there was a confrontation between democratic practice of politics and secular values in the public-political domain. As a result, due to the demands and contingencies of India's democratic politics, Nehruvian secularism had to constantly face the test of democracy.[146] The weakening of Nehruvian type of secularism may be partially attributed to its inability to accommodate a form of electoral politics that was increasingly focusing on religion and other identarian issues, like caste. In the next chapter, with the help of specific cases, we will examine Nehru's position on identity-based politics of caste and religion. In that chapter, we will see that Nehru did indeed come up with an alternative to the Muslim League's (hereafter, the League) politics of religion by initiating the Muslim mass contact campaign in 1937, which sought to increase Muslim membership within Congress, while retaining a leftist secular agenda for the party.

FROM NEHRUVIAN SECULARITY TO NEHRUISM

It is well acknowledged that Nehru's historical success and legacy lay in the establishment and the success of the modern state apparatus. Rajni Kothari has famously argued that during the Nehruvian period – that is, in the first two decades after independence – a political consensus, also called the 'Nehruvian consensus', developed around institutional and ideological axes for an interventionist modernising state committed to democratic socialism, secularism, planned economy, large-scale industrialisation and non-alignment.[147] It is argued that the Nehruvian consensus, which Kothari notes was disturbed since 1962–1963, has withered away, and with it died Nehruvian secularism. Critics of Nehruvian secularism argue that the crisis of secularism in contemporary India that is unable to manage the rise of religious intolerance is due to the state-imposed secularism of the Nehruvian era which failed to see Indian society's inherently tolerant and pluralist heritage of religious and communitarian ways of life. In disagreeing with the critics, I have already pointed out how this argument about tradition of tolerance, which was also part of Nehruvian narrative of Indian secularity, can be problematic. In this section, I shall distinguish Nehru's views on secularism and his conception of modern secularity from the 'Nehruism' of the 1970s in order to rescue what is valuable in Nehruvian secularity. By Nehruism, I understand an ideology, where under Indira Gandhi's rule Nehru's political vision was reduced to a populist gimmick with the rhetoric of socialism and secularism, centralisation of state power and an authoritarian enforcement of the moral and political authority of science.[148]

Nehru's daughter and India's third prime minister, Indira Gandhi progressively weakened the democratic institutional framework of

Indian polity, which culminated in the declaration of twenty-one months Emergency Rule from 1975 to 1977. The consolidation of Indira Gandhi's dictatorial style of rule went alongside her populist rhetoric, where Nehruvian visions of secularism and scientific temper became part of her justification for an authoritarian state. In 1974, a statement on national science policy was written into India's fifth five-year plans. In 1976, during the Emergency, this was followed by several amendments to the Indian constitution, which included the inclusion of the word 'secular' in the preamble of the constitution and the duty of every Indian citizen 'to develop the scientific temper' as part of the fundamental duties.[149] However, these moves reveal more about Indira Gandhi's attempt to consolidate her political position as her father's heir rather than the actual pursuit of science or her commitment to Nehruvian secularism.[150] Regarding Indira Gandhi's propagation of Nehruvian science, Arnold remarks, 'Indira Gandhi and her son Rajiv ... kept alive the idea of a special relationship between the Nehru/Gandhi dynasty and science and technology, as demonstrated by elements of Mrs. Gandhi's "emergency" program in 1975 and Rajiv's attempts to usher in a new age of technological modernity in the 1980s.'[151] Indira Gandhi's rule imbued Nehruvian secularity with new meanings, where it increasingly came to be understood in isolation from democratic ethos and, what I have called, Nehru's humanist-universal narrative of secularity. The 1980s debate on scientific temper, to which I now turn to, is illustrative of this shift in the meaning of Nehruvian secularity.

In October 1980, under the aegis of the Nehru Centre in Bombay, several scientists, public intellectuals, economists and political scientists assembled together to discuss their common concern for what they saw as 'the accelerating pace of retreat from reason' in Indian society. The result of their deliberation was a document titled 'A Statement on Scientific Temper',[152] which was released in July 1981.[153] The document paid homage to Nehru's contribution towards the development of modern science and technology, and observed the value of scientific temper in contemporary times:

> The need of the time is the diffusion of science and technology into the societal fabric at all levels. This can only be achieved by promotion of what Jawaharlal Nehru chose to call the Scientific Temper – a *rational attitude*, the importance of which he emphasized time and

again. Indeed, the Scientific Temper has to be fostered with care at the individual, institutional, social, and political levels. (Emphasis added)[154]

This document identified 'rational attitude' as the sole basis of scientific temper and sociopolitical action.[155] Words like 'humanism' and 'scientific humanism' which, as I have shown, were central to Nehruvian understanding of scientific temper, are missing from this document. The statement insisted that all of India's societal problems needed to be understood and solved with a scientific temper, that is, rationally. In a rather polemical and a sharp rejoinder to this, Nandy wrote a 'Counter-Statement on Humanistic Temper', where he called for a recognition of 'plurality of sciences' and a delinking of modernity with notions of progress and history.[156] This 1980s debate illustrates how in post-colonial India, ideological positions congealed between those who are pro and anti-Enlightenment epistemology, philosophy, and politics, where you are either a 'Nehruvian' or a 'Gandhian'.[157] What this polarisation confounded is the issue that the language of 'modern', 'secular' or 'rational' is not accessible only to the modernist or the secularist;[158] just like the Gandhian religious language, which has been appropriated by right-wing Hindu groups for utterly anti-Gandhian political ends.[159] The rise of the Hindu right in the 1980s and the BJP's ascendency in Indian politics since has amply demonstrated that the language of secularism can be easily appropriated by religious fundamentalists and bigots, such that those preaching tolerance for religious difference and minority religious practices are labelled 'pseudo-secularists'.[160] To put it differently, what this contrived binary between Nehruvians and Gandhians overlooks is the possibility that even the languages of secularism and secularity can be used in ways that are equally dogmatic and intolerant like religious fundamentalism. Second, in such a polarised discourse, to be modern is synonymous with being secular and tolerant and possess an attitude of scientific temper, and to side with tradition or religion is to be anti-modern, anti-science and anti-secular. It, therefore, overlooks the possibility of miscibility of the languages of modernity and tradition and the numerous ideological positions and possibilities this produces.[161] Kaviraj therefore rightly remarks, 'Modernity and tradition are not doctrinal positions, but alphabetical "languages", through the elements of which quite dissimilar doctrinal positions can be fashioned.'[162] Ideological positions like the

Nehruism of the 1970s and 1980s will be unable to accept that traditional and modern values may cohabit side by side, without any contradiction.

A CRITICAL APPRAISAL OF NEHRUVIAN SECULARISM

It seems to me that much of the defence of Nehruvian secularism today is ill-placed because these seek to argue that, unlike Western secularism, it did not mind the presence of religion in the political sphere. At the same time, much of the criticism of Nehruvian secularism, which points to its failure because of its Western origins, has not sufficiently acknowledged how Indian secularism came to be conditioned by democracy and electoral politics, as well as the political ingenuity and improvisation that was involved in applying the concept of secularism in Indian society. Nehruvian secularism, nevertheless, has two major shortcomings due to which it increasingly struggled with electoral politics and seems largely ineffective with the consolidation of majoritarian politics in contemporary India. The first shortcoming is its inability to see the ideals of secularism and nationalism as distinct and autonomous of each other. In Nehru's mind, because of its inclusive character, Indian nationalism and secularism were indissolubly linked:

> In a country like India, which has many faiths and religions, no real nationalism can be built up except on the basis of secularity. Any narrower approach must necessarily exclude a section of the population, and then nationalism itself will have a much more restricted meaning than it should possess. In India we would then have to consider Hindu nationalism, Muslim nationalism, Sikh nationalism or Christian nationalism and not Indian nationalism.[163]

This first criticism also emerges in Bilgrami's remark about the 'Archimedean existence' of Nehruvian secularism.[164] He argues that Nehruvian secularism was indeed an imposition, like Nandy and Madan point out. But Bilgrami clarifies that his criticism of Nehruvian secularism is not the Madan–Nandy type of objection that sees it as an imposition by the modern state upon a traditional society that has never been secular. He is, in fact, in favour of statist reforms by a secular liberal state. Nehruvian secularism, in Bilgrami's view, was an imposition in the sense that it 'stood outside the substantive arena of political commitment'.[165] That is, the doctrine of secularism was not in there with Hinduism and Islam as one among substantive contested political commitments to be negotiated with one another. According to him, the reason for the non-negotiated nature of Nehruvian secularism lies in its historical antecedents – during the nationalist movement. He argues that for two or three decades before independence, the Congress under Nehru refused to let a secular policy emerge through negotiation between different communitarian voices, 'by denying at every step in the various conferrings with the British, Jinnah's demand that the Muslim League represent the Muslims, a Sikh leader represent the Sikhs, and a Harijan leader represent the untouchable community'.[166] He notes that the ground for the denial was simply that as a secular party the Congress could not accept that they did not represent all these communities. Bilgrami therefore remarks, '[S]ecularism thus never got the chance to emerge out of a creative dialogue between these different communities. It was sui generis.'[167] As such, 'this Archimedean existence gave secularism procedural priority but in doing so it gave it no abiding substantive authority. As a result, it could be nothing more than a holding process, already under strain in the time of its charismatic architect, and increasingly ineffective after his death.'[168]

A second shortcoming of Nehruvian secularism is a distrust of religion's involvement in the political sphere. Nehru's distrust with religion's emotional and irrational appeal obstructing reasoned politics led him to identify a separation between religion and politics as desirable politics, exemplified in his rhetoric of socialism and his initial identification of the problem of communalism only in socio-economic terms. It was only in the late 1940s that Nehru understood minority politics in terms of the fear of majority.[169] If we look into group-based representational politics (for instance, Jinnah and the League, or the politics of the depressed classes, most prominently represented by Ambedkar) during the early phases of the national movement, we will discover that that the meaning of sociopolitical terms like 'communal', 'secular', 'minority' and 'democracy' were being constantly debated as a result of the bargaining and negotiation of the political rights of the numerical (like Muslims) and social (lower castes) minorities.[170] It was only during the mature phase of Indian nationalism that some of these terms began developing the fixity of meaning and purpose that reflect contemporary understandings and prejudices. Thus, even before secularism was enshrined in the Indian constitution, it was entangled with minority and group-based identity politics during colonial rule. Shabnum Tejani, for instance, has shown that prior to the Nehruvian nationalist phase, various sociopolitical groups like peasants, Left, non-Brahman and untouchable movements, Khilafat, Non-cooperation and Civil Disobedience campaigns, Congress nationalists, Hindu nationalists, liberals, socialists and Muslim parties had all defined Indian nationalism in myriad and often contradictory ways. She argues that it was the process of constitution-making that hardened the particular meaning of nationalism and communalism. Tejani has further argued that it was not until the 1940s that the term 'secularism' began to be used in Indian political discourse.[171] Moreover, all these aforementioned political concepts and categories developed in relation to each other. Thus, Rochana Bajpai has shown the changing legitimating vocabulary of secularism, and its interplay with ideas of democracy, social justice, national unity and development in post-colonial India. In the next chapter, we will expand on these criticisms by analysing Nehru's engagement with politics and thereby look at his notion of secularity relationally. In that chapter, we will further examine how Nehru's narrative of secularity engaged with competing discourses of nationalism and, later in post-colonial India, with the demands of democracy and electoral politics.

CONCLUSION

Nehruvian secularity has been described as both an asset and an issue for Indian society. Critics of Nehruvian secularity, like Madan and Nandy (who are also against Hindutva politics), have argued that the modern secular state that emerged under Nehru's leadership was a flawed vision as it sought to emulate the West, disregarding the religious nature of Indian society. At the same time, with growing communalisation of society and politics in the 1980s, where secularism appeared an embattled ideology, it is also argued that under Nehru's stewardship, secularism successfully withstood this onslaught and was the 'ruling credo' for over two decades.[172] In this chapter, I have argued that those who are critical of Nehruvian secularism generally confound it with Nehruvian statism and the rhetoric of Nehruism that emerged under Indira Gandhi's rule. This chapter has shown that in criticising Nehru's ideas, it may be important that we do not conflate his ideas with the larger sociopolitical processes. Nehruvian statism has been rightly identified as problematic and needs to be criticised. The critics are also right in arguing that Nerhuvian secularism seems to be rather ineffective in the era of identity politics. But its weakness is not so much because Nehruvian secularism attempted to ape the West, but because it was not a negotiated outcome among competing doctrines. After India's independence, Nehru's inclusive nationalism was redefined as Nehruvian secularism. However, those who are sympathetic towards Nehruvian secularism and argue that Nehru did not seek to limit religion's role in political life, overlook Nehru's concern with politicised religion. Nehru, I have argued, had a definite distrust with regard to religion's inclusion in politics, be it in its institutional or non-institutional forms. And yet his commitment to values of democracy and pluralism ensured that secularism in India was not a statist imposition but a shared ethical ideal that influenced India's popular consciousness through nationalist slogans like 'unity in diversity'.

NOTES

1. Sunil Khilnani, 'Introduction: Ideas of India', in *The Idea of India* (e-book), pp. 35–46 (New Delhi: Penguin, 2004 [1997]), p. 41.
2. According to Judith Brown, by 1936 Gandhi was publicly proclaiming that Nehru was his political heir. Judith M. Brown, *Nehru: A Political Life* (New Delhi: Oxford University Press, 2004), p. 127. Also see M. K. Gandhi, 'Gandhi–Nehru Letters', Supplementary Writings in *Hind Swaraj and Other Writings*, ed. Anthony J. Parel, pp. 149-156 (New York: Cambridge University Press, 2009 [1997]), p. 151. Uma Iyenger and Lalitha Zackariah observe a 'growing closeness' between Gandhi and Nehru from 1925 onwards: '... the two men began to bond through letters ... evident in the changed subscription from "Gandhi" to "Bapu" ... Nehru became dearer to Gandhi as "Jawahar"'. See Uma Iyengar and Lalitha Zachariah (eds.), 'Introduction', in *Together They Fought: Gandhi–Nehru Correspondence 1921–1948*, pp. xxxi–xli (New Delhi: Oxford University Press, 2011), p. xxxiii.
3. Under Gandhi's recommendation, Nehru was elected as the Congress president for the first time in 1929. In 1946, he was sworn in as the prime minister for the provisional government of independent India. For Nehru's political biography, see Brown, *Nehru*; B. N. Pandey, *Nehru*

(Madras: Macmillan India Press, 1976); and Benjamin Zachariah, *Nehru* (London: Routledge, 2004).
4. Nehru retained the ministerial portfolio of scientific research for himself in the first government of independent India. The expenditure on scientific research shot up from 24 million rupees in 1947 to 550 million rupees in 1964. See Zachariah, *Nehru*; and Bhikhu Parekh, 'Jawaharlal Nehru and the Crisis of Modernisation', in *Crisis and Change in Contemporary India*, ed. Upendra Baxi and Bhikhu Parekh, pp. 21–56 (New Delhi: SAGE Publications, 1995). Srirupa Roy argues that in the first few decades after independence, the 'need for science' discourse dominated India's post-colonial project of nation-state formation. For a critical evaluation of Nehru's emphasis on science, rationality and expertise as the bases for the nation-state, see Srirupa Roy, *Beyond Belief: India and the Politics of Postcolonial Nationalism* (Durham: Duke University Press, 2007); and Partha Chatterjee, *Nationalist Thought and the Colonial World: A Derivative Discourse* (London: Zed Books, 1993 [1986]).
5. For Nehru's conception of secularism, see M. Balasubramanian, *Nehru: A Study in Secularism* (New Delhi: Uppal Publishing House, 1980).
6. 'Dalit' is a Marathi and Hindi term that means 'the oppressed'. This term is used for the ex-untouchable groups in India, who are designated the lowest ritual status in the Hindu caste hierarchy.
7. Gandhi, 'Gandhi–Nehru Letters', p. 150.
8. Hand-spun and handwoven cloth.
9. Gandhi, 'Gandhi–Nehru Letters', p. 150.
10. Nehru, 'Gandhi–Nehru Letters', pp. 152–153.
11. Akeel Bilgrami, 'Gandhi (and Marx)', in *Secularism, Identity, and Enchantment*, pp. 122–174 (Cambridge, MA: Harvard University Press, 2014), p. 140.
12. 'The British became dominant in India, and the foremost power in the world, because they were the heralds of the new big-machine industrial civilization. They represented a new historic force which was going to change the world, and were thus, unknown to themselves, the forerunners and representatives of change and revolution; and yet they deliberately tried to prevent change, except in so far as this was necessary to consolidate their position and help them in exploiting the country and its people to their own advantage.' Jawaharlal Nehru, *The Discovery of India* (Delhi: Oxford University Press, 1994 [1946]), p. 312. Also see Jawaharlal Nehru, 'The Need for External Contacts', in *Jawaharlal*

Nehru, an Anthology, ed. Sarvepalli Gopal, pp. 467–468 (Delhi: Oxford University Press, 1980 [1928]), p. 468; and Jawaharlal Nehru, 'Can Indians Get Together?' in *Jawaharlal Nehru, an Anthology*, ed. Sarvepalli Gopal, pp. 322–323 (Delhi: Oxford University Press, 1980 [1942]), p. 322.

13. Sudipta Kaviraj, 'On the Enchantment of State: Indian Thought on the Role of the State in the Narrative of Modernity', in *Trajectories of the Indian State: Politics and Ideas*, pp. 40–77 (Ranikhet: Permanent Black, 2012).
14. The resolution for *purna swaraj*, or complete political independence, from the British rule was taken at the Lahore Congress in 1929.
15. Unlike Gandhi, who had faith in the British empire until the early 1920s, Nehru's ideas and politics were pivoted against imperialism. As early as 1924 in his political career, Nehru stated, 'Personally I said I was for complete independence. I am against the idea of empire and of one country forcibly ruling another.' Jawaharlal Nehru, in Sarvepalli Gopal (ed.), *Selected Works of Jawaharlal Nehru (SWJN)*, series 1, vol. 2, p. 197 (electronic book) (New Delhi: Nehru Memorial Museum and Library, 1988 [1974]), http://nehruportal.nic.in/writings (accessed on 1 September 2021).
16. See Chapter 2 on Gandhi, where I distinguish between two overlapping conceptions of religion in his thought: faith and ethical living.
17. Jawaharlal Nehru, 'What Is Religion', in *An Autobiography*, pp. 370–380 (New Delhi: Oxford University Press, 1982 [1936]), p. 378. Nehru wrote his autobiography during his incarceration in 1934–1935. I have consulted both the UK and India (1982 [1936]) and the US (1941) editions.
18. Ibid. Also see Nehru, *Discovery*.
19. Balasubramanian, *Nehru*, p. 13.
20. Nehru, *An Autobiography*, p. 380.
21. Ibid.
22. Gandhi quoted by Nehru in Ibid.
23. Ibid.
24. Ibid.
25. Nehru, *Discovery*, p. 29.
26. Nehru says, 'I knew that Gandhiji usually acts on instinct (I prefer to call it that than the 'inner voice' or an answer to prayer), and very often that instinct is right.... The reasons which he afterward adduces to justify his action are usually afterthoughts and seldom carry one very far. A

leader or a man of action in a crisis almost always acts subconsciously and then thinks of the reasons for his action. I felt also that Gandhiji had acted rightly in suspending civil resistance. But the reason he had given seemed to me an insult to intelligence and an amazing performance for a leader of a national movement.' Jawaharlal Nehru, *Toward Freedom: The Autobiography of Jawaharlal Nehru* (New York: The John Day Company, 1941), pp. 310–311.
27. Nehru, *Toward Freedom*, p. 240.
28. Ibid., p. 243.
29. Nehru, *Discovery*, p. 26.
30. Ibid, p. 513.
31. Nehru, *Toward Freedom*, p. 240.
32. Ashis Nandy, 'The Politics of Secularism and the Recovery of Religious Tolerance', in *Secularism and Its Critics*, ed. Rajeev Bhargava, pp. 321–344 (New Delhi: Oxford University Press, 2008 [1998]).
33. Nehru, *Toward Freedom*, p. 241 and p. 243.
34. Ibid., p. 241.
35. Ibid., pp. 241–243.
36. Ibid., pp. 242–243.
37. In his narrative of the evolution of the 'secular' in the Western world, Charles Taylor shows how this term which initially was an 'internal' dyad, eventually mutates and becomes an 'external' dyad, where 'secular' and 'religious' become opposed to each other. I am using the oppositional dyad of 'this-world' and 'the other-world' in view of Taylor's analysis. It follows that there can be worldviews where this-worldly views and the other-worldly views are miscible such that no clear separation between the two can be made. See Charles Taylor, *A Secular Age* (Cambridge, MA: Harvard University Press, 2007); and Charles Taylor, 'The Polysemy of the Secular', *Social Research: An International Quarterly* 76, no. 4 (2009): 1143–1166.
38. Nehru, *Toward Freedom*, pp. 242–243. Also see Nehru, *Discovery*, pp. 513–514.
39. Nehru, *Toward Freedom*, p. 240. Nehru laments, 'Was it my fault that I could not enter into the spirit and ways of thinking of my countrymen?' Ibid.
40. Under the British colonial administration, a *zamindar* was a large landholder recognised as a proprietor who paid land revenues to the government.

41. Jawaharlal Nehru, 'Reply to Address of All Bengal Students Association', 25 September 1928, *SWJN* (1), vol. 3, p. 198.
42. Ibid.
43. Chatterjee, *Nationalist Thought*, p. 142.
44. Ibid.
45. Ibid., p. 143.
46. Nehru says: 'Always we had the feeling that, while we might be more logical, Gandhiji knew India far better than we did....'. Nehru, *Toward Freedom*, p. 191.
47. Ibid., p. 67.
48. Ibid., p. 73.
49. Ibid., p. 190.
50. Ibid., p. 237. Referring to Gandhi's twenty-one-day fast unto death against Ramsay MacDonald's communal award, Nehru says, 'Then came news of the tremendous upheaval all over the country, a magic wave of enthusiasm running through Hindu society, and untouchability appeared to be doomed. What a magician, I thought, was this little man sitting in Yeravda Prison, and how well he knew how to pull the strings that move people's hearts!' Ibid.
51. 'Political independence meant, of course, political freedom only, and did not include any social change or economic freedom for the masses.... When it comes, it will bring a large measure of social freedom also.' Nehru, *Toward Freedom*, p. 115.
52. Ibid., p. 190.
53. For Nehru's political struggle with dilemmas and ambiguities of mass nationalism, see Brown, *Nehru*; see especially the chapters under the section titled 'The Ambiguities of Mass Nationalism, 1920–1939'.
54. Nehru, *Toward Freedom*, pp. 71–73.
55. Nehru, *Discovery*, p. 31. Nehru described his worldview in terms of the application of 'scientific temper'. I discuss his notion of scientific temper in detail later in the chapter.
56. Kingdom of God (Rama) on earth; Gandhi's ideal political society.
57. Chatterjee, *Nationalist Thought*, pp. 151–152.
58. Nehru, *Toward Freedom*, pp. 71–73.
59. Ibid., p. 82. Interestingly, even for some of the Muslim nationalists, *ahimsa* (non-violence) could be adopted only as practical politics against colonialism and not as a philosophical justification for the national struggle.

60. Gandhi, however, hoped that the efficacy of non-violence both as a 'creed' and 'policy' would eventually lead the Congress to accept its creedal importance.
61. Nehru, *Toward Freedom*, p. 82.
62. For instance, see Nehru, 'Politics and Religion', in *The Oxford India Nehru*, ed. Uma Iyengar, pp. 217–219 (New Delhi: Oxford University Press, 2011 [1928]).
63. Quoted from Sunil Khilnani, 'Nehru's Faith', *Economic and Political Weekly* 48, no. 30 (2002): 4793–4799, at p. 4793.
64. Nehru, *Discovery*, pp. 512–513. Also see Jawaharlal Nehru, 'Speech at the 40th Session of the Indian Science Congress, Held at Lucknow, 2 January 1953', in *Jawaharlal Nehru on Science: Speeches Delivered at the Annual Sessions of the Indian Science Congress*, ed. Baldev Singh, pp. 33–39 (New Delhi: Nehru Memorial Museum and Library); and Jawaharlal Nehru, 'The Progress of Science', in *The Unity of India: Collected Writings, 1937–1940*, ed. V. K. Krishna Menon, pp. 178–186 (London: Lindsay Drummond, 1948 [1941]).
65. Khilnani, 'Nehru's Faith', p. 4793.
66. Ibid.
67. Nehru, *Discovery*, p. 558.
68. See Chapter 2 for Gandhi's critique of a dominant strand of post-Enlightenment epistemology which separates fact and value and expressed in the Cartesian dualism. For a detailed discussion of the separation of fact and value and Gandhi's criticism of it, see Anuradha Veeravalli, *Gandhi in Political Theory* (Surrey: Ashgate Publishing, 2014).
69. Nehru, *Discovery*, pp. 512–513. Also see Sarvepalli Gopal (ed.), *Jawaharlal Nehru, an Anthology* (Delhi: Oxford University Press, 1980), pp. 493–494.
70. Nehru, *Discovery*, p. 512.
71. Nehru, 'Speech at the 40th Session of the Indian Science Congress', p. 35.
72. Khilnani, 'Nehru's Faith', p. 4794.
73. Nehru, *Toward Freedom*, p. 67.
74. Khilnani, 'Nehru's Faith', 4794.
75. Ibid.
76. Nehru, *Discovery*, p. 558.
77. Khilnani, 'Nehru's Faith', p. 4794.
78. Nehru quoted by David Arnold in 'Nehruvian Science and Postcolonial India', *Isis* 104, no. 2 (2013): 360–370.

79. Jawaharlal Nehru, 'The Roots of Culture', in *Jawaharlal Nehru, an Anthology*, ed. Sarvepalli Gopal, pp. 492–495 (Delhi: Oxford University Press, 1980 [1950]), pp. 493–494. Also see Nehru, '40th Session of the Indian Science Congress'.
80. Arnold, 'Nehruvian Science', p. 362.
81. Nehru, *Discovery*, p. 557.
82. Ibid., p. 558.
83. Nehru, *Discovery*, p. 558. Elsewhere he says, 'The culture of a people must have its roots in the national genius'. Nehru, *Anthology*, p. 467.
84. See Akeel Bilgrami, 'Secularism, Nationalism, and Modernity', in *Secularism and Its Critics*, ed. Rajeev Bhargava, pp. 380–417 (New Delhi: Oxford University Press, 2008 [1998]), p. 381. By the 1970s, the 'Nehruvian state', or more specifically, what Rajni Kothari has called, the 'Congress system', fell into decay, and a different kind political system was revived by Indira Gandhi, Nehru's daughter. Furthermore, by the 1980s, even the restructured system had failed Congress, and Congress's conception of a pluralist Indian nation was being seriously challenged by an aggressive Hindu nationalism. See Sudipta Kaviraj, 'On the Enchantment of State: Indian Thought and the Role of the State in the Narrative of Modernity', in *The Trajectories of the Indian State: Politics and Ideas*, pp. 40–77 (Ranikhet: Permanent Black, 2012).
85. Nandy, 'The Politics of Secularism', p. 322.
86. T. N. Madan, 'Secularism in Its Place', in *Secularism and Its Critics*, ed. Rajeev Bhargava, pp. 297–320 (New Delhi: Oxford University Press, 2008 [1998]).
87. For a more detailed discussion of Madan and Nandy's criticism of secularism, see Chapter 1.
88. V. K. Krishna Menon, 'Foreword to the First Edition', in *The Unity of India: Collected Writings, 1937–1940*, by Jawaharlal Nehru, pp. iv–vi (London: Lindsay Drummond 1948 [1941]), p. v.
89. Neeladri Bhattacharya has argued that secular histories continue to be framed within the terms set in opposition to communal history. He notes, 'Where communal historians can only see the hard lines of the boundaries that separate communities, secular historians have emphasized the porosity and open-endedness of these boundaries. Where communal historians look at the communities as homogeneous and unitary, secular historians point to the heterogeneity and fragmentation within them. Where communal historians look at the

past as a time of communal discord, secular historians have sought to underline the elements of concord, harmony, and togetherness. Where communal historians hear only the voices of orthodoxy and sectarianism, secularists have searched for histories of syncretism and tolerance.' Neeladri Bhattacharya, 'Predicaments of Secular Histories', *Public Culture* 20, no. 1 (2007): 57–73, at 58–59. For an assessment of communal histories, see Romila Thapar, Bipan Chandra and Harbans Mukhia, *Communalism and the Writing of Indian History* (Delhi: People's Publishing House, 1969).

90. Kaviraj remarks, 'I think Nehru's curious inattentiveness to cultural construction cannot be explained without understanding how seriously his generation believed in the story they had told themselves'. Sudipta Kaviraj, *Imaginary Institutions of India: Politics and Ideas* (New York: Columbia University Press, 2010), p. 151. For an analysis of history-writing in relation to projects of nationalism and nation-building, see Rajeev Bhargava 'History, Nation and Community: Reflections on Nationalist Historiography of India and Pakistan', *Economic and Political Weekly* 35, no. 4 (2000): 193–200.

91. Sudipta Kaviraj, 'Religion, Politics, and Modernity', in *Crisis and Change in Contemporary India*, ed. Upendra Baxi and Bhikhu Parekh, pp. 295–316 (New Delhi: SAGE Publications, 1995), p. 301. Romila Thapar argues that Indian history writing in the early twentieth century was inevitably influenced by the nationalist movement. During this time, nationalist historians relied heavily on the work of Orientalists who tended to glorify the ancient past. See Romila Thapar, 'Communalism and the Writing of Ancient Indian History', in *Communalism and the Writing of Indian History*, by Romila Thapar, Harbans Mukhia, and Bipan Chandra, pp. 1–23 (New Delhi: People's Publishing House, 1987 [1969]).

92. Partha Chatterjee, 'The Moment of Arrival: Nehru and the Passive Revolution', in *Nationalist Thought and the Colonial World: A Derivative Discourse*, pp. 131–166 (London: Zed Books, 1993 [1986]).

93. Jawaharlal Nehru, 'India – Old and New', in *Jawaharlal Nehru, an Anthology*, ed. Sarvepalli Gopal, pp. 238–241 (Delhi: Oxford University Press, 1980 [1962], p. 238.

94. Nehru, *Discovery*, p. 70.

95. Ibid.

96. Ibid., p. 71.

97. Ibid., p. 72.

98. Ibid.
99. See Taylor, *A Secular Age*; and Taylor, 'The Polysemy of the Secular'.
100. Nehru, *Discovery*, p. 73.
101. Ibid., pp. 73–74.
102. Ibid., p. 95.
103. Rajeev Bhargava, 'Indian Secularism: An Alternative, Trans-cultural Ideal', in *The Promise of India's Secular Democracy*, pp. 63–105 (New Delhi: Oxford University Press, 2010), p. 77.
104. Nehru, *Discovery*, p. 257.
105. Ibid.
106. Jawaharlal Nehru, 'Our Inheritance', in *Jawaharlal Nehru, an Anthology*, ed. Sarvepalli Gopal, pp. 206–209 (New Delhi: Oxford University Press, 1980 [1948]), p. 207.
107. Ibid.
108. Nehru, *Discovery*, p. 382.
109. Sudipta Kaviraj, 'Disenchantment Deferred' in *Beyond the Secular West*, ed. Akeel Bilgrami, pp. 135–187 (New York: Columbia University Press, 2016), p. 146.
110. Akeel Bilgrami, 'Jawaharlal Nehru, Mohandas Gandhi, and the Contexts of Indian Secularism', in *The Oxford Handbook of Indian Philosophy*, ed. Jonardon Ganeri, pp. 693–717 (New York: Oxford University Press, 2017).
111. Sudipta Kaviraj, 'On the Structure of Nationalist Discourse', in *Imaginary Institutions*, pp. 85–125 (New York: Oxford University Press, 2010), p. 121.
112. Nehru, *Discovery*, p. 262.
113. Ibid., p. 287.
114. Jawaharlal Nehru, 'A Generation Sentenced to Hard Labour', in *Jawaharlal Nehru's Speeches*, vol. 1, September 1946–May 1949 (Delhi: Publications Division [Ministry of Broadcasting and Information], Government of India Press, 1967 [1948]), p. 90.
115. Chatterjee, *Nationalist Thought*, p. 137.
116. Nehru, *Discovery*, pp. 557–558.
117. Ibid.
118. Roy has argued that by identifying the nation-building process within the 'need for science' discourse, the Nehruvian state inserted India within world historical time and could claim world historical agency for the state as the fulfiller of scientific needs. She argues that through this

discourse of science the specificity of Indian needs received less attention than the universal nature of the problems that India faced. She says, 'In the rhetoric of Nehruvian India, science was described as a need that manifested itself with equal urgency in new and old, Western and non-Western, and developed and underdeveloped nations. The discourse of scientific needs was harnessed for the nation state that can be termed ... the project of "universalizing India".' See Roy, *Beyond Belief*, pp. 115–116.
119. See the introduction to this book for an elaboration of the Gandhi-Nehru tradition.
120. Nehru, *Toward Freedom*, p. 116.
121. Ibid., pp. 115–116. However, Nehru's views regarding communalism changed in the late 1930s. In the next chapter, I argue how Nehru's politics from the late 1930s onwards is better understood through the framework of 'liberalism of fear'.
122. For instance, see Nehru, *Anthology*, pp. 82–84; and Nehru, *SWJN* (1), vol. 3, pp. 225–226.
123. Chatterjee, *Nationalist Thought*, pp. 139–140.
124. Ibid., p. 139.
125. Nehru, *Anthology*, p. 82.
126. Ibid.
127. Nehru, *Discovery*, p. 383.
128. Kaviraj, 'On the Structure of Nationalist Discourse'.
129. Ibid., p. 118.
130. Taylor, *A Secular Age*.
131. Kaviraj, 'Disenchantment Deferred'.
132. For a detailed analysis of the Constituent Assembly Debates on secularism, see Shefali Jha, 'Secularism in the Constituent Assembly Debates, 1946–1950', *Economic and Political Weekly* 37, no. 30 (2002): 3175–3180; Shabnum Tejani, *Indian Secularism: A Social and Intellectual History 1890–1950* (Ranikhet: Permanent Black, 2007); and Rochana Bajpai, *Debating Difference: Group Rights and Liberal Democracy in India* (New Delhi: Oxford University Press, 2011).
133. In the debates on secularism in India, the relational nature of secularism and democracy has not been adequately looked into. Due to the presence of democracy, the legitimating vocabulary of Indian secularism has been constantly changing, such that the conception is contextual and therefore historically contingent. See Bajpai, *Debating Difference* for such an argument.

134. Sudipta Kaviraj, 'Languages of Secularity', *Economic and Political Weekly* 48, no. 50: 93–102, at p. 95.
135. Rajeev Bhargava, 'Nehru against Nehruvians: On Religion and Secularism', *Economic and Political Weekly* 52, no. 8 (2017): 34–40. For a counterargument, see Sarvepalli Gopal, 'Nehru and Minorities', *Economic and Political Weekly* 23, nos. 45–47 (1988): 2463–2466.
136. Bhargava, 'Nehru against Nehruvians', p. 36.
137. The term 'depressed classes' was coined by the colonial state for the untouchables, who are designated the lowest status in the Hindu caste hierarchy.
138. Consider this speech by Nehru in 1928: 'Communalism, of course, has to be fought ruthlessly and suppressed. But I really do not think it is such a power as it is made out to be. It may be a giant today but it has feet of clay. It is the outcome largely of anger and passion and when we regain our tempers it will fade into nothingness. It is a myth with no connection with reality and it cannot endure. It is really the creation of our educated classes in search of office and employment.' Jawaharlal Nehru, 'Presidential Address at Punjab Provincial Congress', 11 April 1928, *SWJN* (1), vol. 3, pp. 225–226. Also see the Congress election manifesto of 1936 written by Nehru where he insisted that '… the whole communal problem, in spite of its importance, has nothing to do with the major problems in India – poverty and widespread unemployment. It is not a religious problem and it affects only a handful of people at the top'. Jawaharlal Nehru, 'The Congress Election Manifesto', 22 August 1936, *SWJN* (1), vol. 7: 463.
139. Apart from the fact that, like religious politics, secular politics is not immune to affect.
140. Thus, from a historical process witnessed in the West, secularisation becomes a normative project for the non-western world. Even the eminent sociologist Dipankar Gupta is guilty of seeing secularisation as a prescriptive project for the post-colonial modern state. And this despite his caution that 'one should heed the sociological distinction between secularisation as social process and secularism the ideology'. Secularism, in this view, is inextricably linked to the secularisation process, and the former has become an embattled ideology due to latter's failure to entrench itself in Indian society. In such a view, secularism has failed because the historical process of secularisation is not complete in modern India. See Dipankar Gupta, 'Secularisation and Minoritisation:

Limits of Heroic Thought', *Economic and Political Weekly* 30, no. 35 (1995): 2203–2207.
141. Rajeev Bhargava makes a distinction between two types of secularism: ethical and political secularism. He has argued that Indian secularism is of the latter type. According to him, as a normative stance that justifies the separation of religion from politics, ethical secularism states that derivation of the fundamental bases of moral conduct come from human sources and not from divine sources. He further notes that secularism can be delinked from ethical conceptions and be given a purely political character. See Rajeev Bhargava, 'What is Secularism For?' in *Secularism and Its Critics*, ed. Rajeev Bhargava, pp. 486–555 (New Delhi: Oxford University Press, 2008 [1998]). Also see Chapter 1 in this book.
142. Nehru, *Anthology*, p. 330.
143. Ibid., p. 331.
144. Ibid.
145. Nehru's commitment to and observance of democratic norms and practices has been affirmed by several scholars, despite glaring lapses. For instance, see Sunil Khilnani, *The Idea of India* (New Delhi: Penguin, 2012 [1997]); and Brown, *Nehru*. Commenting on Nehru's sometimes dictatorial style of governance, Brown observed, 'Although he [Nehru] was an articulate and powerful advocate of democracy, and worked to sustain the practice of free and fair elections, to educate voters in the issues at stake in elections, and to nurture the institutions and practices of democratic government, his own style in office tended to be dictatorial and to bypass the norms of cabinet government and ministerial collegiality.' Brown, *Nehru*, pp. 342–343.
146. Nehru's deference towards democratic politics is visible in his engagement with communal or religious politics of the minorities both before and after independence. In the 1936 election manifesto of the Congress, which Nehru drafted, he said, 'The attitude of the Congress is, therefore, not one of indifference or neutrality. It disapproves strongly of the communal decision and would like to end it. But the Congress has repeatedly laid stress on the fact that a satisfactory solution of the communal problem can come only through the goodwill and cooperation of the principle communities concerned.' Nehru, 'The Congress Election Manifesto', p. 462. I discuss Nehru's engagement with minority politics in detail in the next chapter.

147. Rajni Kothari, 'Political Consensus in India: Decline and Reconstruction', *Economic and Political Weekly* 4, no. 41 (1969): 1635–1644.
148. The term 'Nehruism' has been used by Kaviraj, and I have used it in a similar vein as him. See Kaviraj, 'On the Structure of Nationalist Discourse'.
149. See the 42nd Amendment in the Indian Constitution, Article 51A (h) of the Fundamental Duties.
150. Nehruvian secularism, it should be recalled here, is conditioned by democratic and liberal values, for which Indira Gandhi hardly had any regard.
151. Arnold, 'Nehruvian Science', p. 369.
152. *Mainstream*, 'A Statement on Scientific Temper', 12 July 1981, pp. 6–10.
153. P. N. Haksar was one of the public intellectuals in whose name the statement on scientific temper was released. He was Indira Gandhi's principal secretary from 1967 to 1973.
154. *Mainstream*, 'A Statement', p. 6.
155. Ibid.
156. Ashis Nandy, 'Science for Unafraid', *Mainstream*, 26 June 1982, pp. 17–20, at 17.
157. For such an argument, see Meera Nanda, *Prophets Facing Backward: Postmodern Critiques of Science and Hindu Nationalism in India* (New Jersey: Rutgers University Press, 2003).
158. During the Shah Bano controversy in the 1980s, where the debate for a Uniform Civil Code (UCC) irrupted, the Left and the feminists found themselves uncomfortably on the same side as the Hindu right in arguing against the Muslim Personal Law. For the parliamentary debates on the Muslim Women (Protection of Rights on Divorce) Act, 1986, introduced by the Congress government as a result of the Supreme Court judgment in 1985, which called for a UCC, see Sushmita Nath, 'Secularism in Crisis: The Indian State's Codification of the Muslim Personal Law and the Relegation of Muslim Women's Rights', *Studies in Religion* 45, no. 4 (2016): 520–541.
159. Meera Nanda, for instance, criticises that 'the left/postmodernist Gandhians have refused to recognise the vast agreement between the Hindu right wing and the holistic socialism of Gandhi'. She remarks, '… the left/postmodernist Gandhians have closed their eyes to the historical connection between neo-Hinduism [by which she means the modern right-wing ideology propagated by political organizations like

the Rashtriya Swayamsevak Sangh (RSS) and the BJP] and Gandhian thought. They have ... continued to propagate, in theory and in practice (of new social movements), the Gandhian ideas of cultural authenticity, anti-secularism, and "community". Their insistence upon cultivating an "alternative" and "patriotic" science belongs to this overall project'. Nanda, *Prophets Facing Backward*, p. 217.

160. Writing in the 1990s, Partha Chatterjee noted that the political leadership of the Hindu right describes its adversaries as 'pseudo-secularists', thereby conceding to the ideal of the secular state. Chatterjee, 'Secularism and Tolerance.

161. Indeed, various competing narratives of Indian nationalism, from Raja Rammohun Roy to Dadabhai Naoroji to Bankimchandra Chattopadhyay to the twentieth-century nationalists, like Bal Gangadhar Tilak, Lala Lajpat Rai, Rabindranath Tagore, Gandhi, Jinnah, Nehru and Ambedkar are replete with such miscible doctrinal positions.

162. Kaviraj, 'Languages of Secularity', p. 93.

163. Jawaharlal Nehru, 'A Secular State', in *Jawaharlal Nehru, an Anthology*, ed. Sarvepalli Gopal, pp. 330–331 (Delhi: Oxford University Press, 1980 [1961]), p. 330.

164. Bilgrami, 'Secularism, Nationalism, and Modernity', p. 395.

165. Ibid., p. 394. For Nandy and Madan, however, Nehruvian secularism is a cultural or ideological imposition.

166. Ibid., p. 395.

167. Ibid.

167. Ibid., pp. 395–396.

168. I discuss this point further in the next chapter.

170. See Tejani, *Indian Secularism*, for such an argument.

171. Tejani, *Indian Secularism*; and Tejani, 'Defining Secularism in the Particular: Caste and Citizenship in India 1909–1950', *Politics and Religion* 6, no. 4 (2013): 703–729.

172. Gupta, 'Secularisation and Minoritisation', p. 2203.

5

NEHRU AND THE POLITICS OF LIBERALISM OF FEAR

INTRODUCTION

If Gandhi's politics challenged British colonialism and politics, after India's independence, Nehru's political challenge was to create structures and styles of governance which were national rather than imperial.[1] How could the inherited colonial structures and norms of government, which had evolved to meet imperial needs, be geared to serve the needs of a newly independent nation-state? Simultaneously, the newly formed nation-state's problems could not be considered in isolation from the rest of the world. For the first prime minister of independent India, the national problems needed to be understood in the context of a wider picture, that is, 'in a world-setting'.[2] Nehru, Sunil Khilnani remarks, was 'a man whose hand certainly touched the wheel of history'.[3] Not only did Nehru determine the shape and content of the independent state, his political judgements and their effects still shape the contexts in which Indians must today decide for themselves. 'So much so, that much of India's recent politics can be seen as representing a range of evaluations on what Indians have taken to be Nehru's judgements.'[4] As such, to be in a position to make a retrospective historical assessment of Nehru's judgements, one needs to understand the basis of Nehru's own political judgements. In order to gain insight into the circumstances in which Nehru made political decisions, in this chapter, I will engage with his political actions in order to understand the role and relation of religion he envisaged vis-à-vis the state and society.

Nehru's political predilection was towards mass nationalism rather than liberal politics of constitutional reform introduced by the colonial government. Although, as early as 1924, Nehru had declared that he stood for complete independence from the British rule,[5] throughout the late 1920s[6] and 1930s his political vision increasingly came in conflict with the realities of nationalist politics with many Congressmen favouring constitutional reform (including Gandhi) and dominion status.[7] Remarking on Nehru's dilemma, Judith Brown says, '... constitutional action was a snare for protagonists of a mass nationalism aiming for independence'.[8] Nehru feared that the constitutional politics of the Indian National Congress (hereafter, the Congress) would strengthen a reformist mentality in the party and lock it in a collaborative enterprise with the British Raj.[9] Indeed, Indian politics under colonialism continued to be beset with two, often contradictory, processes: ballot-box constitutional politics and mass nationalism.[10] While the colonial government's constitutional politics and governance with its restricted franchise privileged the voice of the Indian elite, it was the mobilisation of disadvantaged groups that generated popular mass movements where Nehru laid his hope for *swaraj*, or complete independence.[11]

In what follows, I have arranged Nehru's engagement with politics around the event of partition of the Indian subcontinent in 1947 as it radically altered previously held political views about democracy, secularism, citizenship and representation. The first section deals with Nehru's engagement with politics prior to partition and India's independence from the British rule. The political issues that I discuss under this section are (*a*) communal or minority question and (*b*) the Muslim mass contact campaign, 1937. After providing a brief overview of the history of group rights in India, on the issue of communal or minority question, I argue how during the 1920s and early 1930s, Nehru deemed group-based representative politics based on separate electorates as communal politics. He believed that the minority question could be solved through a two-pronged approach of state-led economic development and constitutional safeguards for minority communities. However, with growing polarisation in politics on the basis of religion, by the late 1930s Nehru had modified his political opinion on religion's relation to politics. I argue that from the late 1930s onwards, Nehru's political philosophy reflected, what has been called, 'the liberalism of fear', where constitutional rights are not assumed as equally given to every citizen; rather, they need to be safeguarded by the state. In the same section, I proceed to discuss Nehru's political initiative called the 'Muslim mass contact campaign', undertaken in 1937 to increase the Congress's contact with the Muslim masses. This initiative was Nehru's answer to the growing popularity of communal politics. The Muslim mass contact campaign was Nehru's attempt to implement his political idea that the communal problem was essentially an economic issue, which could be solved by placing an economic programme before the masses. I then move on to the second section of the chapter which discusses Nehru's engagement with politics in post-colonial India with regard to (*a*) group-rights for religious minorities and the Scheduled Castes (SCs) and Scheduled Tribes (STs) and (*b*) the Hindu Code Bill controversy. On the issue of group rights, I discuss the limitations of Nehruvian political vision, which has been unable to take on the challenge posed by identity-based politics that has come to dominate post-colonial national politics. On the Hindu Code Bill controversy, I argue that what is revealing about Nehru's position on the Bill is that he did not believe that sociocultural transformations could be brought about by disregarding democratic norms and procedures and by forcing modernisation of religious law by the state. Since Nehru cherished religion's internal plurality and dynamism, he thought that codification of religious laws by the state would arrest the dynamic qualities of religion and culture. That modernists like Nehru did not seek to impose a single or uniform Indian identity upon the new nation is visible in the relegation of the uniform civil code to the directive principles of the state. The last section surmises Nehru's political thought and action in light of the discussions in this and the previous chapter.

NEHRU'S ENGAGEMENT WITH POLITICS BEFORE PARTITION OF INDIA

THE 'COMMUNAL OR MINORITY QUESTION'

Before independence and the division of the Indian subcontinent, the 'communal question' and the 'minority question' were considered the same in the constitutional provisions.[12] This scenario changed after partition and independence as these events seemed to provide an answer to the communal problem – with the partition creating the state of Pakistan, home for India's Muslims. Correspondingly, the secular republic of India was to protect the minorities, where minorities now specifically meant religious and not social minorities, like the SCs. The political issue of what came to be called the communal question can be traced back to 1906 when a debate began over constitutional reform in colonial institutions of representation. This debate culminated in the 1909 Indian Councils Act, famously known as the Morley–Minto reforms, which instituted separate electorates for Muslims. Rochana Bajpai remarks that representation of Indians in colonial representative structures was impelled by 'a cautious liberalism, and the need for better information and more personnel after the Great Uprising of 1857'.[13] As the British rulers decided that representation of Indians could not be individual, 'important' and 'distinctive' interests became the hallmark of colonial constitutionalism.[14] In this framework, minorities defined in religious terms, and later caste and racial terms, were the most prominent groups recognised for the purpose of representation. Groups defined in terms of social and economic criteria – landholders, universities and trade associations – were also accorded representation in legislative bodies. The Morley–Minto constitutional reforms started a long drawn-out contentious debate on group rights in Indian politics over separate and joint electorates, which remained controversial until the partition, as competing modes of electoral representation.[15]

The unfolding of the communal or minority question in the Indian subcontinent challenged the Congress's claim and standing as the party of inclusive nationalism.[16] The communal or minority question sharply pointed out that the inclusive politics of Indian nationalism propagated by the Congress was actually hegemonic. Furthermore, it also demonstrated that political independence was not the primary objective for all anti-colonial struggles. Indeed, with the Congress's sporadic and equivocal attempts at addressing minority or communal concerns, and with colonial reform offering incentives to minority leaders, by the end of the 1920s, the principal organisations of Muslims and the Depressed Classes had become antagonistic to nationalist politics.[17] Bajpai has argued that the Congress's claim to represent all sections of the people in India meant that it was intrinsically antagonistic to separate or special representation mechanisms for minorities.[18] Thus, if in Nehru's view, national unity and democracy were the primary objectives of the Congress,[19] a major challenge as to how they were variously perceived came from the communal or minority question. Through the political organisation of the Muslim League (hereafter, the League),[20] Jinnah sought to represent the interest of Indian Muslims; and Ambedkar,[21] who steadfastly refused the subsumption of the untouchables[22] into the Hindu fold, represented their interest through the colonial state's label of the Depressed Classes.

It was in the nature of colonial politics to claim representation without being representative. But it was also the case that in the colonial state's attempt to expand electoral representation based on group-based representative politics, the political consciousness of various communities as separate and distinct was stimulated. The mid-1920s saw the collapse of the Non-cooperation and the Khilafat movements, and with the weakening of the Khilafat–Congress alliance, violent conflicts between Hindus and Muslims erupted across the subcontinent. In the midst of heightened communal conflicts and the revival of extremist religious ideologies, the terms of political discourse shifted. From now on, legitimate political loyalty towards the Congress and the national movement largely meant a politics based on declared policies and programmes rather than around communitarian affiliations of people. Now, only electoral politics based on formal or virtual representation was seen as 'secular', non-sectarian politics by the Congress. Any demand for mirror representation of communities in the legislative bodies was deemed anti-secular and anti-national politics.[23] In Gyanendra Pandey's opinion, the events of the 1920s brought about a new reversal in nationalist politics, which, he maintains, has in turn helped in moulding contemporary debates and understanding of Indian society and politics. He argues that while in the past 'Hindu' and 'Muslim' political mobilisation had been seen as necessary, even inevitable, in the building of Indian nationalism, they now became 'divisive, primitive and ... the product of a colonial policy of Divide and Rule'.[24] Thus, in *The Discovery of India*, Nehru lamented, 'In political matters, religion has been displaced by what is called communalism, a narrow group mentality basing itself on a religious community but in reality concerned with political power and patronage for the interested group.'[25] By the late 1920s, the discourses that shaped the Congress's ideology and politics had drastically changed as compared to the Lucknow Pact of 1916, where both the Congress and the League called for complete self-government as India's goal and came up with a joint scheme of reforms in the representative bodies. The Lucknow Pact, as has been noted, may be described as one of the last political examples of 'complete accord' between the League and the Congress, which reflected the 'spirit of Hindu–Muslim cooperation'.[26]

Moreover, the term 'communal', which earlier referred to the creation of electorates in imperial and provincial legislative councils, by the mid-1920s had become 'communalism' – a term now used to describe the various violent sectarian conflicts between Hindus and Muslims at the grassroots.[27] Thus, for instance, the Nehru Report in 1928 declared, 'The communal problem in India is primarily the Hindu–Muslim problem'.[28] As communal riots spiralled in various parts of the subcontinent, from the mid-1920s onwards sectarian organisations, like the Hindu Mahasabha, gained new importance. According to Shabnum Tejani, during this period, Mahasabha leaders, like Madan Mohan Malaviya, sought to appropriate the legitimating language of nationalism by aligning Hindu unity with national unity and everything else as communal politics.[29] A range of alternative and inclusive discourses on nationalism which were made available by Khilafat and Non-cooperation leaders, like Gandhi and Mohammad Ali in the early 1920s, now stood delegitimised. As seen in Chapter 3, during the Non-cooperation–Khilafat movements, both Gandhi and Mohammad Ali espoused notions of a 'federated nationalism' rather than a 'totalizing idea of unity'.[30] Tejani has shown how the Khilafat and the Non-cooperation movements were made up of divergent aspirations, and many of them had little to do with either Indian nationalism or Hindu–Muslim unity. According to Gyanendra Pandey, even Gandhi's position changed in the aftermath of the breakdown of the Khilafat–Non-cooperation alliance as he declared '… we are Indians first and Hindus, Musalmans, Parsis, Christians, after'.[31] It is in this context of changing political discourse and politics that we need to understand Nehru's stance on separate electorates before partition and India's independence from British colonial rule.

Early in his political career, Nehru held the view that communalism was not a real political issue as it had nothing to do with the masses. It was an artificial creation of a small upper class based on feudal leadership who sought political power and privileges for themselves. For Nehru, the priority of the Congress and the national movement was to overthrow the British rule as colonialism was responsible for India's economic backwardness. Political independence, he argued, would also do away with restricted representative structures instituted by the colonial government serving imperial interests. Simultaneously, the Congress was to focus on economic problems that affected the large masses as this would provide the party and the national movement with the impetus to conduct mass nationalism. Moreover, Nehru had also hoped that the nation would overcome the problem of communalism by focusing on and implementation of a leftist programme of economic equality, like land reforms and employment:[32]

> There is no place for communalism or dogma-ridden people in it [India]. Communalism, of course, has to be fought ruthlessly and supressed. But I really do not think that it is such a power as it is made out to be. It may be a giant today, but it has feet of clay. It is the outcome of largely anger and passion and when we regain our tempers it will fade into nothingness. It is a myth with no connection with reality and it cannot endure. It is really a creation of our educated classes in search of office and employment.... There is a great deal in common between the Muslim and Sikh and Hindu zamindars; and very little in common between a Muslim peasant and a Muslim zamindar. We must, therefore, begin to think of and act on common economic issues. If we do so, the myth of communalism will automatically disappear. Conflict there may be, but it will be between different classes and not different religions.[33]

In *The Discovery of India*, Nehru opined that religion had played little part in India's political conflicts although he also noted that religion was often used and exploited. He said, 'Religious differences, as such, do not come in the way, for there is a great deal of mutual tolerance for them.'[34] He saw the presence of composite culture in Indian society, the intermixing and synthesis of worldviews and living habits, as a chief characteristic of Indian civilisation and a proof of socio-cultural resources for tolerance among various religious communities. From early on in his political career, Nehru had held on to this secular historiography of the subcontinent and argued that tolerance and inclusiveness were built into India's civilisation.[35] Aided with India's history of a tolerant cultural past, in his early political view, Nehru believed that the problem of communalism could be solved with cultural safeguards for minorities on issues such as language, education and schools.[36] Minorities did not require additional political safeguards (like representation in legislatures, executives and government employment) as this would mean interference of religion in political matters:

> If this question of culture is settled satisfactorily ... what remains of communalism? If in addition we replace our present system of territorial election by some method of selection by economic units, we

not only introduce a more efficient and progressive system, but also do away with joint and separate electorates and the reservation of seats. It is generally recognised now, or it ought to be, that separate electorates, which are meant to protect interest of minorities, really injure them and reduce their effective power in the State.... Personally, I am not in favour of territorial election at all, but if it is retained I am wholly opposed to separate electorates. I do not fancy reservation of seats on a communal basis either, but if this solution pleases people I would agree to it.... It is necessary, however, for such of us as do not believe [sic] in communalism and religion interfering with political and economic matters, to take up a strong attitude now....[37]

During the 1920s and early 1930s, Nehru propagated a politics that sought to circumscribe religion's role in society to cultural issues. On this view, any consideration and involvement of religion outside the cultural sphere would only aid and abate communalism. He believed that cultural safeguards in the constitution for minority religions would provide them with a free environment to preserve, protect and cultivate their culture. In addition, cultural safeguards would also help build up 'a rich and varied and yet a common culture',[38] providing the nation with greater cultural and intellectual resources, apart from fostering traditions of tolerance. This political vision can be seen of piece with, what I have identified in the previous chapter as, Nehru's nationalist narrative of secularity. What must be noted here is that despite his rejection of separate electorates as politics of communalism, Nehru prioritised democratic values over his political ideal of 'secular' politics by maintaining that if a majority of the people wished for separate electorates, he would accept it.[39] Furthermore, although Nehru propagated a politics that sought religion's non-interference in the political sphere, he did not consider the state's involvement in abolishing unjust and unequal social practices, like untouchability, hindering freedom of religion. In Nehru's view, as the practice of untouchability was a social issue and not a religious one, the Congress, as a secular political body, could legitimately interfere in this matter. In fact, Nehru asserted that since untouchability was a social issue, communal organisations concerned with religious issues could not interfere on the matter:

> If the high priests of religion and the shining lights of communal organizations are to decide the question of untouchability and all

other social problems, the division of provinces and the methods of election and similar problems, what exactly is the function of the National Congress or of other political organizations?... Perhaps there is no subject on which it [the Congress] has taken up a stronger attitude than the one of untouchability, and to say today that this is outside the purview of the Congress because it smacks of religion, is an amazing assertion.... The Congress ... much less it is likely to agree to any dictation or interference from religious or communal organisations in the social or economic sphere.[40]

But by the late 1930s, Nehru seems to have modified his political opinion on religion's relation to politics. Stating his views on Hindu and Muslim communalism in 1933, Nehru made a distinction between 'honest communalism' and 'false communalism', and attributed the former's presence in society to a political-psychological reaction of minorities based on 'fear':

It is the fear complex that we have to deal with in these communal problems. Honest communalism is fear; false communalism is political reaction. To some extent *this fear is justified*, or is at least understandable, in a minority community. (Emphasis added)[41]

This seems to be a revised and more nuanced political position on communalism on Nehru's part, as opposed to his earlier political stance of not acknowledging communalism as a political problem at all.[42] By accepting and addressing communalism as a political issue, Nehru, I believe, shifted from a particular secularist discourse of irrelevance of religion in politics, often reflected in his rhetoric of socialism, to a more nuanced political position. By including communalism driven by the minority community's fear of the majority community as a major political issue to be resolved, Nehru's political position from the late 1930s onwards, I argue, reflected the political philosophy of, what Judith Shklar has called, 'the liberalism of fear'.[43] Such a notion of political liberalism is centrally concerned with preventing political violence, cruelty and institutional humiliation of the weak from the powerful as these inhibit liberal freedom. It is about building a political order, where constitutional rights are not assumed as equally given to every citizen. According to Shklar,

... liberalism of fear adopts a strong defense of equal rights and their legal protection. It cannot base itself upon the notion of rights as fundamental and given, but it does see them as just those licenses and empowerments that citizens must have in order to preserve their freedom and to protect themselves against abuse.[44]

This kind of liberal politics actively seeks proper constitutional and institutional measures so as to safeguard the liberal citizenry from the fear of 'abuse of power and intimidation of the defenceless'.[45] It may be argued that the rights of citizens construed through the framework of liberalism of fear provided a multicultural thrust to post-colonial India's constitution, at a time when it was not very common to imagine the nation-state in this way. It provided the possibility to argue that changes in the personal laws of minority religious communities could only be brought about when these communities were 'ready' for them. In contemporary Indian politics, it is this idea of protection of minorities through constitutional and cultural safeguards which has been increasingly attacked by the Hindu right as 'pseudo-secular'.[46] They are seen as preferential policies of multiculturalism that have inhibited the development of the idea of universal identity of citizenship and a common national culture.[47]

With Jinnah as his political interlocutor and adversary, in January 1938, Nehru maintained:

> Whosoever wishes to fight the Congress on the communal issue will have to fight in the air, for the Congress will have nothing to do with such internecine conflicts.... But I should like to assure Mr. Jinnah ... any statement or proposal by Mr. Jinnah will always have the most careful consideration.... So far as the minorities question is concerned, it is the declared and well-established policy not only to do full justice to them, but to go even beyond that in order to *inspire confidence and goodwill* in them. The Congress can conceive of no freedom for India which is not an equal freedom for all the various religious communities which inhabit India and in which all do not share equally and have full opportunities of growth and development. So far as religious and cultural matters are concerned it has given the fullest possible assurances and declared that these should be incorporated in our fundamental rights in the constitution. A further assurance has been given in regard to personal law. In regard to certain political rights,

> the *Communal Award stands for the present and we have stated repeatedly that we seek no change except with the concurrence of those concerned....* Essentially the Congress is a political body acting on the national and political plane, and inevitably dealing with economic questions. All these over-lap communal and religious boundaries. Because of the strength that has come to the Congress from the organized masses of this country, and because of the growing importance of India, the Congress functions also to some extent on the international plane. This is bound to grow. This has also nothing to do with religious or communal questions. (Emphasis added)[48]

By the late 1930s, Nehru realised that Muslims as a numerical (around a quarter of the subcontinent's population) and social minority feared Hindu domination in politics, especially in the wake of independence from the British rule. But he also perceived that in a democratic state, with the promise of proper constitutional safeguards for minority communities on religious and cultural issues, this was an unreasonable fear. Unlike Jinnah or Ambedkar, Nehru did not see inclusion of communal or minority interests in representative bodies as a better mechanism of electoral politics. With regard to Muslim minorities, it was seen necessary by him to the extent that it assuaged the fear of majoritarianism: 'The communal problem, as it was called, was one of adjusting the claims of the minorities and giving them sufficient protection from majority action.'[49] Such measures would, as noted in Nehru's quote, inspire 'confidence and goodwill' among minority communities. On the communal question, we see that in Nehru's political opinion, there is an assumption that protecting minority community interests through constitutional safeguards in the sphere of religion, culture and education is secular politics, whereas safeguarding those very same interests via group-based representative political measures such as separate electorates is deemed as communal politics. Therefore, even as Nehru revised his political opinion in the late 1930s, he still did not see the political demand of separate electorates of groups such as the League as legitimate. Referring to Jinnah, he argued that communal politics 'bear no relation whatever to modern conditions and modern problems, which are essentially economic and political. Religion is both a personal matter and a bond of faith, but to stress religion in matters political and economic is obscurantism'.[50] As such, Nehru continued his insistence that the Congress, acting on a national and increasingly on an international plane, was the only secular political body representative of all sections of the society and that it alone carried the legitimate secular voice of Indian nationalism.

Nehru saw separate representation as further alienating the minority population from the majority. He said:

> ... separate electorates made matters a little worse, for the protected group for the majority electorate [that is, the Hindu community] lost interest in it, and there was little occasion for mutual consideration and adjustment which inevitably takes place in a joint electorate when a candidate has to appeal to every group.[51]

That the provision of separate electorates was not a prudential electoral mechanism for liberal democratic politics was equally visible in Nehru's rejection of it for the Depressed Classes:

> The obvious policy in dealing with groups or minorities which were backward educationally and economically was to help them in every way to grow and make up these deficiencies, especially by a forward educational policy. Nothing of this kind was done either for the Moslems or for other backward minorities, or for the depressed classes who needed it most. The whole argument centred in petty appointments in the subordinate public services, and instead of raising standards all round, merit was often sacrificed. Separate electorates thus weakened the groups that were already weak or backward, they encouraged separatist tendencies and prevented the growth of national unity, they were the negation of democracy, they created new vested interests of the most reactionary kind, they lowered standards, and they diverted attention from the real economic problems of the country which were common to all. These electorates, first introduced among the Moslems, spread to other minorities and groups till India became a mosaic of these separate compartments.... Out of them have grown all manner of separatist tendencies and finally the demand for a splitting up of India.[52]

Nehru toed the line of the dominant nationalist discourse which emerged in the late 1920s, whereby nationalism increasingly came to be defined in opposition to any form of group-based representative politics. This discourse, where national politics is understood in terms of a universal political category of citizen and any political demand based on group rights is seen as threatening to 'national unity',[53] was also invoked after India's independence during the making of the Indian constitution and later during the Shah Bano controversy of 1986.[54] In analysing these aforementioned cases, Bajpai has demonstrated how group rights may be delegitimised or seen antithetical to other political conceptions and values in a liberal democracy, such as secularism, justice and national unity, when the dominant or the legitimising discourse perceives one or some of these latter values as being threatened by the demands of group rights.[55] Although mainstream nationalism, during its mature phase, was inclusive, it was nevertheless a 'totalizing idea of unity'.[56] And although this nationalism was ideologically far removed from the one propagated by right-wing groups, like the Hindu Mahasabha, on the question of electoral representation in the legislative bodies and its relation to national unity, it often shared the same discursive ground.[57] For instance, both mainstream nationalism and right-wing ideological groups, claimed that separate electorates encouraged 'fissiparous tendencies'[58] and 'prevented the growth of national unity'.[59] Nehru's rejection of separate electorates was based on his faith in India's history of secularity that produced mutual toleration in the past through synthesis of various cultures, the provision of fundamental rights and constitutional safeguards for the weaker sections of the society, and in the modern state's focus on socio-economic development that would make class the primary category for social justice. Thus, in Nehru's opinion, it was not separate representation in electoral politics, but 'the legacies of the past, the laws of the present, and future remedies....' which would ensure equal status to different communities.[60]

THE MUSLIM MASS CONTACT CAMPAIGN, 1937

In 1937, Nehru initiated a campaign in the Congress to have greater contact with the Muslim masses. Sarvepalli Gopal notes that this was Nehru's chance of putting to practice his theory that the communal problem was a side issue which could be solved through political action, by placing an economic programme before the masses.[61] According to Mushirul Hasan, the Muslim mass contact campaign constituted the last serious attempt of the Congress to mobilise Muslims in British India in a joint struggle against colonial rule. Hasan remarks that the idea of mass contact was 'Nehru's brainchild and he alone, along with some of his trusted comrades, pressed it relentlessly until it formed part of the Congress programme'.[62] In March 1937, in a circular to provincial Congress committees, Nehru observed:

> During our election campaign and subsequently there has been much discussion about increasing Congress contacts with the Muslim masses. Wherever we went we found a willing response from them, an eagerness to hear the Congress message and a desire to line up with our freedom movement. But the lack of previous work among them and the paucity of trained Muslim workers prevented us from taking a full advantage of this new interest and awakening. Since then the subject has engaged the earnest attention of leading Congressmen and it has been felt that we must take a special effort to enrol Muslim Congressmen members, so that our struggle for freedom may become even more broadbased than it is, and the Muslim masses should take the prominent part in it which is their due.[63]

The campaign of mass contact, conceived after the 1936 elections in which the Congress fared poorly in Muslim constituencies, evinced Nehru's political philosophy. First, this political attempt showed Nehru's public advocacy of the idea that the Congress was an inclusive national movement and a party which represented the interests of all religious communities in India. This campaign showed Nehru's commitment to a broad-based representative politics. Indeed, the Muslim mass contact was a possible alternative to representative politics of separate electorates, which by the late 1920s had become very politically contentious and fractious. Second, the effort of the Congress to increase contact with the Muslim masses, while being 'communally' particular in its goal, was 'secular' in its intent and orientation. Muslims were to be roped in the Congress's common national struggle to fight imperial injustices and excesses on the one hand, and solve social problems of poverty and unemployment that beset the nation on the other:

> Indeed when we look at the vital problems facing the country, the problem of independence and of the removal of poverty and unemployment, there is no difference between the Muslim masses and the Hindu or Sikh or Christian masses in the country. Differences only come to the surface when we think in terms of the handful of upper

class people. Even these differences are no doubt capable of adjustment if approached in a friendly manner and with the larger viewpoint always before us.'[64]

The mass contact with Muslims, in Nehru's view, was not independent of the national cause. It was interdependent on the 'larger viewpoint',[65] where the primary goal was of independence from British colonial rule. When asked to explain how he planned to make millions of Muslims rally behind the Congress party, Nehru declared that he would do so by treating them as 'non-Muslims, i.e., approach them with the economic issue'.[66] Nehru went on to add, 'My appeal will not be to the top leaders but to the masses with whom the economic reality is bound to prevail.'[67] The Congress's mass contact campaign, Hasan opines, was based on a fresh assumption which questioned the efficacy of its previous practice of negotiating with a handful of Muslim politicians for short-term political gains.[68] Furthermore, this initiative of direct contact with the Muslim masses, Hasan notes, was equally a rejection of the earlier religio-political initiatives, such as the Congress support to the Khilafat cause. Although Gandhi and the Congress's support to the Khilafat cause showed the importance of Hindu–Muslim unity for national freedom, such religious politics sits uncomfortably with liberal and secular politics. That is why many political leaders (including within the Congress), both on the Muslim and Hindu sides, were unhappy with the movement. Nehru's mass contact campaign was a fine example of a commitment to both secular politics and Hindu–Muslim unity. As an alternative to both Gandhi's and Jinnah's politics, this campaign provided group representation and voice, where, by increasing their political presence in the national movement and the Congress party, a minority community could seek social and economic justice.

As the campaign's aim was to increase Muslim membership within the Congress and wean the masses away from the League's communal politics, Nehru suggested that each provincial Congress committee appoint a special committee to educate the Muslim masses about the socialist policies and programmes of the Congress and also enrol them from rural and urban areas. These enrolled Muslims would then engage with the day-to-day activities of the Congress in that particular area, and thereby work as Congressmen and not as Muslims.[69] The All India Congress Committee (AICC) set up a cell to control and direct activities relating to Muslims, to propagate the Congress programme through newspaper,[70] articles and pamphlets, and to counteract anti-Congress propaganda. Nehru's 'communist lieutenant',[71] Kunwar Mohammad Ashraf[72] ran the AICC cell for this purpose. Impressed with Nehru's 'language of Marxism', Ashraf opined, 'Any honest and consistent anti-imperialist struggle led by the Congress would wean away the Muslim masses from the growing influence of Jinnah and the revived Muslim League.'[73] Venkat Dhulipala notes that Nehru's chosen 'stalwarts' of the Muslim mass contact campaign, like Ashraf and Z. A. Ahmad, made use of the political vocabulary of Marxism and the idea of a composite culture to capture the imagination of the Muslim community.[74] Dhulipala remarks that the rhetoric of the stalwarts of mass contact programme matched the new nationalist historiography being written in this period, which stressed 'the composite Hindu–Muslim mass culture, the Ganga–Jamuni tehzeeb [Ganga–Yamuna culture]'.[75] As pointed out in the previous chapter, Nehru cherished the syncretic Mughal culture that developed amongst the North Indian elite during the medieval period, and the idea of synthesis and composite culture played a crucial role in his conception of a multi-national nation.

However, within two years of its launching, the mass contact campaign ran into serious trouble. According to Hasan, this was not so much due to the League's opposition or the lack of Muslim support. Instead, it was because of the Congress's own reluctance to pursue it with any vigour or sense of purpose. Not many in the Congress party shared Nehru's enthusiasm for mass contact with the Muslims. Gandhi, for instance, disapproved of the mass contact programme and preferred to proceed cautiously through constructive work among the Muslim masses by both Hindu and Muslim workers. Reservations were also expressed by some of Nehru's socialist allies who argued that their concern was with the masses, not as Hindus or Muslims but as peasants and workers of all communities. The biggest opposition to mass contact, however, came from the Congress right-wing as they feared that with Nehru's backing and Gandhi's grudging support, Muslims would wrest major concessions and influence Congress policies. Furthermore, several leading Congressmen had unpleasant memories of the Khilafat and Non-cooperation days which they saw as Gandhi's pandering to the religious sentiments of the Muslims and dictating Congress policies. Hasan remarks, '... the Congress right wing, in alliance with the Hindu Mahasabha, fiercely attacked the mass contact programme and spared no efforts to thwart its success'.[76] The success of the mass contact campaign depended on the active backing of provincial and district Congress committees and this was not easily forthcoming. Part of the reason, Hasan argues, was that these bodies were often controlled by men with anti-Muslim proclivities who had close links with the Hindu Mahasabha and other overtly communal organisations. In hindsight, one may argue that the failure of the mass contact programme should have sent warning signals to Nehru about the increased influence of the right-wing groups within the Congress. Its failure seriously questioned the Congress's claim of being representative of the entire nation and gave greater impetus to the League's politics.

NEHRU'S ENGAGEMENT WITH POLITICS IN POST-COLONIAL INDIA

The event of partition and the establishment of a secular state significantly defined Nehru's national politics in post-colonial India. In 1947, in a note to the Cabinet Ministers, he said:

> The secession of certain parts of India and the formation of Pakistan has left India very predominantly non-Muslim, though it has still a considerable Muslim population. We have guaranteed in the constitution we are making the fullest rights to all minorities.... It is clear, however, that the part that Muslims have played in India has been very greatly reduced by the establishment of Pakistan. Such part as they can play can only be a cooperative part, and not one of compulsion which the great majority will never tolerate. There has been this element of compulsion in the past or threats, and this has led to present unhappy situation and anger between the various communities....[77]

After partition, the changed demographic and political composition of independent India had a serious influence on Nehru's political thought and practice. While, on the one hand, constitutional protection of the rights of minority religious communities became a central concern, on the other hand, Nehru blamed the present circumstance of a divided India and the creation of a new nation-state on the basis of religion on pre-partition electoral politics of separate representation. As already argued in the previous chapter, like Gandhi, Nehru believed that religious difference was not a cause of conflict, and therefore he did not think that Indian nationalism needed to emulate European-style nation-state formation. He believed that India's religious diversity was its strength, and the subcontinent's history of assimilation and synthesis demonstrated its propensity towards toleration of difference. This was what Nehru saw as unique to India, or, as he often called it, the 'genius of the nation'.[78] As such, the partition of India and the creation of Pakistan on the basis of religion were a historical contradiction and went against the 'main trends of India's history':

> Are we to aim at or to encourage trends which will lead to the progressive elimination of the Muslim population in India, or are we to consolidate, make secure and absorb as full citizens the Muslims who remain in India? That, again, involves our conception of India; is it going to be, as it has been in a large measure, a kind of composite state [nation-state] where there is complete cultural freedom for various groups, but at the same time a strong political unity, or do we wish to make it, as certain elements appear to desire, definitely a Hindu or a non-Muslim state?... The whole of India has been one of assimilation and synthesis. That has been both the strength and the weakness of India. The Muslim League movement of separatism was a throwback and a contradiction of India's history. The establishment of Pakistan is a further contradiction and, perhaps, many of the troubles we are facing today are due essentially to this attempt to go against the main trends of India's history.... It seems to me clear, therefore, that we cannot encourage this business of Muslims leaving India.... I feel convinced that culturally India will be the poorer by any such divorce and all wrong tendencies will hold the field then.[79]

Partition challenged Nehru's deeply held conviction that India was 'the melting pot of so many races and cultures'.[80] Indeed, as seen in his nationalist narrative of secularity in the previous chapter, Nehru's idea of India, his political imagination, was based on such a conviction.

As throughout his political career, Nehru steadfastly and consistently refused religion's inclusion in electoral politics, the Muslim minority now reduced both in number and political power posed a serious issue. How was the newly found sovereign nation-state, whose formation was based on inclusive and secular politics, supposed to assuage and assure the minorities that the rights guaranteed in the constitution *would be* protected? That India would not, as many had claimed, become a 'Hindu Raj?' The paucity of Nehru's 'liberalism of fear' was that beyond constitutional safeguards and a commitment to secularism, there were not many options left for secular democratic politics, which considers religion's politicisation as dangerous to liberal politics. In her analysis of the Constituent Assembly debates, Shefali Jha notes that in India there is an inclination to favour a conception of a secular state as equal respect of all religions, as opposed to a Western notion that may seek religion's exclusion from the public-political sphere. She asks, 'Can the Constituent Assembly debates throw any light on whether this conception requires not only that religion be defined broadly by the state, but also that minorities must be granted political safeguards. Is this the only way that the state can prevent itself from becoming a Hindu state or will this added provision worsen the situation for Indian democracy?'[81] Jha's question highlights the tension between the state's commitment to liberal values and representative politics in post-colonial India. Although Rajeev Bhargava has pointed out the ingeniousness of India's constitutional design with regard to the normative considerations of Indian secularism as being different from Western secularism's 'wall of separation' doctrine,[82] in the face of majoritarian and heightened communal politics, one may further ask whether today we need to reimagine Indian secularism in its relationship to group-based representative politics. With the entrenchment of identity-based politics and the rise and domination of the Hindu right in electoral politics, secularism is more and more perceived to be ineffective in contemporary Indian politics. Does a political conception of secularism today also not require that the political safeguards for minority religious communities be expanded and extended beyond religious, cultural and educational rights, which include group-based representative politics?

Since the late 1920s, the Congress and Nehru did not see communal electorates being compatible with secular liberal politics. After independence, and especially with the horrors witnessed during partition, the option of communal electorates in legislative bodies was no longer available. This despite the fact that many leaders had already realised the real dangers that majoritarian politics now posed. However, Nehru continued his emphasis on the same political possibilities suggested by him prior to independence that lay outside the pale of representative politics of group representation. These were constitutional measures that would ensure 'confidence and goodwill' among minority religious communities.[83] A secular state was one such a solution:

> We have called our state a secular state, and there has been some misunderstanding of this, as if this was something opposed to religion or morality. Some misguided people in our country have even demanded something in the nature of a communal state here. But so far as this House is concerned and the vast majority of the people in our country, we have definitely adopted the idea of a secular state and we intend to adhere to it in full measure. This does not mean that religion ceases to be an important factor in private life of the individual. It means that the state and religion are not tied up together. It simply means the repetition of the cardinal doctrine of modern democratic practice that is the separation of the state from religion and the full protection of every religion....[84]

Such a state would not be anti-religious, it would indeed further Nehru's ideal of a 'composite nationality'.[85] This latter ideal itself was imbued with values of religious freedom and toleration that secularism sought to promote. The importance of pluralism and composite national culture for religious toleration is exemplified in one of the several reasons that Nehru gave regarding the 'Kashmir problem':

> Kashmir is going to be a drain on our resources, but it is going to be a greater drain on Pakistan.... The position however is this that even if we were somewhat weaker than we are, we cannot desert the people of Kashmir to whom we have given our pledge. Kashmir gives us an example of communal unity and cooperation. This has had a healthy effect in India....[86]

Given the Indian government's position on Kashmir today, a Nehruvian conception of nation and its relevance for Indian secularism shows the continued importance of Nehruvian thought today. Apart from declaring the separation of religion and state and providing constitutional safeguards to minority groups, what political safeguards did the Indian constitution provide? What was Nehru's political stance on the communal or minority question after independence? I now turn to

Nehru's engagement with the question of political rights of the religious and social minorities in India.

GROUP RIGHTS FOR RELIGIOUS MINORITIES AND THE SCs AND STs

The Constituent Assembly debates (1946–1949), wherein the content of sovereign India's constitution was deliberated upon and formed, was the founding moment for India's road to a secular liberal democracy. Before the first general election (1951–1952), the Constituent Assembly also acted as the interim legislature. During the Constituent Assembly debates, both the religious minorities and lower-caste groups were considered minorities, and their claims for cultural safeguards (like religious, cultural and educational rights) and political rights (like separate electorates, and reservation in legislative bodies, ministries, and the civil, military and judicial services of the government) were considered together. However, by the time the constitution was ratified in 1950, these claims had been separated.[87] Reservation in legislatures for religious minorities was abandoned. For the untouchables and tribal communities, now known as the SCs and the STs, reservation was retained temporarily for a limited period until these communities were deemed to have reached a level where they no longer required such support. The temporally limited validity of group-based political representation of SCs and STs in post-colonial Indian politics showed the lack the legitimacy wielded by the state policy of affirmative action.

When, in the draft constitution, political safeguards in the form of separate electorates and reservation of seats were eventually abandoned for Muslims and Christians, Nehru noted:

> I think that doing away with this reservation business is not only a good thing in itself, good for all concerned, more especially for the minorities, but psychologically too it is a very good move for the nation and the world. It shows that we are really sincere about this business of having a secular democracy.[88]

A secular democracy for Nehru could not be based on robust forms of representative politics that relied on mechanisms of group-based representation in legislatures because historical experience showed that it exacerbated social-psychological condition of people being differentiated on the basis of their communal identity. He was of the same view with regard to the provision of reservation for social minorities, that is, the SCs and the STs:

> I would like you to consider this business, whether it is reservation or any other kind of safeguard for the minority, objectively. There is some point in having a safeguard of this type or any other type where there is autocratic rule or foreign rule. As soon as you get something that can be called political democracy, then this kind of reservation, instead of helping the party to be safe-guarded and aided, is likely to turn against it....[89]

Nehru maintained that any kind of group-based political safeguard, such as reservation of seats in legislatures and government jobs, by a democratic state to its citizens was not a salubrious solution as it divided them on the basis of communal identities of caste and religion. In other words, in the arena of representative politics, a citizen was to be identified as an individual and not in terms of group identity. Nehru's disdain for identity-based politics in a democratic society led him to identify only that politics as secular which focused on social and political issues based on declared policies and programmes. Thus, he considered identity-based representative political safeguards, such as reservation of seats in legislatures as generally harmful for a secular democracy. By the time India was born as an independent nation-state, in the dominant political discourse, the term 'secular' signified the universal homogeneous category of the citizen, and 'communal' referred to any form of communitarian politics that focused on identitarian issues of caste and religion. A secular democracy was now increasingly identified with the universal category of the citizen. While Jha has suggested that in the course of the Constituent Assembly debates any notion of 'contempt for religion' was marginalised, scholars like Tejani and Bajpai, who have taken a longer historical view, show how group rights were limited in the making of the Indian constitution. According to Bajpai, the founding of the post-colonial Indian state marked 'a moment of containment' for group rights as the separation of the demands of religious and caste reservations led to an attenuation of the rights of religious minorities.[90] Tejani attests to this view and goes on to show how in the colonial era the term 'communal electorate' did not necessarily involve a pejorative meaning and signified a variety of groups and not just religious minorities.⁹¹ In rejecting political safeguards for religious minorities and attenuated political rights for the backward groups of the SCs and STs, a lot came to be expected from Nehruvian secularism in protecting the rights of minorities in the wake of growing identity politics, which, ultimately, it could not fulfil.

THE HINDU CODE BILL CONTROVERSY

After India's independence, under the chairmanship of the then law minister Ambedkar, in April 1948, the Hindu Code Bill was introduced in the parliament to reform and codify the Hindu personal law.[92] This Bill was debated extensively in the parliament between the years 1948–1951. According to Reba Som, Nehru was confident that the Hindu Code Bill would be easily passed following the easy acceptance of the Fundamental Rights resolution ensuring sex equality at the Karachi Congress in 1931 and, subsequently, by the constitution in 1947. In 1949, Nehru stated, 'We stand committed to the broad approach of the Bill as a whole and the Government will stand or fall on it.'[93] However, by the early 1950s, this initiative at social reform through the means of law was temporarily dropped due to considerable opposition to it in the parliament. Som remarks that in the course of these debates, Nehru 'painfully realized that while accepting the principle of sex equality on paper, there had been no serious contemplation of what it implied and hence the outburst on seeing the specific clauses of the Bill'.[94] As Ambedkar resigned from the post of law minister over the abandonment of the Bill in 1951, it was Nehru who reintroduced the Bill in the parliament after the Congress won the first general election. As a result, he came to be identified as the prominent leader supporting the passage of the Bill. The Hindu Code Bill was finally passed in the mid-1950s but only after it was broken up into four separate acts: the Hindu Marriage Act, 1955, the Hindu Succession Act, 1956, the Hindu Minority and Guardianship Act, 1956, and the Hindu Adoptions and Maintenance Act, 1956.[95]

The parliamentary stalemate on the passing of the Hindu Code Bill, which Nehru remarks was of 'dilatory nature', demonstrates the considerable influence that conservative and the right-wing members had both within and outside the Congress party.[96] The democratic norms and procedures, like a clause by clause discussion of this massive Bill in the parliament, resulted in both delaying and diluting the contents of this progressive Bill.[97] As there was considerable opposition to the passing of the Bill both 'in the House and in the country', Nehru explained to Ambedkar that if the Bill was passed by riding roughshod over majority opinion, there would be obstruction in the implementation of the Bill.[98] Whatever may be the criticisms against Nehru over his failure on the question of the Hindu Code Bill, it must be acknowledged the he did not think that codification and modernisation of religious law could be undertaken by disregarding majority opinion both within the parliament and outside it. In a 1951 presidential address, Nehru observed:

> In India, as elsewhere, we have these conflicts between reactionary and static elements and dynamic and progressive forces. Essentially it is on the economic plane, but it touches the social life of the people in many ways. Thus, the Hindu Code Bill, which has given rise to much argument, became a symbol of the conflict between progress and reaction in the social domain.... This [the Bill] was a spirit of liberation and of freeing our people, and more especially, our womenfolk from outworn customs and shackles that bound them. We cannot progress along one front and remain tied up on other fronts. We have, therefore, to keep in view this idea of integrated progress on all fronts, political, economic, and social. That progress cannot be based on a rejection of our past, out of which we have grown, nor can it be mere copying of what others do; it must be based on our genius and cultural inheritance....[99]

Despite the Bill's dilution as a result of parliamentary amendments to it, Nehru considered it a progressive step due to the 'spirit underlying the Bill', which sought women's liberation from 'outworn customs and shackles that bound them'.[100] What is revealing in Nehru's position on the Bill is that, while in the political and economic spheres he advocated overcoming pre-modern social formations like a village economy through large scale industrialisation,[101] in the social sphere, he sought changes through a gradual process of reform that needed to follow democratic procedures. In other words, it was Nehru's view that socio-cultural transformations could not be brought about through forced modernisation of religious law by the state. Part of the reason why Nehru thought reform of religious and cultural laws needed gradual reform instead of state imposed progressive laws is because he cherished religion's internal plurality and dynamism, which he thought could be marred by codification and homogenisation of religious laws by the modern state.

As we know, the Congress party was composed of both conservative and progressive elements. During the debates on the Hindu Code Bill, these contradictory ideological positions came in direct conflict with each other, making any progress on the Bill especially difficult. It must be noted here that the disagreement over the Bill was largely ideological. The recurrent objection that appeared from the conservative and right-wing parliamentary members through the years of debate was that the Hindu *shastras*[102] were hallowed by tradition, and any attempt to tamper with them was presumptuous and undesirable.[103] The Hindu Mahasabha, consistently in various meetings and resolutions, condemned the proposed reform as its members saw it subverting Hindu ideas, culture and religion. According to Som, they also feared that Nehru's ideological influence would be a menace to India's religious identity and bring about a 'Godless State'.[104] Writing in the 1990s, Partha Chatterjee claimed that the Hindu right has demonstrated a considerable shift in their political conception of Hindutva.[105] He argued that these groups are unlikely to pit themselves against the idea of a secular state – that is, anti-secular demands of the type seen during the debates on the Hindu Code Bill are not crucial to the political thrust or even the public appeal of their campaign. As such, Chatterjee raised doubts about whether secularism is 'an adequate, or even appropriate, ground on which to meet the political challenge of Hindu majoritarianism'.[106] He thus warned that there is a 'very real possibility of a Hindu right locating itself quite firmly within the domain of the modernising state and using all of the ideological resources of that state to lead the charge against people who do not conform to its version of the "national culture"'.[107] According to Chatterjee, from this position, the Hindu right can not only deflect accusations of being anti-secular but can even use the arguments for interventionist secularisation to promote intolerance and violence against minorities. The Hindu right's use of the modern state to further its exclusionary politics has sadly become a truism in Indian political life today. However, as we shall see in the following pages, Nehru's pluralist conception of Indian civilisation, along with his conception of a dynamic cultural life, provides political possibilities to offset such a danger. At the same time, however, Nehru's unreflective assumption of a continuous dynamic and tolerant culture, coupled with his lack of interest in social reform, diminished the possibility of a pluralist path that the modernising post-colonial Indian state could have adopted.

According to Narendra Subramanian, cosmopolitan and Hindu majoritarian discourses of the Indian nation have influenced family law in India. He argues that early post-colonial political elites with their Hindu majoritarian, as well as cosmopolitan and pluralist orientation, linked their vision and ideal of the universal Indian citizen with the project of changing the Hindu society. As a result, these political elites focused more on Hindu law than on the already existing secular laws, like the Special Marriage Act (SMA) or the minority laws. The SMA, notes Subramanian, appeared more compatible than the personal laws with the Indian state's professed secularism, as it did not apply to particular religious groups or draw overtly from religious norms. He remarks that couples who opted to be governed by this Act could indeed be considered forerunners of a secularised future. Although members of all religious groups could register their marriage under the SMA, it was the Hindu Code Bill that became the basis to reform Hindu society. The focus on Hindu law along with state's non-interference in minority religions, however, led to a public perception of Muslim appeasement by the state. Subramanian outlines the various reasons that the parliamentarians provided for their focus on Hindu law. First, many of them felt that as the executive and legislature were largely drawn from Hindus, it would be best for them to change Hindu law and leave changes in other family laws to the initiative of the concerned groups. Second, it was also argued that this focus was natural as Hindus accounted for the vast majority of the population. Third, some valued consolidation of Hindus and called it a goal of Hindu law reform. Fourth, some claimed that Hindus were ready for reform as opposed to other religious groups (especially Muslims). Fifth, some said that Hindu law was more backward than Muslim and Christian laws, and so particularly in need of reform. Sixth, the greater diversity of legally recognised customs among Hindus was considered a reason to prioritise the consolidation and codification of Hindu law.[108] This focus on Hindu law both as the object and reason for reform has led some scholars to conclude that when the Hindu Code Bill was finally passed in the mid1950s, the terms of reference had been altered. While initially it was supposed to be a step towards legal reform, it was later transformed into a grand project of modernisation of religious law, where Hindus as the majority community were to set an example in the interest of building a secular society.[109] The focus on Hindu law reform, as opposed to a common code, also led to resentment that the Muslim Personal Law remained untouched. The Mahasabha leaders, for instance, argued that the Hindu Code was, after all, a communal measure, and in order to give effect to the secular ideals, a uniform civil code should have been made instead.[110]

Subramanian identifies Nehru and Ambedkar as among those 'cosmopolitan nationalists' who were the most influential agents of early post-colonial family law.[111] He notes that the claim about the presence and representation of Hindus in the state machinery as a legitimating basis for Hindu law reform was made by these leaders. According to Subramanian, although secularists like Nehru and Ambedkar did not value Hindu solidarity, they nevertheless claimed that homogenisation of Hindu law would enable Indian solidarity. The consolidation of Hindu law, they claimed, was a step towards a UCC. But at the same time, they remained silent on the content of the UCC. Since secularists like Nehru and Ambedkar considered the reform of Hindu law as a means to 'form the citizen', they sought consolidation of Hindu law, which varied considerably until then by region and caste.[112] Modernists like Ambedkar also advanced an argument about uniformity in religious law, as he associated uniformity with modernity and effective state regulation. Subramanian points out that these features of family law policy were congruous with other policies introduced around the same time. For instance, Hindus belonging to the SCs were accorded preferential treatment in legislative bodies and special civil rights protections. But the same protection was not extended to lower castes who were considered non-Hindus, although there was ample evidence that this latter group faced much the same constraints and indignities as low-caste Hindus. It may be argued that one of the consequences this dominant cosmopolitan and Hindu majoritarian discourse that influenced religious laws has been that it aided in hardening the distinction between religious minority and social backwardness, a distinction not made in undivided British India. As such, while preferential treatment by the state was later extended to Sikh, Buddhist and Jain SCs, by provisions in law, minority religious groups like Muslims and Christians remained outside such consideration.[113] The distinction and separation of religious and social minorities that was sharpened and hardened during the Constituent Assembly debates, after India's independence, has been cemented through laws such as the 1950 Presidential Order.

In Subramanian's opinion, the state's efforts to reduce enduring inequalities focused on Hindus because it was influenced by an 'uneasy coexistence of majoritarian and pluralist outlooks' among the political elite.[114] He further notes that Ambedkar and Nehru differed in the relative importance they gave to statutes, texts of religious law and customs. Nehru was more open than Ambedkar to the recognition of customs, especially those of tribal groups. The pressures that tribal-group representatives exerted to maintain tribal customary law ensured that these groups were excluded from the purview of Hindu law statutes. The initial proposals, which faced strong opposition, were modified later in the 'eclectic ways' that Nehru favoured more than Ambedkar.[115] Nehru's openness to unwritten customary practices and preference for eclecticism emanated from his faith in the dynamism he attributed to Indian civilisation that in the past had led to 'cultural synthesis and fusion'.[116] Such being the basis of Indian culture, Nehru assumed that Indian society would easily absorb the prospective socio-legal changes. Thus, Som remarks, whereas Ambedkar dwelt on the static quality of Hindu society, Nehru was never tired of emphasising its dynamism: 'Hindu law had never been rigid', 'Hindu law had certain dynamic quality'.[117] Thus, with regard to Hindu law, in *The Discovery of India*, Nehru noted:

> The British replaced this elastic customary law by judicial decisions based on the old texts, and these decisions became precedents which had to be rigidly followed. That was, in theory, an advantage, as it produced greater uniformity and certainty. But, in the manner it was done, it resulted in the perpetuation of the ancient law unmodified by subsequent customs. Thus, the old law which, in some particulars [sic] and in various places, had been changed by custom and was thus out of date, was petrified, and every tendency to change it in the well-known customary way was suppressed. It was still open to a group to prove a custom overriding the law, but this was extraordinarily difficult in the law courts. Change could only come by positive legislation, but the British Government, which was the legislating authority, had no wish to antagonize the conservative elements on whose support it counted. When later some legislative powers were given to partially elected assemblies, every attempt to promote social reform legislation was frowned upon by the authorities and sternly discouraged.[118]

In Nehru's view, as Hindu law was largely based on custom, it was dynamic. As customs changed, societal customary law also changed and was applied in different ways to fit changing customs. However, it seems that Nehru assumed this inherent dynamism in Indian culture to be continuous and ceaseless with only intervening periods of stultification.[119] Unlike Gandhi, who, through his constructive work, sought to reform society and 'build up the nation from the very bottom upward',[120] social reform was never really an important aspect of Nehru's political vision. Modernist leaders like Nehru sought radical social change through the post-colonial 'transformative constitution' and therefore put faith in the modern state and the bureaucracy.[121] While Nehru believed that the plurality in India's religion and culture provided internal dynamism to them, he at the same time, did not sufficiently consider that such dynamism would also require efforts in social reform. In reviewing the effect of the reformed Hindu law, Som argues that unlike customary law, which had been simple, inexpensive and geared to local requirements, the separate Acts had nuances which were never fully explained or understood at the local level. Furthermore, she notes that in many cases, those guilty of violating the laws could not be easily brought to book as the offence was very often not cognisable, as in the case of the Child Marriage Restraint Act, 1929. Thus, Som remarks that Nehru's victory in reforming the Hindu law was largely 'symbolic'.[122] This was as much conceded by Nehru: '... they are not in any way revolutionary in the changes they bring about and yet there is something revolutionary about them. They have broken the barrier of ages and cleared the way somewhat for our womenfolk to progress.'[123]

CONCLUSION

In this chapter, I highlighted the varied political positions that Nehru took on religion's relation to state and society in pre- and post-independence India. If Nehru had any disdain for religion's involvement in politics, it was challenged in his engagement with Indian politics. Early in his political career, and prior to partition, Nehru did not consider religion's involvement in politics manifested in the problem of communalism a real political issue. By the late 1930s, however, with increasing polarisation and politicisation of religion, he had to reconsider his political position regarding the state's relationship to religion. Moreover, by the 1940s, as the question of a secular state itself came to be questioned in the form of the demand for Pakistan, it became a historical necessity to elaborate upon a conception of political secularism that sought separation of state and religion. In Nehru's political thought and action, this took the shape in extending expansive religious and cultural rights to minority religious communities in the post-colonial state. Nehru's discomfort with religion's involvement in politics was visible in his political position with regards to the question of mechanisms of representative politics. He assumed that any involvement of religion in representative politics would lead to religion's politicisation, which, in turn, would hinder the formation of a 'secular' citizen. An effect of rejecting political safeguards for religious minorities and attenuated political rights for the backward groups of the SCs and STs has been that democratic practices have not sufficiently aided in promoting liberal values of freedom and equality. As today a major threat to secularism comes from growing Hindu majoritarianism, there is a need to seriously reconsider the relationship between the practice of political secularism and the ideal of a secular democracy.

Towards the end of her biography on Nehru's political life, Brown remarked:

> Of the many ironies in Nehru's life, one was the association of a young man fired by a left-wing and secular vision of a new India with a figure who was an icon of Hinduism, deeply rooted in Indian tradition and committed primarily to moral renewal.[124]

This irony that describes Nehru is also his resolution of religion's place and role – first, in the secular-nationalist movement and, later, in a liberal democratic secular polity. In Chapter 4, I argued that in Nehru's reconstruction of Indian history, its culture and philosophy are shown as both predominantly secular and inherently pluralistic. He considered these two qualities to be a dominant feature of ancient Indian civilisation, as opposed to the presence of transcendent and the supernatural elements in ancient religions. In Nehru's retelling, with the coming of the Mughals in the subcontinent, there was also a gradual process of intermixing between the cultures of these foreign conquerors with the existing indigenous culture. Through this gradual process of 'synthesis of thought and ways of living', a composite culture developed, which has been responsible for much of India's tolerant past.[125] Nehru saw the continued presence of this composite culture in the subcontinent – in Kashmir, 'the life and vigour and beauty of the present',[126] and in the United Provinces of Agra and Oudh, the 'heart of Hindustan'[127] – as an affirmation that this is what truly defined Indian culture and civilisation. The tolerance that this pluralist and composite culture produced was both a mark of pride for a nationalist like Nehru and an effective tool to resolve communal and sectarian issues in contemporary India. The two chapters on Nehru (Chapters 4 and 5) together hopefully demonstrate that while Nehru's idea of composite and tolerant cultures visible in his nationalist narrative of secularity opened up possibilities, his reluctance over religion's involvement in political life also led to closures. Furthermore, Nehru's unreflective belief in the continuation of traditions of tolerance, reflected in cultural synthesis as being an inherent trait of Indian civilisation, led him justify and deny the resolution of the minority or communal question in the political domain of representation. At the same time, the assumption of dynamism that he attributed to composite cultures inclined him towards the idea of religion's reform from within. Such being Nehru's conception of Indian history, culture and society, instead of an active intervention of a modernising state to reform religions, a supporting role of the state in the form of socio-legal reforms seemed a desirable solution. In a country with a dominant Hindu majority, the state was to intervene in reforming minority religions when its communities were 'ready' for it. It may be argued that this vision of Nehru's secularity influenced how Indian secularism came to be conceived and practised in post-independence India, and how it can be differentiated from aggressive forms of secularism practised in Kemalist Turkey, or modern-day France or much of post-Soviet East European countries. Nehru's conception of a dynamic, pluralist and composite culture provided the political possibility to offset uniformity and homogenisation of religions and cultures that are demanded by the driving ideologies of a modern state. To the dismay of many modernists and secularists, the fate of a uniform civil code for all Indians was resigned to the directives for the state, but in doing that the secular constitution of India left open the possibility for pluralist traditions to develop an Indian secularity.

NOTES

1. Nehru's writings are accessed from Jawaharlal Nehru, *Selected Works of Jawaharlal Nehru*, series 1 and 2, ed. Sarvepalli Gopal (electronic book)

(henceforth *SWJN* (1) and *SWJN* (2)). New Delhi: Nehru Memorial Museum and Library, http://nehruportal.nic.in/writings (accessed on 1 October 2021).
2. Jawaharlal Nehru, 'The Solution to India's Problems', Presidential Address to the Indian National Congress, Lucknow, 12 April 1936, in *Jawaharlal Nehru, An Anthology*, ed. Sarvepalli Gopal, pp. 296–302 (Delhi: Oxford University Press, 1980), p. 299.
3. Sunil Khilnani, 'Nehru's Judgement', in *Political Judgement*, ed. Richard Bourke and Raymond Guess, pp. 254–278 (New York: Cambridge University Press, 2009), p. 257.
4. Ibid.
5. In 1924, Nehru stated, 'Personally I said I was for complete independence. I am against the idea of empire and of one country forcibly ruling another.' Nehru, *SWJN (1)*, vol. 2, p. 197.
6. As per the Government of India Act 1919, in 1927, the next wave of constitutional reforms began with the Simon Commission, which was to review India's political development towards future self-government.
7. See Gandhi's letter to Nehru, 17 January 1928, and Nehru's reply to it, 23 January 1928, in *Together They Fought: Gandhi–Nehru Correspondence 1921–1948*, ed. Uma Iyengar and Lalitha Zackariah (New Delhi: Oxford University Press, 2011), pp. 55–59.
8. Judith M. Brown, *Nehru: A Political Life* (New Delhi: Oxford University Press, 2004), p.78.
9. In 1923, when Nehru got elected to the Allahabad Municipal Board, he reminded UP Congressmen not to forget that their goal was political independence: 'Let us be careful that we do not forget this or else our capturing municipalities will become a curse to us rather than a blessing.' Nehru quoted from Brown, *Nehru*, p. 78.
10. For differences between elite national politics and the mass movements of the subaltern groups, see Ranajit Guha, 'On Some Aspects of the Historiography of Colonial India', in *Subaltern Studies 1: Writings on South Asian History and Society*, ed. Ranajit Guha, pp. 1–8 (Delhi: Oxford University Press,1982).
11. For instance, see Nehru, *SWJN (1)*, vol.3, p. 224–225.
12. For a detailed analysis on how Muslims came to be regarded as communal minorities from an earlier perception of a distinct religious community, see Shabnum Tejani, *Indian Secularism: A Social and Intellectual History 1890–1950* (Ranikhet: Permanent Black, 2007), ch. 3.

13. Rochana Bajpai, *Debating Difference: Group Rights and Liberal Democracy in India* (New Delhi: Oxford University Press, 2011), p. 32.
14. Ibid.
15. For debates on group-differentiated rights within India's liberal democratic framework, see Bajpai, *Debating Difference*; and Gurpreet Mahajan, *The Multicultural Path: Issues of Diversity and Discrimination in Democracy* (New Delhi: SAGE Publications, 2002). For a detailed analysis of the same in relation to secularism, see Tejani, *Indian Secularism*.
16. Both Gandhi and Nehru saw the Congress as representing all Indians. In the Round Table Conference on communal electorates, Gandhi said, 'Congress is only one of the many parties that are said to be represented here. The organic fact, however, is that it is the only representative body speaking for the vast masses in India.' M. K. Gandhi, 'Speech at Birmingham Meeting', 18 October 1931, *CWMG*, vol. 54, p. 45.
17. The first census of 1872 classified Indians according to their religious identity. Subject to the practice of untouchability, successive censuses brought together the myriad caste groups into a single all-India category of Depressed Classes. This created the basis for the latter group for subsequent political mobilisation as untouchables. See Bajpai, *Debating Difference*.
18. Ibid., p. 41.
19. Jawaharlal Nehru, *The Discovery of India* (Delhi: Oxford University Press, 1994 [1946]), p. 384.
20. The League was formed in December 1906, the same year when the debates over electoral reforms began.
21. Ambedkar came from the Mahar caste – the largest caste of untouchables in Maharashtra.
22. The word 'untouchable' was used for those members of the Hindu caste system who were deemed lowest members in the caste hierarchy and also those deemed to be outside the fourfold *varna* scheme.
23. The Nehru report of 1928 (the committee was headed by Motilal Nehru), delineating the Congress's position on constitutional reform, denounced special representation. This report is generally seen as the 'parting of ways' between the Congress and minority parties. Until 1920s, however, it was not uncommon to be members of both the Congress and the League. Jinnah was member of the League and the Congress until the end of 1920. See Bajpai, *Debating Difference*.

24. Gyanendra Pandey, *The Construction of Colonialism in Colonial North India* (Delhi: Oxford University Press, 1997 [1990]), p. 235.
25. Nehru, *Discovery*, p. 382.
26. Hugh F. Owen, 'Negotiating the Lucknow Pact', *Journal of Asian Studies* 31, no. 3 (1972): 561–587.
27. For an argument about how the term 'communal' transformed into a pathological condition which described tensions between Hindus and Muslims in mid 1920s, see Tejani, *Indian Secularism*; and Pandey, *Construction of Colonialism*, ch. 1.
28. Quoted from Pandey, *Construction of Colonialism*, p. 9.
29. Tejani, *Indian Secularism*, p. 179.
30. Ibid, p. 23.
31. Gandhi quoted in Pandey, *Construction of Communalism*, p. 233.
32. For Nehru's reasons for complete independence from the British rule, see for instance, The Congress Election Manifesto, 1937, drafted by Nehru in *SWJN (1)*, vol. 7, pp. 459–464. Also see Nehru's draft manifesto for the Central assembly elections written in 1945 in *SWJN (1)*, vol. 14, pp. 105–109.
33. Nehru, *SWJN (1)*, vol. 3, pp. 225–226.
34. Nehru, *Discovery*, p. 382.
35. See the previous chapter for a detailed discussion of the same. Also see Jawaharlal Nehru, 'Synthesis Is Our Tradition', *Jawaharlal Nehru, An Anthology*, ed. Sarvepalli Gopal, pp. 225–230 (Delhi: Oxford University Press, 1980). For a critical engagement with the notion of composite culture in the Indian subcontinent, see Javeed Alam, 'The Composite Culture and Its Historiography', *South Asia: Journal of South Asian Studies* 22, no. 1 (1999): 29–37.
36. Nehru, *SWJN (1)*, vol. 3, p. 226.
37. Ibid., 226–227. Also see Nehru, *SWJN (1)*, vol. 4, p. 260; and Jawaharlal Nehru, 'The Aims of Congress', *Jawaharlal Nehru, An Anthology*, ed. Sarvepalli Gopal, pp. 80–84 (Delhi: Oxford University Press, 1980 [1929]), pp. 81–82.
38. Nehru, *SWJN (1)*, vol. 3, p. 226.
39. Jawaharlal Nehru, 'Congress and Communalism', in *The Oxford India Nehru*, ed. Uma Iyengar, pp. 239–242 (New Delhi: Oxford University Press, 2007), pp. 240–241.
40. Jawaharlal Nehru, 'Untouchability', in *Jawaharlal Nehru, an Anthology*, ed. Sarvepalli Gopal, pp. 79–80 (Delhi: Oxford University Press, 1980 [1928]), p. 79.

41. Nehru, *SWJN* (1), vol. 6, p. 164.
42. Consider Nehru's own admission: 'For a long time past I had remained quiet on the subject [communal problem] because I wished to ignore this aspect of Indian public life and hoped that national activities would gradually divert people's attention from it.' Nehru, *SWJN* (1), vol. 6, p. 158.
43. Judith Shklar, 'The Liberalism of Fear', in *Political Liberalism: Variations on a Theme*, ed. Shaun P. Young, pp. 149–166 (Albany: State University of New York Press, 2004 [1989]).
44. Ibid., p. 164.
45. Ibid., p. 155.
46. Partha Chatterjee, 'Secularism and Tolerance', in *Secularism and Its Critics*, ed. Rajeev Bhargava, pp. 345–379 (New Delhi: Oxford University Press, 2008 [1998]).
47. For instance, see the debates on Muslim Personal Law vis-à-vis the demand for a Uniform Civil Code.
48. Nehru, 'Congress and Communalism', pp. 240–241. Also see Nehru, *Discovery*, p. 383.
49. Nehru, *Discovery*, p. 382.
50. Nehru, *SWJN* (1), vol. 8, p. 120.
51. Nehru, *Discovery*, p. 383.
52. Ibid., p. 355.
53. Ibid.
54. See Bajpai, *Debating Difference*.
55. Ibid.
56. Tejani, *Indian Secularism*, p. 23.
57. For instance, see the criticism of Mahasabha leaders like M. R. Jayakar and Madan Mohan Malaviya against separate electorates in Tejani, *Indian Secularism*.
58. Mahasabha leader, M. R. Jayakar, quoted in Tejani, *Indian Secularism*, p. 178.
59. Nehru, *Discovery*, p. 355.
60. Khilnani, 'Nehru's Judgement', pp. 267–268.
61. Sarvepalli Gopal, 'Nehru and Minorities', *Economic and Political Weekly* 23, no. 45–47 (1988): 2463–2466, at p. 2465.
62. Mushirul Hasan, 'The Muslim Mass Contact Campaign: An Attempt at Political Mobilisation', *Economic and Political Weekly* 21, no. 52 (1986): 2273–2282, at p. 2279.

63. Nehru, *SWJN* (1), vol. 8: 122–123.
64. Ibid.
65. Ibid.
66. Nehru, *SWJN* (1), vol. 7: 277.
67. Ibid.
68. Nehru said, 'We have lost faith in the old style all parties conferences, in a few persons, representing communal organisations with no common political background.... We have had enough experience of these in the past, and that experience does not call for repetition.' Nehru quoted in Hasan, 'The Muslim Mass Contact Campaign', p. 2274.
69. Nehru, *SWJN* (1), vol. 8, p. 123.
70. Like the Urdu newsweekly, *Hindustan*.
71. Venkat Dhulipala, *Creating a New Medina: State Power, Islam, and the Quest for Pakistan in Late Colonial North India* (Delhi: Cambridge University Press, 2015), p. 52.
72. Ashraf, a dedicated communist, joined the Congress Socialist party before joining the AICC office in 1936. Ashraf was a Meo from Alwar, a community which was famous for being neither fully Muslim nor Hindu, borrowing from the traditions and practices of both these religious communities. Before taking to communism as a young man, Ashraf had been a devout Muslim and in the habit of saying his prayers regularly and keeping fasts. See Dhulipala, *Creating a New Medina*.
73. Hasan, 'The Muslim Mass Contact Campaign', p. 2274.
74. Dhulipala, *Creating a New Medina*, p. 65.
75. Ibid., note 35. For a criticism of this new secular nationalist historiography, see Pandey, *Construction of Communalism*, especially ch. 7. According to Pandey, the new nationalist appeal to history was based on a binary opposition between nationalism and communalism that was set up in the 1920s.
76. Hasan, 'The Muslim Mass Contact Campaign', p. 2279.
77. Jawaharlal Nehru, 'Muslim Population in India', in *The Oxford India Nehru*, ed. Uma Iyengar, pp. 303–306 (New Delhi: Oxford University Press, 2007 [1947]), pp. 304–306. The Congress Working Committee issued a statement on 24 September 1947, assuring the implementation of the following promises: abolition of separate electorates and elections on the basis of joint electorates, reservation of seats for the different recognised minorities on the basis of their population, and safeguards and non-justiciable principles to the fundamental rights.

78. Nehru, *Discovery*, p. 265.
79. Nehru, 'Muslim Population in India', pp. 304–306. Also see Jawaharlal Nehru, 'Pakistan and the Indian States', in *The Essential Writings of Jawaharlal Nehru*, vol. 1, ed. Sarvepalli Gopal and Uma Iyengar, pp. 171–175 (New Delhi: Oxford University Press, 2003 [1948]), pp. 172–175.
80. Nehru, *Discovery*, p. 58.
81. Shefali Jha, 'Secularism in the Constituent Assembly Debates, 1946–1950', *Economic and Political Weekly* 37, no. 30 (2002): 3175–3180, at p. 3180.
82. Rajeev Bhargava, 'What is Secularism For?' in *Secularism and Its Critics*, ed. Rajeev Bhargava, 486–555 (New Delhi: Oxford University Press, 2008 [1998]).
83. Nehru, 'Congress and Communalism', pp. 240–241.
84. Ibid., p. 361.
85. Brown, *Nehru*, p. 177.
86. Nehru, *SWJN* (2), vol. 4, p. 347.
87. Jha 'Secularism in the Constituent Assembly Debates'; Tejani, *Indian Secularism*; Bajpai, *Debating Difference*.
88. Nehru quoted in Jha, 'Secularism in the Constituent Assembly Debates', p. 3179. Also see Jawaharlal Nehru, *Jawaharlal Nehru's Speeches*, vol. 1, September 1946–May 1949 (Delhi: Publications Division [Ministry of Broadcasting and Information], Government of India Press, 1967 [1949]), p. 77.
89. Jawaharlal Nehru, 'Reservations for Backward Groups', Speech in the Constituent Assembly, 26 May 1949, *Oxford India Nehru*, p. 355. Also see, Jawaharlal Nehru, 'Politics and Religion', in *Jawaharlal Nehru's Speeches*, vol. 1, September 1946–May 1949, pp. 73–78 (Delhi: Publications Division [Ministry of Broadcasting and Information], Government of India Press, 1967 [1949]).
90. Bajpai, 'Introduction', in *Debating Difference*, p. 1.
91. Tejani, *Indian Secularism*.
92. The precursor to the Hindu Code Bill was the Hindu Law Committee formed prior to India's independence in 1941. It is also known as the Rau Committee.
93. Nehru quoted by Reba Som, 'Jawaharlal Nehru and the Hindu Code Bill: A Victory of Symbol Over Substance', *Modern Asian Studies* 28, no. 1 (1994): 165–194, at p. 181.
94. Ibid.

95. For a detailed examination of the history, reform and codification of Hindu Personal Law, and the controversy around the Hindu Code Bill, see Narendra Subramanian, *Nation and Family: Personal Law, Cultural Pluralism, and Gendered Citizenship in India* (Stanford, CA: Stanford University Press, 2014).
96. Nehru, *SWJN* (2), vol. 10, p. 325.
97. 'We have had one speech lasting four hours on a particular clause of a Bill'. Jawaharlal Nehru, 4 October 1951, *Letters to Chief Ministers, 1950–1952*, vol. 2, ed. G. Parthasarthy (New Delhi: Government of India, 1986), p. 500.
98. Nehru, *SWJN* (2), vol. 10, p. 326.
99. Jawaharlal Nehru, 'Moulding Our Destiny', Presidential Address, 57th Session of India National Congress, New Delhi, 18 October 1951, in *Oxford India Nehru*, p. 384.
100. Ibid.
101. See Chapter 4 for a discussion on Nehru's idea of modernity.
102. *Shastra* is a general term which refers to a large body of Hindu scriptures.
103. Som, 'Nehru and the Hindu Code'.
104. A member of Hindu Mahasabha in the Lok Sabha, quoted in Som, 'Nehru and the Hindu Code', p. 174.
105. The ideological position of right-wing Hindu groups that calls for cultural and political domination of Hindus. The term was coined by V. D. Savarkar in 1923.
106. Chatterjee, 'Secularism and Tolerance', p. 345.
107. Ibid.
108. Narendra Subramanian, 'Making Family and Nation: Hindu Marriage Law in Early Postcolonial India', *The Journal of Asian Studies* 69, no. 3 (2010): 771–798. Also see Subramanian, *Nation and Family*.
109. Jivanta Schoettli, *Vision and Strategy in Indian Politics: Jawaharlal Nehru's Policy Choices and the Designing of Political Institutions* (Oxon: Routledge, 2011).
110. Som, 'Nehru and the Hindu Code'.
111. Subramanian, 'Making Family and Nation', p. 777.
112. Ibid.
113. See the Constitution (Scheduled Castes) Order, 1950, also known as the 1950 Presidential Order, published by the Ministry of Law Notification No. S.R.O. 385, 1950, Gazette of India, Extraordinary, 1950, Part II, Section 3, p. 163.

114. Subramanian, 'Making Family and Nation', p. 778.
115. Ibid., p. 786.
116. Nehru, *Discovery*, p. 73.
117. Nehru quoted in Som, 'Nehru and the Hindu Code', p. 187.
118. Nehru, *Discovery*, p. 330.
119. See Nehru's *Discovery* for such a view.
120. M. K. Gandhi, *Constructive Programme: Its Meaning and Place* (Ahmedabad: Navajivan Trust, 1945 [1941]), p. 2.
121. Sandipto Dasgupta, 'Legalizing the Revolution', PhD dissertation, Columbia University, 2014. Dasgupta has argued that the Indian constitution differed from the French and the American constitution in that the Indian national leaders sought social transformation through a constitutional path rather than seeing the constitution itself as providing the imprimatur for the completion of a revolution. Also see Gautam Bhatia, *The Transformative Constitution: A Radical Biography in Nine Acts* (Noida: HarperCollins, 2019).
122. Som, 'Nehru and the Hindu Code', p. 191.
123. Nehru quoted in Ibid.
124. Brown, *Nehru*, p. 339.
125. Nehru, *Discovery*, p. 257.
126. Ibid., p. 51
127. Ibid., p. 58

CONCLUSION

On the idea of India, nationalist slogans, like 'unity in diversity' and *sarva dharma samabhava*, brought together the varied philosophy and politics of nationalist leaders like M. K. Gandhi and Jawaharlal Nehru. Despite their distinctive epistemology and politics, Gandhian and Nehruvian narratives came together on the question of the design of the new nation-state. Post-colonial India was to be an 'unnational'[1] and secular state based on religious plurality and religious non-discrimination. What is the relationship that Gandhi and Nehru envisaged among religion, state and society under conditions of (colonial) modernity? In this book, I pursued this question to demonstrate how these prominent national leaders influenced and contributed to the discourse of secularity in modern and contemporary India. I also considered clichéd slogans and phrases, such as the Gandhi–Nehru tradition, *sarva dharma samabhava* and 'unity in diversity', as central to India's social imaginary of secularity in order to address the issue of understanding narratives of secularity in its historical context. Gandhi and Nehru are prominently seen to exemplify modern India's secular ideal, but puzzlingly, they are also considered as the epitome of traditionalism and modern Western secularity, respectively. Thus, both leaders are often invoked to defend or decry the value of secularism in contemporary India. How can Gandhi and Nehru's vision be secular and Indian, but also expressed in traditional and Western terms, such that the former's ideas and ideals are a storehouse for religious tolerance and alternatives to secularism, and the latter's vision is seen as an influence on Indian secularism, as well as its derivativeness? I sought to unravel this puzzle, apart from showing the points of affinity and departure from the

Western construal of the secular and its cognates. The goal was to show that a serious theoretical reflection on Gandhian and Nehruvian thought and politics would bring to relief the varied narratives of secularity that have influenced debates on secularity in contemporary India.

Two distinctive narratives of secularity emerged in Gandhian and Nehruvian political thought and practice, which together influenced India's secular imaginary as expressed in the Gandhi–Nehru tradition, and idea(l)s of *sarva dharma samabhava* and 'unity in diversity'. The first secularity narrative, found in Gandhian thought and practice, I argued, evinces a counter-narrative to secularisation and secularity, and yet it does not stand in opposition to a liberal conception of political secularism understood as a value-based ideal which seeks religious non-discrimination by the state. Such an observation, I believe, can have serious theoretical and practical implications for the relative independence of the cognates of the secular. Chapters 2 and 3 focused on Gandhi's political thought and practice and demonstrated how the Gandhian holistic vision of society does not elicit an adversarial position towards political secularism. This may be seen as an important insight about Indian secularity vis-à-vis debates on the global intellectual history in secularity. While narratives of secularity in the Western world (Euro-America) have shown that the 'secular age' may have been unique to that region,[2] the debates in the Arab world have demonstrated that although Islamic reformism generally rejected secularism, it articulated a conception of secularity within Islam.[3] The dominant narratives of secularity in modern India, by contrast, not only articulated holistic visions of society (that is, a counter-narrative to secularity) but also did not reject a secular state for independent India.

A central claim in Chapter 2 is that Gandhi understood religion through multiple values that the notion of *ahimsa* (non-violence) connoted for him, like truth and non-violence, love, compassion and social service. As a result of this capacious understanding of religion, Gandhi did not think, at least in the early part of the twentieth century, that religion required the support of the doctrine of secularism to maintain a tolerant society. Chapter 2 thus demonstrated how and why Gandhi's religion could not be separated from his politics. In this chapter, I elaborated upon Gandhi's conception of religion by making a conceptual distinction between religion as 'faith' and religion as the 'discovery' of the absolute truth, seen as attainable through a practice of ethical living. I argued that while religious faith required unquestioning abidance of the faithful, religion as ethical living was based on experimentation, and it was demonstrated in exemplary living. I noted that both these overlapping ideas of religion as faith and ethical living were essential to Gandhi's notion of religion and were practised in the *ashram*. The *satyagrahi ashramite* was simultaneously the embodiment of ethical living and exemplary action. Gandhi's religious faith also involved spiritual activities, such as spinning, fasting, praying and celibacy, which had sociopolitical significance. These activities sought to cultivate values and attitudes such as patience, self-knowledge, self-discipline and sacrifice, which Gandhi considered as essential to engage in non-violent politics. Chapter 3 followed upon these arguments and further demonstrated how in Gandhi's politics, religion was essential to conduct politics based on the principles of *ahimsa*. In that chapter, I distinguished between two types of religious politics: religion *in* politics and politics *of* religion to argue how Gandhi's religious politics was far apart from ethno-nationalist and exclusionary politics, such as communalism, which also involve religion in politics.

In both the chapters on Gandhi, I also noted how an elaboration of the idea of secularism in contemporary India as *sarva dharma samabhava*, that is, equal respect for all religions, by political actors makes the discourse of secularity very complex. This indigenous construal of secularism as equality of all religions is associated with the notion of tolerance, where India's long tradition of peaceful co-existence of diverse communities is seen as a justification for the practice of secularism in contemporary India.[4] This justificatory vocabulary, however, can easily slip into arguments of the superiority of Hinduism vis-à-vis other religions because it can be claimed that Hinduism inherently values religious diversity and accommodates difference. Furthermore, in these arguments on tolerance, religious differences may be subsumed in notions of syncretic traditions and composite cultures that exhibit qualities of assimilation and synthesis of religions and cultures. The discussions on Gandhi's notion of religious tolerance, however, demonstrated that his perfunctory narrative of Indian history could easily be placed within a communal historiography with his emphasis on absolute and unassimilable religious difference. The point of this observation was to argue that, in Gandhi's political thought, the basis of tolerance cannot be found in the already existing tradition of tolerance in the subcontinent, as exhibited in nationalist arguments of composite cultures. Rather, I argued that Gandhi sought societal tolerance by simultaneously engaging in three forms of associationalism in the sociopolitical field through which tolerance was to be *forged* in society. I argued that it is in these associational activities in the social and political sphere where Gandhi saw the political possibility of forging equality and unity among various communities without subsuming difference and diversity to these ideals.

A very different narrative of secularity emerged in Nehru's political thought and practice. In Chapter 4 on Nehruvian secularity, I argued that Nehru's notion of secularity should be seen within the framework of liberal secularism, where it is not only desirable to separate religion and politics but also possible. However, this observation should not lead us to assume that Nehru sought an anti-religious secular state in independent India. In this chapter, I argued that Nehru cherished and valued India's religious and cultural diversity, which he thought needed constitutional protection. His political vision, where religious and cultural diversity were seen as an asset and not a hindrance to national unity, may have influenced the Indian constitution, which exhibited values of multiculturalism at a time when it was not common to imagine the nation-state in those terms. The chapter went on to identify two strands of arguments in Nehru's conception of secularity. One argument, I argued, can be located in Nehru's nationalist narrative about its cultural familiarity and suitability for the Indian society. The other argument, I maintained, relies on the origin and success of secularity in the West, where its secular-humanist ideals gave it universal validity. Because secular-humanist ideals animated Western secularity, it not only needed emulation but was indeed desirable. I called the first secularity narrative 'nationalist' and the second 'humanist-universal', and argued that both these strands of arguments were brought together by Nehru to construct a narrative of Indian secularity and to also argue that secularity as such is an universalisable ideal.

The last chapter, on Nehru, examined how he put his ideas into political practice. I evaluated Nehru's politics by focusing on the communal or minority question and the Muslim mass contact campaign in colonial India, and the question of group rights for minorities, and the Hindu Code Bill controversy in post-colonial India. On the issue of communal or minority question in colonial India, I argued that during the 1920s and 1930s, Nehru deemed group-based representative politics of separate electorates as politics of communalism. In his view, the minority question could be solved through a two-pronged approach of state-led economic development and constitutional safeguards for minority communities.

However, with growing politicisation of religion, by the late 1930s Nehru modified his political opinion on religion's relation to politics. From the late 1930s onwards, Nehru's political philosophy reflected, what has been called, 'the liberalism of fear', where constitutional rights are not assumed as equally given to every citizen; rather, they need to be actively safeguarded by the state. It is in this changed political context, as well as the shift in Nehru's opinion, that one should understand his politics and support for a secular state in post-independence India. Nehru's political project of increasing contact with the Muslim masses in 1937 should be seen as his solution to the minority question and an answer to the communal politics of separate electorates, which he unequivocally rejected. However, the paucity of Nehruvian politics of 'liberalism of fear'[5] was revealed in post-colonial India, when identity-based politics started to assert itself in the 1980s. Nehruvian secularism does not possess adequate resources to respond to electoral politics based on majoritarianism and issues raised by identity politics. Finally, on the Hindu Code Bill controversy, what is revealing about Nehru's position on the Bill is that he did not believe that sociocultural transformations could be brought about in society by disregarding democratic norms and procedures and by forcing modernisation of religious law by the state. Since Nehru cherished religion's internal plurality and dynamism, he thought that codification of religious laws by the state would arrest the dynamic qualities of religion and culture. That modernists like Nehru did not seek to impose a single or uniform Indian identity upon the new nation is visible in the relegation of the uniform civil code to the directive principles of the state.

In this book, I examined the Gandhi–Nehru tradition of secularity without relegating either of the national leaders, who lent their names to this tradition, to a seamless and monochromatic position of tradition or modernity, where they are necessarily opposed doctrinal positions. I also attempted to engage in a discursive field, where one examines embedded concepts and ideas, such as secularity, in their proper historical and cultural context to show how they are engaged with by indigenous actors both combatively and creatively. As such, the aim in this book was not to search for the authentic or the indigenous, or to reveal the derivativeness of embedded ideas, but to engage with the global intellectual history of secularity in a way which may illuminate a comparative study in social and political theory.

NOTES

1. Rajendra Prasad quoted from Faisal Devji, *Muslim Zion: Pakistan as a Political Idea* (London: Harvard University Press, 2013), p. 30.
2. Charles Taylor, *A Secular Age* (Cambridge, MA: Harvard University Press, 2007).
3. Florian Zemmin, 'Secularism, Secularity and Islamic Reformism', in *Companion to the Study of Secularity*, ed. Humanities Centre of Advanced Studies (HCAS) 'Multiple Secularities: Beyond the West, Beyond Modernities', Leipzig University, 2019, pp. 1–14.
4. As opposed to secularism being considered as separation of religion and politics and expressed in state neutrality.
5. Judith Shklar, 'The Liberalism of Fear', in *Political Liberalism: Variations on a Theme*, ed. Shaun P. Young, pp. 149–166 (Albany: State University of New York Press, 2004 [1989]).

BIBLIOGRAPHY

PRIMARY DOCUMENTS

LAWS AND CASES

Dr. Ramesh Yeshwant Prabhoo v. Prabhakar K. Kunte, AIR (1996) SC 1113.
Manohar Joshi v. N. B. Patil, AIR (1996) 796.
The Constitution (Scheduled Castes) Order, 1950.

M. K. GANDHI'S WRITINGS

Gandhi, M. K. 1968 (1928). 'Satyagraha in South Africa', translated by Valji Govindji Desai. In *The Selected Works of Mahatma Gandhi*, vol. 2, edited by Shriman Narayan, pp. 1–312. Ahmedabad: Navajivan Trust.
———. 1932. *From Yeravda Mandir*. Ahmedabad: Navajivan Trust.
———. 1945 (1941). *Constructive Programme: Its Meaning and Place*. Ahmedabad: Navajivan Trust.
———. 1940. *An Autobiography or the Story of My Experiments with Truth*, translated by Mahadev Desai. Ahmedabad: Navajivan Trust.
———. 1955. *Ashram Observance in Action*, translated by Valji Govind Desai. Ahmedabad: Navajivan Trust.
———. 2009 (1997). 'Indian Home Rule or Hind Swaraj', translated by M. K. Gandhi. In *M.K. Gandhi: Hind Swaraj and Other Writings*, edited by Anthony J. Parel, pp. 1–125. Cambridge: Cambridge University Press.

JAWAHARLAL NEHRU'S WRITINGS

Nehru, Jawaharlal. 1941. *Toward Freedom: The Autobiography of Jawaharlal Nehru*. New York: The John Day Company.

———. 1982 (1936). *An Autobiography*. New Delhi: Oxford University Press.

———. 1994 (1946). *The Discovery of India*. Delhi: Oxford University Press.

———. 2004 (1934–1935). *Glimpses of World History: Being Further Letters to His Daughter, Written in Prison, and Containing a Rambling Account of History for Young People*. New Delhi: Penguin.

COLLECTED WORKS, BIOGRAPHIES, AND NEWSPAPER AND MAGAZINE ARTICLES

Ambedkar, B. R. 2014 (1936). 'Annihilation of Caste: Speech Prepared for the Annual Conference of the Jat-Pat-Todak Mandal of Lahore but Not Delivered'. In *Annihilation of Caste: The Annotated Critical Edition*, edited by S. Anand, pp. 181–356. London: Verso.

———. 1999 (1933). 'Appendix X: Discussion with B. R. Ambedkar', 4 February 1933. In *The Collected Works of Mahatma Gandhi* (CWMG), vol. 59. New Delhi: Government of India.

Anand, S. (ed.). 2016 (2014). *Annihilation of Caste: The Annotated Critical Edition*. London: Verso.

Bhattacharya, Sabyasachi (ed.). 1997. *The Mahatma and the Poet: Letters and Debates between Gandhi and Tagore 1915–1941*. New Delhi: National Book Trust.

Candler, Edmund. 1922. 'Mahatma Gandhi'. *The Atlantic*, July. https://www.theatlantic.com/magazine/archive/1922/07/mahatma-gandhi/306373/. Accessed on 12 August 2021.

Desai, Mahadev. 1946. *The Gospel of Selfless Action or The Gita According to Gandhi*. Ahmedabad: Navajivan Trust.

Desai, Narayan. 2009. *My Life Is My Message: Satyagraha (1915–1930)*, vol. 2, translated by Tridip Suhrud. New Delhi: Orient Blackswan.

Gandhi, M. K. 1963. *The Way to Communal Harmony*, edited by U. R. Rao. Ahmedabad: Navajivan Trust.

———. 1999. *The Collected Works of Mahatma Gandhi* (CWMG), 98 volumes (electronic book). New Delhi: Government of India. https://www.gandhiashramsevagram.org/gandhi-literature/collected-works-of-mahatma-gandhi-volume-1-to-98.php. Accessed on 6 August 2021.

Jinnah, M. A. 1940 (1983). *Address by Quaid-i-Azam Muhammad Ali Jinnah at Lahore Session of Muslim League, March, 1940*. Islamabad: Directorate of Films and Publishing, Ministry of Information and Broadcasting, Government of Pakistan. http://www.columbia.edu/itc/mealac/pritchett/00islamlinks/txt_jinnah_lahore_1940.html. Accessed on 20 August 2021.

Mainstream. 1981. 'A Statement on Scientific Temper'. 25 July, pp. 6–10.

Nehru, Jawaharlal. 1948 (1941). *The Unity of India: Collected Writings, 1937–1940*, edited by V. K. Krishna Menon. London: Lindsay Drummond.

———. 1967 (1948). *Jawaharlal Nehru's Speeches*, vol. 1, September 1946–May 1949. Delhi: Publications Division (Ministry of Broadcasting and Information), Government of India Press.

———. 1986. *Letters to Chief Ministers, 1950–1952*, vol. 2, edited by G. Parthasarthy. New Delhi: Government of India.

———. *Selected Works of Jawaharlal Nehru* (*SWJN*), series 1, vols. 1–15, edited by Sarvepalli Gopal (electronic book). New Delhi: Nehru Memorial Museum and Library. http://nehruportal.nic.in/writings. Accessed on 1 October 2021.

———. *Selected Works of Jawaharlal Nehru* (*SWJN*), series 2, vols. 1–61, edited by Sarvepalli Gopal (electronic book). New Delhi: Nehru Memorial Museum and Library. http://nehruportal.nic.in/writings. Accessed on 1 October 2021.

Iyengar, Uma, and Lalitha Zackariah (eds.). 2011. *Together They Fought: Gandhi–Nehru Correspondence 1921–1948*. New Delhi: Oxford University Press.

Iyengar, Uma (ed.). 2007. *The Oxford India Nehru*. New Delhi: Oxford University Press.

Parel, Anthony J. (ed.). 2009 (1997). *M.K. Gandhi: Hind Swaraj and Other Writings*. New York: Cambridge University Press.

Sarvepalli, Gopal (ed.).1980. *Jawaharlal Nehru, an Anthology*. Delhi: Oxford University Press.

Sarvepalli, Gopal, and Uma Iyengar (eds.). 2003. *The Essential Writings of Jawaharlal Nehru*, vol. 1. New Delhi: Oxford University Press.

Savarkar, V. D. 2007. 'Essentials of Hindutva'. In *Selected Works of Veer Savarkar*, vol. 4. New Delhi: Abhishek.

Singh, Baldev (ed.). 1986. *Jawaharlal Nehru on Science: Speeches Delivered at the Annual Sessions of the Indian Science Congress*. New Delhi: Nehru Memorial Museum and Library.

Tagore, Rabindranath. 1997 (1934). 'The Bihar Earthquake'. In *The Mahatma and the Poet: Letters and Debates between Gandhi and Tagore 1915–1941*, edited by Sabyasachi Bhattacharya, pp. 157–158. New Delhi: National Book Trust.

SECONDARY SOURCES

BOOKS, CHAPTERS IN BOOKS, JOURNAL ARTICLES AND WORKING PAPERS

Abraham, Arvind K. 2021. 'Essential Religious Practices Test and the First Amendment: A Comparative Analysis of the Free Exercise of Religion in India and the United States'. In *The Indian Yearbook of Comparative Law 2019*, edited by Mathew John, Vishwas H. Devaiah, Pritam Baruah, Moiz Tundawala and Niraj Kumar, pp. 279–301. Singapore: Springer.

Adcock, C. S. 2014. *The Limits of Tolerance: Indian Secularism and the Politics of Religious Freedom*. New York: Oxford University Press.

———. 2018. 'Cow Protection and Minority Rights in India: Reassessing Religious Freedom, *Asian Affairs* 49 (2): 340–354.

Alam, Javeed. 1999. 'The Composite Culture and Its Historiography'. *South Asia: Journal of South Asian Studies* 22 (1): 29–37.

Alter, Joseph. 2000. *Gandhi's Body: Sex, Diet, and the Politics of Nationalism*. Philadelphia: University of Pennsylvania Press.

Amin, Shahid. 1995. *Event, Metaphor, Memory: Chauri Chaura 1922–1992*. California: University of California Press.

Arnold, David. 2013. 'Nehruvian Science and Postcolonial India'. *Isis* 104 (2): 360–370.

Asad, Talal. 2003. *Formations of the Secular: Christianity, Islam, Modernity*. Stanford, CA: Stanford University Press.

———. 2006. 'Responses'. In *Powers of the Secular Modern: Talal Asad and His Interlocuters*, edited by David Scott and Charles Hirschkind, pp. 206–241. Stanford: Stanford University Press.

Bakhle, Janaki. 2013. 'Putting Global Intellectual History in Its Place'. In *Global Intellectual History*, edited by Samuel Moyn and Andrew Sartori, pp. 228–253. New York: Columbia University Press.

Balasubramanian, M. 1980. *Nehru: A Study in Secularism*. New Delhi: Uppal Publishing House.

Bajpai, Rochana. 2011. *Debating Difference: Group Rights and Liberal Democracy*. New Delhi: Oxford University Press.

Batabyal, Rakesh. 2016. 'In Search of Secular Template: History Writing in India in the First Decade of the Republic'. *Studies in People's History* 3 (2): 216–228.

Baxi, Upendra, and Bhikhu Parekh (eds.). 1995. *Crisis and Change in Contemporary India*. New Delhi: SAGE Publications.

Benhabib, Seyla (ed.). 1996. *Democracy and Difference: Contesting the Boundaries of the Political*. New Jersey: Princeton University Press.

———. 1996. 'Introduction: The Democratic Moment and the Problem of Difference'. In *Democracy and Difference: Contesting the Boundaries of the Political*, edited by Seyla Benhabib, pp. 3–18. New Jersey: Princeton University Press.

Bhargav, Vanya. 2018. 'Between Hindu and Indian: The Nationalist Thought of Lala Lajpat Rai'. PhD dissertation. University of Oxford.

Bhargava, Rajeev (ed.). 2008 (1998). *Secularism and its Critics*. New Delhi: Oxford University Press.

———. 2008 (1998). 'What is Secularism For?' In *Secularism and its Critics*, edited by Rajeev Bhargava, pp. 486–555. New Delhi: Oxford University Press.

———. 2000. 'History, Nation and Community: Reflections on Nationalist Historiography of India and Pakistan'. *Economic and Political Weekly* 35 (4): 193–200.

———. 2006. 'Political Secularism'. In *The Oxford Handbook of Political Theory*, edited by John S. Dryzek, Bonnie Honig and Anne Phillips, pp. 636–655. Oxford: Oxford University Press.

———. 2010. *The Promise of India's Secular Democracy*. New Delhi: Oxford University Press.

———. 2017. 'Nehru against Nehruvians: On Religion and Secularism'. *Economic and Political Weekly* 52 (8): 34–40.

Bhattacharya, Neeladri. 2008. 'Predicaments of Secular Histories'. *Public Culture* 20 (1): 57–73.

Bilgrami, Akeel. 2008 (1998). 'Secularism, Nationalism, and Modernity'. In *Secularism and Its Critics*, edited by Rajeev Bhargava, pp. 380–417. New Delhi: Oxford University Press.

———. 2011. 'Gandhi's Religion and Its Relation to His Politics'. In *The Cambridge Companion to Gandhi*, edited by Judith M. Brown and Anthony J. Parel, pp. 93–116. New York: Cambridge University Press.

———. 2012. 'A Different Notion of Fraternity'. *The Immanent Frame: Secularism, Religion and the Public Sphere*, September 7. https://tif.ssrc.org/2012/09/07/a-different-notion-of-fraternity/. Accessed on 19 August 2021.

———. 2012. 'Gandhian Fraternity'. *The Immanent Frame: Secularism, Religion and the Public Sphere*, September 13. https://tif.ssrc.org/2012/09/13/gandhian-fraternity/. Accessed on 19 August 2021.

———. 2014. *Secularism, Identity, and Enchantment*. Cambridge, MA: Harvard University Press.

——— (ed). 2016. *Beyond the Secular West*. New York: Columbia University Press.

———. 2016. 'Jawaharlal Nehru, Mohandas Gandhi, and the Contexts of Indian Secularism'. In *The Oxford Handbook of Indian Philosophy*, edited by Jonardon Ganeri, pp. 693–717. New York: Oxford University Press.

Bhatia, Gautam. 2019. *The Transformative Constitution: A Radical Biography in Nine Acts*. Noida: HarperCollins.

Bose, Sugata, and Ayesha Jalal. 2004 (1997). *Modern South Asia: History, Culture, Political Economy* New Delhi: Routledge.

Brown, Judith M. 1972. *Gandhi's Rise to Power: Indian Politics 1915–1922*. London: Cambridge University Press.

———. 2008 (1977). *Gandhi and Civil Disobedience: The Mahatma in Indian Politics 1928–1934*. Cambridge: Cambridge University Press.

———. 2004. *Nehru: A Political Life*. New Delhi: Oxford University Press.

———. 2011. 'Gandhi as a Nationalist Leader, 1915–1948'. In *The Cambridge Companion to Gandhi*, edited by Judith M. Brown and Anthony Parel, pp. 51–70. New York: Cambridge University Press.

Brown, Judith M., and Anthony Parel (eds.). 2011. *The Cambridge Companion to Gandhi*. New York: Cambridge University Press.

Brown, Wendy, Jan Dobbernack, Glen Newey, Andrew F. March, Lars Tønder and Rainer Forst. 2015. 'What is Important in Theorizing Tolerance Today'. *Contemporary Political Theory* 14 (2): 1–38.

Burchardt, Marian, and Monika Wohlrab-Sahr. 2012. 'Multiple Secularities: Toward a Cultural Sociology of Secular Modernities'. *Comparative Sociology* 11 (6): 875–909.

Burchardt, Marian, Monika Wohlrab-Sahr and Matthias Middell (eds.). 2015. *Multiple Secularities beyond the West: Religion and Modernity in the Global Age*. Boston, Berlin and Munich: De Gruyter.

Casanova, José. 1994. *Public Religions in the Modern World*. Chicago: University of Chicago Press.

———. 2008. 'Public Religions Revisited'. In *Religion: Beyond the Concept*, edited by Hent de Vries, pp. 101–119. New York: Fordham University Press.

———. 2011. 'The Secular, Secularizations, Secularisms'. In *Rethinking Secularism*, edited by Craig Calhoun, Mark Juergensmeyer and Jonathan VanAntwerpen, pp. 54–74. New York: Oxford University Press.

———. 2019. *Global Religious and Secular Dynamics: The Modern System of Classification*. Leiden: Brill.

Cesari, Jocelyne. 2018. *What is Political Islam?* Boulder, CO: Lynne Rienner.

Chakrabarti, Anindita, and Sudha Sitharaman (eds.). 2020. *Religion and Secularities: Reconfiguring Islam in Contemporary India*. Hyderabad: Orient Blackswan.

Chakrabarty, Dipesh. 2000. *Provincializing Europe: Postcolonial Thought and Historical Difference*. Princeton: Princeton University Press.

Chandrachud, Abhinav. 2020. 'Secularism and the Citizenship Amendment Act', *Indian Law Review* 4 (2): 138–162.

———. 2020. *Republic of Religion: The Rise and Fall of Colonial Secularism in India*. New Delhi: Penguin Random House India.

Chandra, Bipan. 1984. *Communalism in Modern India*. New Delhi: Vikas Publishing House.

Chatterjee, Margaret. 1983. *Gandhi's Religious Thought*. Indiana: University of Notre Dame Press.

Chatterjee, Partha. 1993 (1986). *Nationalist Thought and the Colonial World: A Derivative Discourse*. London: Zed Books.

———. 2008 (1998). 'Secularism and Tolerance'. in *Secularism and Its Critics*, edited by Rajeev Bhargava, pp. 345–379. New Delhi: Oxford University Press.

Chatterji, Rakhahari. 2013. *Gandhi and the Ali Brothers: Biography of a Friendship*. New Delhi: SAGE Publications.

Chatterji, Joya. 1995. *Bengal Divided: Hindu Communalism and Partition 1932–47*. Cambridge: Cambridge University Press.

Chiriyankandath, James. 1992. '"Democracy" under the Raj: Elections and Separate Representation in British India'. *Journal of Commonwealth and Comparative Politics* 30 (1): 39–64.

Cohn, Bernard S. 1996. *Colonialism and Its Forms of Knowledge: The British in India*. Princeton: Princeton University Press.

Connolly, William E. 1999. *Why I Am Not a Secularist*. Minneapolis, University of Minnesota Press.

Cultural Anthropology. 2011. 'Secularism' 26 (4).

Dalton, Dennis. 2012 (1993). *Mahatma Gandhi: Nonviolent Power in Action*. New York: Columbia University Press.

Dasgupta, Sandipto. 2014. 'Legalizing the Revolution'. PhD dissertation. Columbia University, New York.

———. 2017. 'Gandhi's Failure: Anti-colonial Movements and Post-colonial Futures'. *Perspectives on Politics* 15 (3): 647–662.

de Vries, Hent (ed.). 2008. *Religion: Beyond the Concept*. New York: Fordham University Press.

Desai, Ashwin, and Goolam Vahed. 2016. *The South African Gandhi: Stretcher-Bearer of Empire*. Stanford: Stanford University Press.

Devji, Faisal. 2012. *Impossible Indian: Gandhi and the Temptation of Violence*. Cambridge, MA: Harvard University Press.

———. 2013. *Muslim Zion: Pakistan as a Political Idea*. London: Harvard University Press.

Dhulipala, Venkat. 2015. *Creating a New Medina: State Power, Islam, and the Quest for Pakistan in Late Colonial North India*. Delhi: Cambridge University Press.

Dirks, Nicholas B. 2001. *Castes of Mind: Colonialism and the Making of Modern India*. Princeton: Princeton University Press.

Dreyfus, Hubert, and Charles Taylor. 2015. *Retrieving Realism*. Cambridge, MA: Harvard University Press.

Dryzek, John S., Bonnie Honig and Anne Phillips (eds.). 2006. *The Oxford Handbook of Political Theory*. Oxford: Oxford University Press.

Eisenstadt, S. N. 1964. 'Social Change, Differentiation and Evolution', *American Sociological Review* 29 (3): 375–386.

———. 2000. 'Multiple Modernities'. *Daedalus* 129 (1): 1–29.

Freeden, Michael, and Andrew Vincent (eds.). 2013. *Comparative Political Thought: Theorizing Practices*. Oxon: Routledge.

———. 2013. 'Introduction: The Study of Comparative Political Thought'. In *Comparative Political Thought: Theorizing Practices*, edited by Michael Freeden and Andrew Vincent, pp. 1–23. Oxon: Routledge.

Frykenberg, Robert E. 1993. 'Constructions of Hinduism at the Nexus of History and Religion'. *Journal of Interdisciplinary History* 22 (3): 523–550.

Ganeri, Jonardon (ed). 2017. *The Oxford Handbook of Indian Philosophy*. New York: Oxford University Press.

Gray, John. 2000. *Two Faces of Liberalism*. New York: The New Press.

Guha, Ranajit. 1982. 'On Some Aspects of the Historiography of Colonial India'. In *Subaltern Studies I: Writings on South Asian History and Society*, edited by Ranajit Guha, pp. 1–8. Delhi: Oxford University Press.

Gupta, Dipankar. 1995. 'Secularisation and Minoritisation: Limits of Heroic Thought'. *Economic and Political Weekly* 30 (35): 2203–2207.

Habermas, Jürgen. 2010. 'An Awareness of What Is Missing'. In *An Awareness of What Is Missing: Faith and Reason in a Post-Secular Age*, edited by Jurgen Habermas et al., translated by Ciaran Cronin, pp. 15–23. Cambridge: Polity Press.

Habermas, Jürgen et al. (eds.). 2010. *An Awareness of What Is Missing: Faith and Reason in a Post-Secular Age*, translated by Ciaran Cronin. Cambridge: Polity Press.

Hardiman, David. 2021. *Noncooperation in India: Nonviolent Strategy and Protest, 1920–22*. New York: Oxford University Press.

Hassan, Mona. 2016. *Longing for the Lost Caliphate: A Transregional History*. New Jersey: Princeton University Press.

Hasan, Mushirul. 1986. 'The Muslim Mass Contact Campaign: An Attempt at Political Mobilisation'. *Economic and Political Weekly* 21 (52): 2273–2282.

———. 2006. *The Mushirul Hasan Omnibus: Comprising Nationalism and Communal Politics in India, 1885–1930; A Nationalist Conscience: M.A. Ansari, the Congress and the Raj; Islam in the Subcontinent: Muslims in a Plural Society*. New Delhi: Manohar Publications.

Howard, Veena. 2013. *Gandhi's Ascetic Activism: Renunciation and Social Action*. Albany: State University of New York Press.

Iqbal, Mohammad. 1934. *The Reconstruction of Religious Thought in Islam*. Oxford: Oxford University Press.

———. (eds.). 2018. *Tolerance, Secularization, and Democratic Politics in South Asia*. New York: Cambridge University Press.

Iyer, Raghavan. 1973. *The Moral and Political Thought of Mahatma Gandhi*. New York: Oxford University Press.

Iyengar, Uma, and Lalitha Zachariah (eds.). 2011. 'Introduction'. In *Together They Fought: Gandhi–Nehru Correspondence 1921–1948*, pp. xxxi–xli. New Delhi: Oxford University Press.

Jahanbegloo, Ramin. 2013. *The Gandhian Moment*. Cambridge, MA: Harvard University Press.

Jalal, Ayesha. 1999 (1985). *The Sole Spokesman: Jinnah, the Muslim League and the Demand for Pakistan*. New York: Cambridge University Press.

Jenco, Leigh. 2010. *Making the Political*. Stanford: Stanford University Press.

Jensen, Rasmus Thybo, and Dermot Moran. 2013. 'Editor's Introduction'. In *The Phenomenology of Embodied Subjectivity*, edited by Rasmus Thybo Jensen, and Dermot Moran. New York: Springer.

———. (eds.). 2013. *The Phenomenology of Embodied Subjectivity*. New York: Springer.

Joas, Hans. 2016. 'Dangerous Nouns of Process: Differentiation, Rationalization, Modernization'. In *The Art and Science of Sociology: Essays in Honor of Edward*

A. *Tiryakian*, edited by Ronald Robertson and John Simpson, pp. 149–162. London and New York: Anthem Press.

Joshi, P. C. 2007. 'Gandhi–Nehru Tradition and Indian Secularism'. *Mainstream* 45 (48). https://www.mainstreamweekly.net/article432.html. Accessed on 7 April 2021.

Jha, Shefali. 2002. 'Secularism in the Constituent Assembly Debates, 1946–1950'. *Economic and Political Weekly* 37 (30): 3175–3180.

Kaviraj, Sudipta. 1995. 'Religion, Politics and Modernity'. In *Crisis and Change in Contemporary India*, edited by Upendra Baxi and Bhikhu Parekh, pp. 295–316. New Delhi: SAGE Publications.

———. 2005. 'An Outline of a Revisionist Theory of Modernity'. *European Journal of Sociology* 46 (3): 497–526.

———. 2010. *Imaginary Institutions of India: Politics and Ideas*. New York: Columbia University Press.

———. 2010. 'On Thick and Thin Religions: Some Critical Reflections on Secularisation Theory'. In *Religion and Political Imagination*, edited by Ira Katznelson and Gareth Stedman Jones, pp. 336–355. New York: Cambridge University Press.

———. 2012. *Trajectories of the Indian State: Politics and Ideas*. Ranikhet: Permanent Black.

———. 2013. 'Languages of Secularity'. *Economic and Political Weekly* 48 (50): 93–102.

———. 2014. 'Modernity, State and Toleration in Indian History: Exploring Accommodations and Partitions'. In *Boundaries of Toleration*, edited by Alfred Stepan and Charles Taylor, pp. 233–266. New York: Columbia University Press.

———. 2014. 'The Curious Persistence of Colonial Ideology'. *Constellations* 21 (2): 186–198.

———. 2016. 'Disenchantment Deferred'. In *Beyond the Secular West*, edited by Akeel Bilgrami, pp. 135–187. New York: Columbia University Press.

Katznelson, Ira, and Gareth Stedman Jones (eds.). 2010. *Religion and the Political Imagination*. New York: Cambridge University Press.

Khilnani, Sunil. 2002. 'Nehru's Faith'. *Economic and Political Weekly* 48 (30): 4793–4799.

———. 2009. 'Nehru's Judgement'. In *Political Judgement*, edited by Richard Bourke and Raymond Guess, pp. 254–278. New York: Cambridge University Press.

———. 2012 (1997). *The Idea of India* (e-book). New Delhi: Penguin.

Kleine, Christoph, and Monika Wohlrab-Sahr. 2016. 'Research programme of the Humanities Centre of Advanced Studies (HCAS), "Multiple Secularities: Beyond the West, beyond Modernities"'. Leipzig University. https://www.multiple-secularities.de/. Accessed on 7 April 2021.

———. 2021. 'Historicizing Secularity: A Proposal for Comparative Research from a Global Perspective'. *Comparative Sociology* 20: 287–316.

Kothari, Rajni. 1969. 'Political Consensus in India: Decline and Reconstruction'. *Economic and Political Weekly* 4 (41): 1635–1644.

Kumar, Aishwary. 2015. *Radical Equality: Ambedkar, Gandhi and the Risk of Democracy*. Stanford: Stanford University Press.

Kumar, Ravinder. 1969. 'Class, Community or Nation? Gandhi's Quest for a Popular Consensus in India'. *Modern Asian Studies* 3 (4): 357–376.

Künkler, Mirjam, John Madeley and Shylashri Shankar (eds.). 2018. *A Secular Age beyond the West: Religion, Law and the State in Asia, the Middle East and North Africa*. New York: Cambridge University Press.

Lal, Vinay (ed.). 2009. *Political Hinduism: The Religious Imagination in Public Spheres*. New Delhi: Oxford University Press.

Lelyveld, Joseph. 2011. *Great Soul: Mahatma Gandhi and His Struggle with India*. New York: Alfred A. Knopf.

Maclure, Jocelyn, and Charles Taylor (eds.). 2011. *Secularism and Freedom of Conscience*, translated by Jane Marie Todd. Cambridge, MA: Harvard University Press.

Madan, T. N. 2008 (1998). 'Secularism in Its Place'. In *Secularism and Its Critics*, edited by Rajeev Bhargava, pp. 297–320. New Delhi: Oxford University Press.

Mahajan, Gurpreet, and Helmut Reifeld (eds.). 2003. *The Public and the Private: Issues of Democratic Citizenship*. New Delhi: SAGE Publications.

Mahajan, Gurpreet. 2002. 'Secularism as Religious Non-Discrimination: The Universal and the Particular in the Indian Context'. *India Review* 1 (1): 33–51.

———. 2002. *The Multicultural Path: Issues of Diversity and Discrimination in Democracy*. New Delhi: SAGE Publications.

Mantena, Karuna. 2012. 'Another Realism: The Politics of Gandhian Nonviolence'. *American Political Science Review* 106 (2): 455–470.

———. 2012. 'Gandhi and the Means–Ends Question in Politics'. Unpublished Paper. Karunamantena, https://karunamantena.files.wordpress.com/2011/04/mantena-gandhimeansends.pdf. Accessed on 16 March 2021.

———. 2012. 'On Gandhi's Critique of the State: Sources, Contexts, Conjectures'. *Modern Intellectual History* 9 (3): 535–563.

Mahmood, Saba. 2016. *Religious Difference in a Secular Age: A Minority Report*. Princeton, NJ: Princeton University Press.

Mehta, Uday Singh. 1999. *Liberalism and Empire: A Study in Nineteenth Century British Liberal Thought*. Chicago: University of Chicago Press.

———. 2011. 'Patience, Inwardness and Self-knowledge in Gandhi's Hind Swaraj'. *Public Culture* 23 (2): 417–429.

Menon, V. K. Krishna. 1948 (1941). 'Foreword to the First Edition'. In *The Unity of India, Collected Writings: 1937–1940*, by Jawaharlal Nehru, pp. iv–vi. London: Lindsay Drummond.

Minault, Gail. 1982. *The Khilafat Movement: Religious Symbolism and Political Mobilization in India*. Delhi: Oxford University Press.

Moyn, Samuel, and Andrew Sartori (eds.). 2013. *Global Intellectual History*. New York: Columbia University Press.

———. 2013. 'Approaches to Global Intellectual History'. In *Global Intellectual History*, edited by Samuel Moyn and Andrew Sartori, pp. 3–30. New York: Columbia University Press.

Nanda, Meera. 2003. *Prophets Facing Backward: Postmodern Critiques of Science and Hindu Nationalism in India*. New Jersey: Rutgers University Press.

Nandy, Ashis. 1982. 'Science for Unafraid'. *Mainstream*, 26 June, pp. 17–20.

———. 1995. 'An Anti-secularist Manifesto'. *India International Centre Quarterly* 22 (1): 35–64.

———. 2008 (1998). 'The Politics of Secularism and the Recovery of Religious Tolerance'. In *Secularism and its Critics*, edited by Rajeev Bhargava, pp. 321–344. New Delhi: Oxford University Press.

Nath, Sushmita. 2016. 'Secularism in Crisis: The Indian State's Codification of the Muslim Personal Law and the Relegation of Muslim Women's Rights'. *Studies in Religion* 45 (4): 520–541.

Needham, Anuradha Dingwaney, and Rajeswari Sunder Rajan (eds.). 2007. *The Crisis of Secularism in India*. Durham: Duke University Press.

Owen, Hugh F. 1972. 'Negotiating the Lucknow Pact'. *Journal of Asian Studies* 31 (3): 561–587.

Pandey, B. N. 1976. *Nehru*. Madras: Macmillan India Press.

Pandey, Gyanendra. 1997 (1990). *The Construction of Colonialism in Colonial North India*. Delhi: Oxford University Press.

Pantham, Thomas. 1995. 'Gandhi, Nehru, Modernity'. In *Crisis and Change in Contemporary India*, edited by Upendra Baxi and Bhikhu Parekh, pp. 98–121. New Delhi: SAGE Publications.

Parekh, Bhikhu, and R.N. Berki. 1973. 'The History of Political Ideas: A Critique of Q. Skinner's Methodology'. *Journal of the History of Ideas*, 34 (2): 163–184.

Parekh, Bhikhu C. 1989. *Colonialism, Tradition, and Reform: An Analysis of Gandhi's Political Discourse*. New Delhi: SAGE Publications.

———. 1995. 'Jawaharlal Nehru and the Crisis of Modernisation'. In *Crisis and Change in Contemporary India*, edited by Upendra Baxi and Bhikhu Parekh, pp. 21–56. New Delhi: SAGE Publications.

Phillips, Anne. 1995. *The Politics of Presence*. Oxford: Clarendon Press.

Pitkin, Hanna. 1972. *The Concept of Representation*. Berkeley: University of California Press.

Pocock, J. G.A. 1964 (1962). 'The History of Political Thought: A Methodological Inquiry'. In *Philosophy, Politics and Society*, series 2, edited by Peter Laslett and W. G. Runciman, pp. 183–202. Oxford: Basil Blackwell.

Qureshi, M. Naeem. 1999. *Pan Islam in British Indian Politics: A Study of the Khilafat Movement, 1918–1924*. Leiden: Brill.

Rawls, John. 1971. *A Theory of Justice*. Cambridge, MA: Belknap Press of Harvard University Press.

———. 1993. *Political Liberalism*. New York: Columbia University Press.

Rodrigues, Valerian. 2017. 'Ambedkar as a Political Philosopher'. *Economic and Political Weekly* 52 (15): 101–107.

Roy, Srirupa. 2007. *Beyond Belief: India and the Politics of Postcolonial Nationalism*. Durham: Duke University Press.

Rudolph, Susanne H., and Lloyd I. Rudolph. 2003. 'The Coffee House and the Ashram: Gandhi, Civil Society and Public Spheres'. Working Paper no. 15. South Asia Institute, Department of Political Science, Heidelberg University.

Sarkar, Sumit. 2002 (1983). *Modern India 1885–1947*. New Delhi: Macmillan India.

Sarvepalli, Gopal. 1988. 'Nehru and Minorities'. *Economic and Political Weekly* 23 (45–47): 2463–2466.

Schneider, Nadja-Christina. 2020. 'Tea for Interreligious Harmony? Cause Marketing as a New Field of Experimentation with Visual Secularity in India'. Working Paper Series of the HCAS 'Multiple Secularities: Beyond the West, beyond Modernities' 20. Leipzig University. https://www.multiple-secularities.de/media/wp_20_schneider_teaforinterreligiousharmony_web.pdf. Accessed on 7 April 2021.

Schoettli, Jivanta. 2011. *Vision and Strategy in Indian Politics: Jawaharlal Nehru's Policy Choices and the Designing of Political Institutions*. Oxon: Routledge.

Scott, David, and Charles Hirschkind (eds.). 2006. *Powers of the Secular Modern: Talal Asad and His Interlocuters*. Stanford: Stanford University Press.

Shankar, Shylashri. 2018. 'Secularity and Hinduism's Imaginaries in India'. In *A Secular Age beyond the West: Religion, Law and the State in Asia, the Middle East and North Africa*, edited by Mirjam Künkler, John Madeley and Shylashri Shankar, pp. 128–151. New York: Cambridge University Press.

Shklar, Judith. 2004 (1989). 'The Liberalism of Fear'. In *Political Liberalism: Variations on a Theme*, edited by Shaun P. Young, pp. 149–166. Albany: State University of New York Press.

Sheikh, Farzana. 1989. *Community and Consensus in Islam: Muslim Representation in Colonial India, 1860–1947*. Cambridge: Cambridge University Press.

Sitharaman, Sudha. 'Limits of Syncretism: Bababudhan Dargah in South India as a Paradigm for Overlapping Religious Affiliations and Co-existence'. In *Rituale als Ausdruck von Kulturkontakt: 'Synkretismus' zwischen Negation und Neudefinition*, Studies in Oriental Religions, vol. 67, edited by A. Pries, L. Martzolff, R. Langer and C. Ambos, pp. 70–109. Wiesbaden: Harrassowitz Verlag, 2013.

Skaria, Ajay. 2002. 'Gandhi's Politics: Liberalism and the Question of the Ashram'. *South Atlantic Quarterly* 101 (4): 955–986.

———. 2009. 'No Politics without Religion, of Secularism and Gandhi'. In *Political Hinduism: The Religious Imagination in Public Spheres*, edited by Vinay Lal, pp. 173–210. New Delhi: Oxford University Press.

———. 2016. *Unconditional Equality: Gandhi's Religion of Resistance*. Minneapolis: University of Minnesota Press.

Skinner, Quentin. 2002 (1969). *Visions of Politics, Vol. 1: Regarding Method*. New York: Cambridge University Press.

Sorabji, Richard. 2012. *Gandhi and the Stoics: Modern Experiments on Ancient Values*. Chicago: University of Chicago Press.

Som, Reba. 1994. 'Jawaharlal Nehru and the Hindu Code Bill: A Victory of Symbol Over Substance'. *Modern Asian Studies* 28 (1): 165–194.

Sparling, Robert. 2009. 'M.K. Gandhi: Reconciling Agonism and Deliberative Democracy'. *Representation* 45 (4): 391–403.

Stepan, Alfred, and Charles Taylor (eds.). 2014. *Boundaries of Toleration*. New York: Columbia University Press.

Subramanian, Narendra. 2010. 'Making Family and Nation: Hindu Marriage Law in Early Postcolonial India'. *Journal of Asian Studies* 69 (3): 771–798.

———. 2014. *Nation and Family: Personal Law, Cultural Pluralism, and Gendered Citizenship in India*. Stanford, CA: Stanford University Press.

Suhrud, Tridip. 2011. 'Gandhi's Key Writings: In Search of Unity'. In *The Cambridge Companion to Gandhi*, edited by Judith M. Brown and Anthony Parel, pp. 71–92. New York: Cambridge University Press.

———. 2018. 'The Story of Antaryami'. *Social Scientist* 46 (11–12): 37–60.

Tambiah, Stanley J. 2008 (1998). 'The Crisis of Secularism in India'. In *Secularism and Its Critics*, edited by Rajeev Bhargava, pp. 418–453. New Delhi: Oxford University Press.

Taylor, Charles. 1995. 'Two Theories of Modernity'. *Hastings Centre Report* 25 (2): 24–33.

———. 2004. *Modern Social Imaginaries*. Durham: Duke University Press.

———. 2007. *A Secular Age*. Cambridge, MA: Harvard University Press.

———. 2009. 'The Polysemy of the Secular'. *Social Research: An International Quarterly* 76 (4): 1143–1166.

———. 2016. 'A Secular Age outside Latin Christendom: Charles Taylor Responds'. In *Beyond the Secular West*, edited by Akeel Bilgrami, pp. 246–260. New York: Columbia University Press.

Tejani, Shabnum. 2007. *Indian Secularism: A Social and Intellectual History 1890–1950*. Ranikhet: Permanent Black.

———. 2013. 'Defining Secularism in the Particular: Caste and Citizenship in India 1909–1950'. *Politics and Religion* 6 (4): 703–729.

Terchek, Ronald J. 1998. *Gandhi: Struggling for Autonomy*. New York: Rowman and Littlefield.

Thomson, Mark. 1993. *Gandhi and His Ashrams*. Mumbai: Popular Prakashan.

Thapar, Romila. 1987 (1969). 'Communalism and the Writing of Ancient Indian History'. In *Communalism and the Writing of Indian History*, edited by Romila Thapar, Harbans Mukhia and Bipan Chandra, pp. 1–23. New Delhi: People's Publishing House.

Thapar, Romila, Bipan Chandra and Harbans Mukhia (eds.). 1987 (1969). *Communalism and the Writing of Indian History*. Delhi: People's Publishing House.

Tully, James (ed.). 1988. *Meaning and Context: Quentin Skinner and His Critics*. Princeton and New Jersey: Princeton University Press.

Uberoi, J. P. S. 1978. 'The Structural Concept of the Asian Frontier'. In *History and Society: Essays in Honour of Niharranjan Ray*, edited by Debiprasad Chattopadhyaya, pp. 67–76. Calcutta: K. P. Bagchi and Company.

van der Veer, Peter. 1994. 'Syncretism, Multiculturalism, and the Discourse of Tolerance'. In *Syncretism/Antisyncretism: The Politics of Religious Synthesis*, edited by Charles Stewart and Rosalind Shaw, pp. 185–199. London and New York: Routledge.

Veeravalli, Anuradha. 2014. *Gandhi in Political Theory*. Surrey: Ashgate Publishing.

Williams, Melissa. 1998. *Voice Trust and Memory: Marginalized Groups and the Failings of Liberal Representation*. New Jersey: Princeton University Press.

Wilson, Bryan R. 1966. *Religion in Secular Society*. London: C.A. Watts & Co. Ltd.

Wohlrab-Sahr, Monika. 2016. 'Secularity, Non-religiosity, Atheism: Boundaries between Religion and its Others'. *Annual Review of the Sociology of Religion* 7: 251–271.

Wolin, Sheldon. 1996. 'Fugitive Democracy'. In *Democracy and Difference: Contesting the Boundaries of the Political*, edited by Seyla Benhabib, pp. 31–45. New Jersey: Princeton University Press.

Wolpert, Stanley. 2002 (2001). *Gandhi's Passion: The Life and Legacy of Mahatma Gandhi*. New York: Oxford University Press.

Young, Iris Marion. 1990. *Justice and the Politics of Difference*. New Jersey: Princeton University Press.

Zachariah, Benjamin. 2004. *Nehru*. London: Routledge.

Zemmin, Florian. 2019. 'How (Not) to Take 'Secularity' beyond the Modern West: Reflections from Islamic Sociology'. Working Paper Series of the HCAS 'Multiple Secularities: Beyond the West, beyond Modernities' 9. Leipzig University.

———. 2019. 'Secularism, Secularity and Islamic Reformism'. *Companion to the Study of Secularity*, edited by HCAS 'Multiple Secularities: Beyond the West, beyond Modernities'. Leipzig University, https://www.multiple-secularities.de/publications/companion/css_zemmin_islamicreformism.pdf. Accessed on 7 April 2021.

INDEX

adivasis (tribals), 73
ahimsa, 8, 10, 47, 49, 50, 52, 57–60, 64, 66–69, 73, 75, 87*n*91, 91*n*141, 98, 99, 101, 102, 104, 105, 120, 121, 138*n*93, 153, 182*n*59, 232, 233
Ali brothers, 107, 119
All India Congress Committee (AICC), 206
Alter, Joseph, 74, 88*n*94
Ambedkar, B. R., 19*n*43, 73, 130*n*3, 139*n*112, 139*n*114
ancient Hindu scriptures, 120
anti-colonial struggle, 151
anti-Congress propaganda, 207
anti-Government, 111
anti-secularist, 35
Arnold, David, 157
artificial incompatibilities, 116
Aryans, 162
Asad, Talal, 23
ashram, 10, 48
ashramites, 47, 57, 65, 73, 233
Ashram Observance in Action (1955), 57, 79*n*13, 80*n*13
associational activities, 70, 93*n*161, 99, 104, 106, 126, 234

associationalism, 99
associational activity, 10, 70, 93*n*161, 99, 104, 106, 126, 234
associational living, 10, 93*n*161, 99, 104, 110, 111, 118
associational politics, 10, 70, 86*n*66, 93*n*161, 99, 103–108, 114, 125–127, 129
political unity, 103–104

Bajpai, Rochana, 9, 195
ballot-box constitutional politics, 193
Bentham, Jeremy, 61
Bhagavad Gita, 62, 77
Bharatiya Janta Party (BJP), 3, 39, 191*n*159
  Hindutva, ideological project of, 6
  right-wing groups, 21
Bhargava, Rajeev, 32, 128, 169
Bilgrami, Akeel, 11*n*1, 38, 56, 58, 61, 65, 66, 68, 90*n*127, 92*n*150, 111, 131*n*11, 145, 158, 159, 164, 175, 176
biomoral/biomorality, 63, 73, 75, 77, 118, 138*n*95

brahmacharya, 57, 63, 77
British colonialism, 81n17, 89n106, 91n139, 91n142, 92n145, 94n165, 132n17, 136n65, 137n87, 138n87, 139n104, 145, 166, 182n59, 192, 193, 197
    British Raj, 4, 82n27, 193
    divide and rule, 71, 196
    Gandhi's politics, 192
    India's path to modernity, 145n12
British colonial rule, 51, 75, 166, 206
British India
    representative government in, 115
    struggle against colonial rule, 204
    undivided, 218
    Westphalian model, 20
British rule, 150
    as colonialism, 197
    complete independence, 193, 202. *See also* purna swaraj
brotherhood, 93n161, 99, 101–104, 109–111, 115, 125, 127, 136n58
Buddhism, Vedic religions/heterodox traditions, 5
Buddhist, 218

canonical Hinduism, 60, 119–120
Cartesian dualism, 63, 89n114, 90n117–118, 183n68
Casanova, José, 4, 21
    secularisation, 27
    functional differentiation, 27, 29, 42n42, 50, 78
caste system, 17n34, 88n95, 96n181, 99, 120, 123, 127, 160, 163, 224n22
Castoriadis, Cornelius, 16n30
Chatterjee, Partha, 39, 46n96, 62–63, 67–68, 84n45, 129, 130n6, 151, 153, 156, 160, 166–167, 179n4, 185n92, 191n160, 216
Child Marriage Restraint Act (1929), 220
Christian culture, 34
Christianity, 4, 13n10, 14n13, 17n34, 34
Christian masses, 205
Church of England, 13n10, 149
church-state separation, 8, 32
Civil Disobedience, 53, 67, 68, 101, 177
colonial rule, 20, 47, 51, 58, 75, 82n25, 102, 106, 137n87, 141, 144–145, 146, 151, 156, 166, 177, 197, 204, 206
communal award, 122, 182n50, 202
communalism, 113, 197, 199
    communal award, 122, 182n50, 202
    communal electorate, 115, 116, 210, 213, 224n16
    communal politics, 71, 99, 102, 158, 167, 193, 194, 197, 202, 206, 210
    communal riots, 77, 118, 146, 197
    false communalism, 200
    communal unity, 69, 73, 104, 106, 109, 110, 112, 211
    communal historiography, 15n20, 70, 93n163, 233. *See also* historiography
    demand for Pakistan, 114–118
    Hindu–Muslim unity, 71, 87n76, 99, 104, 105, 107, 108, 113–115, 118, 119, 121, 132n18, 133n25, 197, 206,
    Khilafat movement/non-cooperation movement (1919–1922), 107–114
    partition of India (1947), 118–119
    separate electorates, 114–118
    unity within religion, 98, 99, 119

composite culture, 70, 95n174, 160, 163, 165, 198, 207, 221, 222, 225n35, 233
composite nationality, 211
Congress party. *See* Indian National Congress (INC)
Constituent Assembly debates (1946–1949), 212
constitutional guarantees, 100
constructive programme/work, 48, 67, 70, 72, 73, 79n8, 92n156, 99, 104, 106, 117, 127, 134n34, 144, 146, 230n120
cosmopolitan nationalists, 218
counter-narrative, 2, 10, 27, 30, 47–97, 232
Counter-Statement on Humanistic Temper, 174
Comparative political theory, 9, 19n49
cow protection, 14n14, 86n67, 88n92, 100, 119, 120, 125, 126, 140n123
criticisms, against Gandhi, 55
cultural inadaptability thesis, 34

Desai, Narayan, 47
Devji, Faisal, 52, 101
Dewey, John, 147
dharma, 8, 50, 65, 83, 98
*dharmashastra*s, 61
Discovery of India, The, 10, 160, 196, 198, 219
disenchantment, 26, 41n34, 43n51, 92n155, 168, 186n109
disinterested unity, 110
dispositional politics, 56, 74, 76, 96n188
Dravidians, 162
Dyer, General, 108

economic development, 145, 193, 204, 234
economic equality, 73, 167, 198
Emergency Rule (1975–1977), 12, 40n1, 173
ethical living, 49, 54–56, 58, 62, 65, 68, 85n61, 146, 232–233
ethical politics, 68
European nationalism, 164–165
European secularity, 29
European-style social democracy, socio-economic models of, 166
Enlightenment, 45n67, 60, 61, 89n114, 110, 165, 174

French Revolution, 22
friendship, Gandhi's politics of, 105

Gandhian *satyagrahi*, 53, 74–75
Gandhi, Indira, 10, 12n6, 40n1, 143, 172, 173, 177, 184n84, 190n50
  Emergency Rule, 12n6, 40n1, 173,
Gandhi, M. K.
  ashram/Ashram, 10, 47–50, 52–54, 56–59, 63, 66, 68, 70, 72–75, 77, 78, 79n2, 79n13, 86n66, 86n70, 88n99, 90n126, 101, 111, 132n19, 233
  ahimsa/non-violence, 66–68
  religions, tolerance/equality of, 68–73
  religious politics, 56–77
  satya/truth, 59–66
  spiritual/ascetic 'biomoral' practices, 73–77
  fraternity, 111
  'holistic vision' of society, 2
  non-violence, policy of, 67

politics, 103
   dispositional, 56, 74, 76, 96n188
   moral, 49, 114
   Non-cooperation movement, 107, 108, 111, 133n24, 135n42, 152, 197
   political thought, 10, 47, 49, 111
   religious, 50, 56, 99, 143, 147, 150, 153
   spiritual practices, 75
   religious language, 174
Gandhi–Nehru tradition, 2, 3, 5–9, 12n8, 13n12, 17n32, 21, 24, 39, 41n26, 118, 142, 187n119, 231, 232, 235
Ganga–Jamuni tehzeeb, 72, 95n174, 207
ganja (cannabis), 75
Gopal, Sarvepalli, 204
Great Uprising of 1857, 195n13

Habermas, Jürgen, 4, 15n21, 97n197
   Habermasian, 77, 86n66
Hasan, Mushirul, 204, 206–208
himsa, 67
Hind Swaraj, 8, 51, 53, 82n26, 84n49, 178n2
'Hindu' and 'Muslim' political mobilisation, 196
Hindu belief, 62
Hindu Code Bill, 194, 214–220, 228n93, 229n95, 234, 235
Hinduism, Gandhi's reinterpretation, 99
Hindu law, 219
Hindu Mahasabha, 102, 113, 197, 204, 207, 208, 216, 229n104
Hindu Marriage Act (1955), 214
Hindu Minority and Guardianship Act (1956), 214

Hindu-Mohammedan unity, 69
Hindu–Musalman ki jai, 107
Hindu–Muslim relations, 112
Hindu–Muslim unity, 71, 87n76, 99, 104, 105, 107, 108, 113–115, 118, 119, 121, 132n18, 133n25, 197, 206
Hindu nationalists, 32, 177
Hindu Raj, 4, 210
Hindu right, 3, 6, 21, 39, 49n95, 70, 129, 174, 190n158, 190n159, 191n160, 201, 210, 216
   generosity of Hindu traditions, 70
   pseudo-secular, 3, 21, 39, 201
   argument, 70
   claim, 3, 6
Hindus
   hereditary privilege of, 109
   upper-caste, 123
Hindutva, 3, 6, 15n17, 18n38, 39, 85n61, 216
   political conception, 39
   votes based on exclusionary politics, 3
historiography
   communal, 15n20, 70, 93n163, 94, 233
   secular, 70, 160, 198
humanism
   exclusive humanism, 23, 29, 43n49, 50, 168
   secular humanism, 143, 157, 159

identity politics, 177, 178, 214, 235
immanent religion, 62
India
   idea of, 1
   nationalism in, 107–108, 175–177, 191, 195–197, 203, 209

non-violent nationalism, 1
religious diversity in, 209
secularism in, 21, 24, 30, 33, 35, 128–129
Indian civilisation, 161, 216
Indian culture, 163, 164
Indian constitution, 3, 4, 7, 12n6, 20, 28, 32, 39, 40n1, 70, 73, 78, 100, 127, 128, 168–171, 173, 177, 190n149, 199, 201, 204, 208, 210–214, 220, 222, 229n113, 230n121, 234
Indian national movement, 4, 38, 80n16, 170
Indian Muslims, Khilafat movement, 107
Indian National Congress (INC), 12n6, 20, 40n1, 48, 51, 68, 82n27, 102, 108, 112, 117, 121, 142, 150–152, 172, 176, 177, 193, 195–197, 199–202, 200, 204–208, 210, 214, 216, 223n2, 224n16, 224n23, 227n72
  mass contact campaign, 206
  nationalists, 177
Indian Political Thought, 1–2, 12n5, 24
Indian politics, contemporary, 21
Indus Valley Civilisation, 160–162
intellectual history, 1, 7, 9–10, 12
  global intellectual history, 8, 9, 18n37, 19n46, 21, 232, 235
inter/intra-religious diversity, 4
Iqbal, Mohammad, 54, 84n52

Jainism, 218
  Vedic religions/heterodox traditions, 5

Jallianwala Bagh massacre (1919), 108–109, 112
Jawaharlal Nehru, 1, 15n20, 17n31, 37, 92n152, 96n151, 141, 173, 179n4, 179n12, 180n15, 180n17, 182n41, 183n64, 184n79, 184n88, 185n93, 186n106, 186n110, 186n114, 188n138, 191n163, 222n1, 223n2, 225n37, 228n79, 231
Jayakar, M. R., 113
Jinnah, Mohammad Ali, 108, 113n71, 116, 117, 138n90, 176, 195, 197, 201, 202, 206, 207
  on Gandhi's attempts at forging Hindu–Muslim unity, 113
  Khilafat and Non-cooperation leaders, 197
  as president of the Congress party, 112

Kant, Immanuel, 65
  categorical imperative, 66
  Kantian model, 65, 66
  universalism, 66
Karachi Congress, 214
karmabhumi, 57, 77, 87n75
Kashmir problem, 211
Kaviraj, Sudipta, 13n11, 14n16, 26, 29, 32, 48, 92n155
  on agreement between Gandhi and Nehru, 2, 13n11, 38
  competitive diversity, 164
  enterprise of 'universal history, 45
  fuzzy communities, 7, 116
  on religious and austerity practices, 48
  revisionist theory of modernity, 31
  sequential reading, 31, 32

study of religious difference in the Vedic and post-Vedic religious traditions, 164
swajatiyata, 110
on Weber's conception of rationalisation, 41n34
khadi, 73, 129, 140n135, 144
Khilafat-Congress alliance, 196
Khilafat movement, 99, 103, 104, 107, 110, 112, 114, 125, 133n24, 135n40, 169, 196, 197
of Indian Muslims, 107
Khilafat-Non-cooperation alliance, 113
Khilnani, Sunil, 141, 154, 192

laïcité, 2, 22, 170
Latin Christendom, 16n26, 21–22
liberal democracy, 9, 116, 204, 212
liberal secularism, 10, 50, 78, 81n21, 98, 110, 129, 234
liberal politics, 20, 52, 77, 100, 101, 102, 104, 115, 129, 192, 201, 210
liberalism of fear, 20, 40n2, 192–230, 200n43, 235
Lyall, Arthur, 71

Macaulay, T. B., 61
Macdonald Award of 1931, 122
MacDonald, Ramsay, 121
Madan, T. N., 33, 158
Mantena, Karuna, 19n49, 56, 76, 82n31, 96n188
majoritarian, 2, 3, 7, 14n12, 38, 39, 78, 80n16, 128, 167, 175, 202, 210, 216–219, 221, 235
Malaviya, Madan Mohan, 197
Marxism, 207
Menon, V. K. Krishna, 159

Mill, J. S., 61, 65
minority appeasement, politics of, 3
minority religions, 199
modernity, 1, 2, 5, 14n14, 14n16, 18n40, 24–27, 30–32, 35–37, 39, 97n198, 116, 141–142, 144–146, 158, 161, 165, 166, 169, 173, 174, 218, 231, 235
in *swaraj*, 144–146
modus vivendi, 125
moral politics, Gandhian acts of, 52
moral-psychological attitudes, 76
Morley, John, 61
Morley-Minto constitutional reforms, 195
Motilal Nehru, 113, 224n23
Mughal era, 163
Mukhopadhyay, Bhudev, 110
multiculturalism, political theory of, 9, 20, 95n175, 170, 201, 234
multiple secularities, 1, 11n1, 11n2, 12n3, 14n16, 17n33, 19n48, 29, 31, 32, 42n39, 43n52, 43n53, 43n54, 43n55, 44n56, 44n62, 236n3
music before mosque, 100, 126
Muslim League, 102, 172, 176, 195, 207, 209
Muslim masses, 172, 193, 194, 204–208, 226n62, 227n76, 234
Muslim minorities, 202
Muslim rule, 'Gandhi's assessment of, 71

Nandy, Ashis, 16n29, 140n129
on alternatives to secularism, 127
charge against secularism, 35
Counter-Statement on Humanistic Temper, 174

criticism of
  Nehruvian statecraft, 158
  secularism in India, 127–128
on distinction between religion as faith and ideology, 85n60, 148
on emergence of religious fundamentalism, 36
on independence of religion from modern statecraft, 128
on modern state's push for secularisation, 158
on state intervention for societal change, 129
on transformation of religion from faith to ideology, 35
views on religious tolerance, 35–36
national culture, 21, 39, 201, 211, 216
nationalism
  Hindu nationalism, 2, 13n12, 15n17, 32, 38, 158, 163, 175, 177, 184n84
  Indian nationalism, 107, 108, 175–177, 191n161, 195–197, 203, 209
  secular nationalism, 70
national unity, 72, 177, 195, 197, 203–204, 234
Nehruism, 10, 143, 169–175, 177, 190n148
Nehruvian
  Nehruvian secularism, 8, 10, 17n32, 143, 158, 159, 169–173, 175–178, 190n150, 191n165, 214, 235
  secularist ideal, 2, 13n12, 93n160
  Nehruvian secularity, 10, 143, 156, 172, 173, 177, 234
Nehru, Jawaharlal
  autobiography, 147

Discovery of India, The, 10, 15n20, 160, 196, 198, 219
engagement with
  post-colonial India, 208–220
  religious minorities, 212–214
  rights of SCs/STs, 212–214
humanist-universal narrative, 165–169
idea of religion, 143
national genius, 157, 166, 184n83
nationalist narrative of secularity, 159–165
political philosophy, 193
political thought, 142, 156
rhetoric on socialism, 170
statecraft, 158
Nehruvian Secularism, 8, 10, 17n32, 143, 156, 158, 159, 169–173, 175–178, 190n150, 191n165, 214, 235
  Archimedean existence of, 175
  critical appraisal of, 175–177
  critics of, 172
  to Nehruism, 172–175
neighbourliness, 99, 103, 105, 106, 132n20
Non-cooperation-Khilafat movements, 70, 103, 112, 114, 118, 169
Non-cooperation movement, 107, 108, 111, 133n24, 135n42, 152, 197
non-violence, 8, 10, 47–50, 56, 58–60, 64, 66–68, 76, 77, 86n75, 90n118, 91n144, 92n151, 94n164, 98, 102–105, 112, 114, 115, 118, 126, 129, 138n95, 144, 153, 232
experiment, 127
nationalism, 1

non-Western societies/democracies, 3, 7, 14n16, 23, 28, 29, 33, 34, 37, 45, 158, 187n118, 188n140

organised religion, 147–149

*panchayat*s (village councils), 75
Pandey, Gyanendra, 196
*pandit*s, 62, 89n105
partition of India, 20, 32, 35, 99, 104, 117, 118, 119, 122, 133n24, 159, 167, 170, 193, 194, 195, 197, 208, 209, 210, 220
Patanjali's Yoga Sutra, 121
pluralism, 78, 100, 178, 211
political alliances, 99, 106, 108, 117
political consensus, through public deliberation, 101
political economy, 153
political secularism, 2–3, 35, 36, 38, 80n16, 100, 128, 158, 171, 189n141, 221, 232
political unity, 93n161, 99, 102, 103, 108, 110, 114–116, 121, 209
  in forms of associationalism, 103–104
  within religion, 119–124
  between religions, 104–119
politics
  communal question, 194–204
  of friendship, 104, 106, 108, 110, 111, 126, 133n20
  Gandhi's conception of, 52
  minority question, 194–204
  Muslim mass contact campaign, 1937, 204–208
  Nehru's engagement, 194–208
    in post-colonial India, 208–220
  political, 50

radical construal, 53
  of religion, 99–103, 130n3, 132n15, 154, 172, 233
post-colonial India, Nehru's engagement, 208–220
post-colonial studies, 2
post-Enlightenment, 23, 62, 63, 89n114, 154, 156, 183
post-secular society, 4
post-Vedic religious, 164
policy of reservation, 17n34, 170, 199, 207, 212, 213, 227n77
  reservation of seats, 170, 199, 212, 213, 227n77
Prasad, Rajendra, 6, 17n35
principled distance, 34, 128
pro-Khilafat Muslims, in India, 107
pseudo-secular/pseudo-secularist, 3, 21, 39, 174, 201
  Hindu right as, 21, 191n160, 201
  minority rights, 3, 39
public-political roles, 4
public religions, 4, 23, 25
purna swaraj, 72, 146, 180n14. *See also* complete independence

Rai, Lala Lajpat, 113
Rawls, John
  Rawlsian, 77
Ramrajya, Gandhi's ideal of, 153
Rashtriya Swayamsevak Sangh (RSS), 191n159
rational attitude, 173, 174
rational monism, 155
religion, 54–56
  privatisation of, 26, 27, 37, 77
  as discovery, 49, 54
  Gandhi's inclusion of, 98
  in Nehru's political thought, 146–150

in politics, 100–103
resurgence of, 4
tolerance/equality of, 68–73
religious conversion, 17, 77, 124
religion-state-society relationship, 4, 8, 21, 30, 37, 50
religious diversity, 4–5, 37, 164, 209, 233
religious fundamentalism in society, emergence of, 36
religious majoritarianism, 3, 78
religious minorities, group rights, 212–214
religious-moral politics, 98
religious music, 125–126
religious outlook, 149, 152–153
religious politics, 24, 30, 38, 48, 50, 56–78, 80n16, 98, 99, 101–104, 106, 110, 113, 129, 133n24, 143, 147, 148, 150–154, 158, 169, 188n139, 189n146, 206, 233
  Gandhi's *ashram*, 56–77
  Gandhi's practice of, 143
  Nehru's political thought, 146–150
  reason, 154–159
religious-secular distinctions, 31
religious tolerance, 6, 35–36, 69, 99–100, 124–127, 158, 165, 231, 233
reservations, 207, 212
  caste, 212–214
  group-based, 213
  religious minorities, 170
  social minorities, 213
right-wing politics, 3
Risley, Herbert, 71
Rowlatt Act (1919), 107–108, 112, 134n38
Royal Society of England, 165

Sabarmati *ashram*, 48, 77, 79n2
samaduhkhasukhata, 111
sanatani Hindu, 60, 61, 119, 120
Sarva Dharma Samabhava, 2, 6, 17n31, 69, 70, 231–233
satya, 50, 59
satyagraha, 10, 48, 49, 56, 57, 59, 76, 79n13, 80n14, 82n28, 83n39, 91n144, 96n192, 112
satyagrahi ashramite, 65, 233
*satyagrahi*s, 52, 103
Savarkar, V. D., 7, 102
Scheduled Castes (SCs), 194
Scheduled Tribes (STs), 194
science of non-violence, 64
scientific temper, 142, 143, 154–156, 159, 173, 174, 182n55, 190n153
secular, 21–24
  age, 3, 4, 22
  ideology, 158
  imaginary, 5, 232
  liberal politics, 210
secularisation, 4, 9, 10, 16n24, 16n27, 21, 24–30, 33–35, 42n38, 42n41, 50, 77, 78, 158, 159, 168, 170, 171, 188n140, 216, 232
  European societies, 27
  of Western society, 33
secularism, 2–6, 8–10, 12n8, 14n14, 15n18, 15n23, 16n25, 16n29, 17n31, 19n48, 20, 21, 23, 24, 30–39, 40n20, 42n41, 44n56, 45n68, 45n71, 46n82, 49, 50, 69, 70, 78, 80n14, 80n16, 81n21, 93n159, 93n160, 100, 102, 127–129, 131n9, 142, 143, 158–160, 163, 169–177,

187n132, 188n140, 189n141, 190n150, 193, 204, 210, 211, 214, 216, 217, 221, 222, 224n15, 228n81, 228n88, 231–235
Nehru against Nehruism, 169–172
Nehruvian secularism, critics of, 172
secularist, 8
secularity, 1–5, 7–10, 11n1, 11n2, 13n8, 15n16, 16n27, 17n33, 21, 23, 27, 29, 30–33, 36–38, 41n33, 43n49, 44n56, 44n57, 47, 49, 50, 77, 78, 81n20, 100, 118, 141–143, 156, 159–162, 164–166, 168, 170–175, 177, 199, 204, 209, 222, 231–235
Gandhi-Nehru ideal of, 4
Gandhi-Nehru tradition, 2, 9, 118, 232
multiple secularities, 1, 11n1–2, 12n3, 14n16, 17n33, 19n48, 29, 31, 32, 43n55
narrative of, 2
Nehru's humanist-universal narrative, 165–169
Nehru's nationalist narrative, 159–165
Nehruvian, 10
Western conception, 1
self-constraint, 77
self-discipline, 23, 77
sacrifice of (the) self, 52, 54
shankaracharyas, 61
shastris, 61
Sikhs, 205, 218
social imaginary, 5–6, 16n30, 28–29, 50, 231
socialism, Nehru's rhetoric of, 170
social reform, 124, 220
socio-cultural transformations, 215

socio-economic reforms, 146
Special Marriage Act (SMA), 217
spirit of the age, 143, 157, 166
spiritual/ascetic 'biomoral' practices, 73–77
Subramanian, Narendra, 217
Skaria, Ajay, 12n5, 38, 49, 58, 63, 105, 106, 134n31
*sudra*s of Hindu community, 60, 61
swadeshi, 58
swajatiyata, 110
swaraj/swarajya, 74, 104, 105, 108, 112, 114, 115, 118, 119, 121, 133n25, 134n28–29, 144–146, 151, 152, 193
fight for, 151
in modernity, 144–146
syncretic culture/syncretism, 70, 72, 163, 207, 233

Tagore, Rabindranath, 55–56, 85n62, 191n161
tapasya/tapas, 52, 76, 83n39, 98, 102
Taylor, Charles, 4, 21, 32
A Secular Age, 28
social imaginary, 5, 6, 16, 28, 29, 50, 231
modernity, 5, 14n14, 14n16, 18n40, 24–27, 30–32, 35–37, 39, 97n198, 116, 141–142, 144–146, 158, 161, 165–166, 169, 173–174, 218, 229n101, 231, 235
Tejani, Shabnum, 107, 113, 177, 197, 213
tolerance
equality of religions, 68–73
tradition of tolerance, 6, 36, 70, 93n160, 162, 163, 172, 233

religious tolerance, 5, 6, 14n14, 21, 23, 35, 36, 50, 58, 68–73, 91n132, 92n155, 92n156, 93n160, 99, 100, 120, 124–128, 158, 162–165, 172, 174, 185n89, 198, 199, 222, 231, 233, 234
transformative constitution, 220
Turko-Afghan invasions, 160

udyog mandir (temple of industry), 56
Uniform Civil Code (UCC), 72, 190n158, 194, 218, 222, 226n47, 235
Unity in Diversity, 2, 6, 178, 231, 232
unnational, 6, 7, 231
untouchability, 56, 58, 73, 99, 100, 119–124, 132n18, 133n25, 139n105, 147, 148, 182n50, 199, 200, 224n17, 225n40

varnashrama dharma, 88n92, 119, 120
Vedic religions, 5, 164

Veeravalli, Anuradha, 58, 63, 90n118, 118, 122, 123, 130n6, 132n18
vote-bank politics, 3

wall of separation, 34, 46n77, 128, 210
Weber, Max, 26
    disenchantment, 26, 41n34, 168
    rationality, 26, 55, 75, 157, 179n4
Western character, 33
Western modernity
    on India, 141
    vision, 144
Western Political Theory, 1
Western secularism, 23, 37, 175, 210
Western-style modern secularity, 164
Western trajectory, 26
Westphalian model, 4, 119
    Westphalian nation-state, 2, 4, 6, 13n10, 20, 36, 118, 119

zamindari system, 150
zamindars, 198